D1601508

SOCIAL SYSTEM ACCOUNTS

KARL A. FOX

Department of Economics,
Iowa State University

SOCIAL SYSTEM ACCOUNTS

Linking Social and Economic Indicators
through Tangible Behavior Settings

D. REIDEL PUBLISHING COMPANY

A MEMBER OF THE KLUWER   ACADEMIC PUBLISHERS GROUP

DORDRECHT / BOSTON / LANCASTER

Library of Congress Cataloging in Publication Data

Fox, Karl August, 1917–
    Social system accounts.

    (Theory and decision library)
    Bibliography: p.
    Includes index.
        1. Social accounting.   2.   Social indicators.   3.   Economic
    indicators.   I.   Title.   II.   Title: Behavior settings.   III.   Series.
    HN60.F69   1985   302   85-2384
    ISBN 90–277–2020–7

Published by D. Reidel Publishing Company,
P.O. Box 17, 3300 AA Dordrecht, Holland.

Sold and distributed in the U.S.A. and Canada
by Kluwer Academic Publishers,
190 Old Derby Street, Hingham, MA 02043, U.S.A.

In all other countries, sold and distributed
by Kluwer Academic Publishers Group,
P.O. Box 322, 3300 AH Dordrecht, Holland.

Printed in The Netherlands

To ROGER G. BARKER

who pioneered the fields of ecological

psychology and eco-behavioral science,

and developed basic concepts and

methods for measuring the

environment of human

behavior

CONTENTS

*By James R. Prescott, Professor of Economics, Iowa
State University.

PREFACE

This book results from a research program on which I have
spent most of my time since 1974. It addresses two of the
major problems facing social system accounting: how to
measure and account for nonmarket activities and how to
combine social and economic indicators. The solution I
propose is accounts based on behavior settings, a concept
originated by Roger G. Barker more than thirty years ago.
Behavior settings are the natural units of social activity
into which people sort themselves to get on with the business of daily life--grocery stores, school classes, religious services, meetings, athletic events, and so on. The
descriptive power of behavior settings has been established
in surveys of complete communities in the United States and
England, of high schools ranging in size from fewer than
100 to more than 2000 students, of rehabilitation centers
in hospitals, and of several other types of organizations.
    Behavior settings are empirical facts of everyday
life. A description of a community or an organization in
terms of behavior settings corresponds to common experience. In many cases, small establishments are behavior
settings; the paid roles in behavior settings are occupations; and the buildings and equipment of establishments
are the buildings and equipment of behavior settings.
Hence, social system accounts based on behavior settings
can be firmly linked with industries in the SIC (Standard
Industrial Classification) system, with occupations in the
SOC-DOT (Standard Occupational Classification-Dictionary of
Occupational Titles) system, and with categories of structures, equipment, and consumer durable goods in the estimates of stocks of physical capital recently (1981) published by the U.S. Bureau of Economic Analysis. Behavior
setting concepts and measures can be applied uniformly to
market and nonmarket activities and to paid and unpaid
participants.
    My proposed accounts imply an exhaustive allocation of
time among behavior settings. Individual well-being in a

community or society can be increased through improvements
in the capacities of individuals (e.g. health, skills),
improvements in behavior settings (which constitute the
immediate physical and social environments of human activity and experience), and improvements in the allocation
of time among behavior settings and roles. I am able to
show that eight of the 33 indicators in The OECD List of
Social Indicators (published in June 1982) measure changes
in the environment (i.e. in behavior settings), that
certain others measure changes in the attributes of individuals, and that still others measure changes in the allocation of time.

Publication of The OECD List of Social Indicators
after more than a decade of work seems to reflect a new
level of maturity and consensus in the development of objective social indicators. The OECD indicators are firmly
linked with established social, economic, and demographic
data systems of high quality. Social system accounts based
on behavior settings can be developed in such a way as to
complement the OECD social indicators and to take advantage
of the multi-billion dollar investments already made in
official data systems in many countries.

Chapter 8 goes well beyond the accounting emphasis of
the book as a whole. It was contributed by James R.
Prescott, who identifies fourteen characteristics of behavior settings which link them with recognized concepts in
organization theory and microeconomics. He proceeds to
outline a computable dynamic model of a community based on
its behavior settings and drawing on 'state of the art'
simulation techniques. If implemented, such a model would
throw considerable light on causal relationships within and
between market and nonmarket behavior settings at the local
level and also generate estimates or conditional forecasts
of social accounting tables for the community.

I take full responsibility for the rest of the volume.
Most of the research underlying it was supported by the
National Science Foundation under research grants SOC 74-
13996 and SOC 76-20084. A Senior Research Fellowship
jointly sponsored by the American Statistical Association
and the U.S. Bureau of the Census gave me time and opportunity during 1980-81 to catch up with recent developments in
many data systems relevant to social accounting and measures of individual well-being. A faculty improvement
leave from Iowa State University and an appointment as
William Evans Visiting Professor at the University of Otago

enabled me to spend August–December 1981 in New Zealand considering the applicability of behavior setting concepts to that environment. The support of all these organizations is gratefully acknowledged.

Several staff members of Iowa State University's Department of Economics helped in preparation of the manuscript. Shu Huang programmed the computations underlying several tables. The original versions of some tables were typed by Lois Roberts, and Jane Larsen typed the semi-final version of the text on the word processor. Carolyn Millage and Lyn Van De Pol handled the exacting task of preparing the final version of the manuscript in camera-ready form.

My indebtedness to the published works of Roger Barker and his associates will be apparent throughout the book; annotated references to several of these works are presented in Appendix I. An anonymous reviewer for D. Reidel suggested the basic strategy for extracting this volume from a larger manuscript; discussions with Jati Sengupta and Paul van Moeseke helped me translate the reviewer's suggestion into a working outline. Selected chapters of the larger manuscript, contributed by Jati Sengupta, James Prescott, and Arnold Faden or coauthored with Syamal Ghosh and Walter Ollor, are listed in Appendix II. Some articles based on these chapters have already been published (Items 7 through 11 in Appendix II) and others should be forthcoming during the next two years. An earlier article coauthored with Paul van Moeseke is cited at several points in the present text.

Karl A. Fox
Distinguished Professor
in Sciences and
Humanities and Professor
of Economics

Iowa State University
Ames, Iowa
November 1984

CHAPTER 1

BEHAVIOR SETTINGS AS A
BASIS FOR SOCIAL SYSTEM ACCOUNTS

Economic science advanced rapidly from economic indicators
and index numbers in the 1920s to national income accounts
and econometric models in the 1930s. These developments
were facilitated by economic theory, but they were pro-
pelled by public concern about economic instability and
unemployment; hence, public funds were made available for
a major expansion in economic data systems for the objective measurement of these phenomena and, hopefully, for
their explanation, prediction, and control. Without these
data systems, the great advances of recent decades in
empirical economic research would have been impossible.
      The range of public concerns in many countries broad-
ened during the 1960s. The development of social indicators addressed to the new concerns was pursued with vigor,
and a long-term goal of comprehensive social system
accounts was stated by Gross (1966). However, no one
social science provided a conceptual framework for such
accounts which would have satisfied the practitioners of
any other, and many social scientists took comfort from the
thought that the issues could be deferred until work within
the social indicators tradition was far advanced.
      Publication of The OECD List of Social Indicators in
June 1982 represents a new level of maturity and consensus
in specifying objective social indicators and relating them
to well-established official data systems. The OECD List
is intended to be both comprehensive and systematic and is
recommended for implementation by OECD member countries as
their circumstances permit. It establishes at least a
temporary plateau for objective social indicators.
      It is time now to commence the active development of
social system accounts. For this we need a criterion of
comprehensiveness (what range of human activities should be
included?), an objective method of classification that
applies equally to market and nonmarket activities, and an
objective unit for sampling and recording the contributions

1

(inputs) people make to the social system and the rewards
(outputs or outcomes) they receive from it.

We can meet these requirements by viewing human societies from the perspective of 'eco-behavioral science,' a
term introduced by Roger G. Barker in 1969 after 22 years
of pathbreaking research within a somewhat narrower framework which he called 'ecological psychology'. His basic
unit of observation is a 'behavior setting'. A system of
social accounts based on behavior settings can incorporate
most of the existing official data systems without impair-
ing their separate usefulness.

In adapting behavior setting concepts to the requirements of objective social accounts, we believe we are help-
ing to extend the foundations of eco-behavioral science and
to provide it with a data base which takes advantage of the
many billions of dollars already invested in official data
systems. If the social system of (say) the United States
is viewed as a comprehensive array of behavior settings
each with its own internal dynamics and its external relations with other settings, collectively incorporating all
of the living-time, behavior, and experience of the U.S.
population in a given year, we believe the contexts and
consequences of most private and public decisions will look
somewhat different than they now do from the perspective of
any existing social science. To the extent that social
scientists concern themselves with real people in real
social systems, they should be interested in the accounting
and modeling implications of this new view.

In most of this book we will refer to the U.S. data
systems and society with which we are familiar. However,
closely comparable data systems and arrays of behavior
settings exist in many other countries, and proposals
framed in terms of the U.S. should be generally adaptable
in them.

1.1. SOCIAL SYSTEM ACCOUNTING: TWO PROBLEMS AND A
      PROPOSED SOLUTION

Social system accounting faces two major problems: how to
measure and account for nonmarket activities and how to
combine social and economic indicators. Our proposed solution is accounts based on behavior settings.

Behavior settings provide the most comprehensive
framework we have yet encountered for describing nonmarket

as well as market activities. To make clear what behavior settings are and how they might be used as a basis for social accounts, we begin our exposition at the level of a community and a complete census of its behavior settings. Similar accounts for a nation or a metropolitan region would be based on samples of behavior settings, linked with, and interpreted in conjunction with, existing data systems.

Behavior settings were discovered by Roger Barker, who adapted methods derived from the traditions of experimental psychology to the observation and measurement of naturally-occurring behavior in a complete community (Midwest, Kansas) which he studied intensively from 1947 to 1972. Examples of behavior settings would include a bank, a Boy Scout troop meeting, the county recorder's office, a Sunday worship service, or a high school mathematics class. Each of these settings has a distinctive program of activities and (hence) a distinctive pattern of behavior by its occupants. It has a definite location in space, and each of its occurrences has a definite beginning, duration, and end in time (e.g. the high school mathematics class occurs in Room 15 between 9:00 and 9:55 a.m. on weekdays). An empty classroom or a closed bank is not a behavior setting.

The five settings listed belong to five different 'authority systems'--private enterprise, voluntary association, government, church, and school--based on the legal status of the person or board with ultimate responsibility for their control. Only the first of these sytems is market-oriented; the other four are engaged in nonmarket activities. Barker applied uniform methods of observation and measurement to behavior settings in all five systems, market and nonmarket alike. Thus, his work provides a unique starting point for efforts to combine social and economic indicators and to measure and account for nonmarket activities.

Behavior settings with identical or closely similar programs (different banks or different high school math classes) are classified by Barker into categories which he calls 'genotypes' (Banks; High School Mathematics Classes). Barker and Schoggen measured social change in Midwest between 1954-55 and 1963-64 partly in terms of the introduction of new genotypes and the disappearance of old ones; in each year they measured differences between Midwest and an English town partly in terms of the arrays of genotypes which were present in one town but not in the other.

Barker and Gump compared large and small high schools
partly in terms of the arrays of genotypes they provided.

Behavior settings can be linked with time budgets and
economic accounts to form the basis for more comprehensive
social system accounts. Barker's private enterprise genotypes can be identified with industries in the Standard
Industrial Classification (SIC) system. The paid roles in
Barker's genotype programs can be identified with occupations in the Dictionary of Occupational Titles (DOT) and
the Standard Occupational Classification. Barker's ratings
of behavior settings on 'action patterns' and 'behavior
mechanisms' suggest linkages (1) with categories of buildings by purposes (commerce, education, religion, government) in the new Bureau of Economic Analysis (BEA) time
series on stocks of physical capital and (2) with DOT
ratings of the complexity of worker functions in relation
to data, people, and things and the level of physical
strength required.

Much exploratory and developmental work would be needed to implement a system of social accounts based on behavior settings. Most of the building blocks already exist in
the form of published data systems, and historical time
series incorporating behavior setting concepts could be
constructed from these and supplementary sources. The
explanatory power of accounts incorporating all nonmarket
as well as market activities should greatly increase our
ability to measure the effects of current social and economic policies and to predict the consequences of proposed
alternatives.

1.2. THE PLAN OF THE BOOK

The concept of behavior settings is becoming widely, but
for the most part rather superficially, known. Our first
task is to show that the concept is concrete, operational,
and useful for describing human activities in a complete
community.

We begin this in Chapter 2 by describing Barker's
method of behavior setting surveys and using the results of
his 1963-64 survey of the town of Midwest to give specific
quantitative illustrations of the terms he developed for
this purpose (action patterns, behavior mechanisms, inhabitant-setting intersections, occupancy times, and several
others). New concepts require new names; it is the

concepts, not the names, which call for and justify intellectual effort on the reader's part.   Perhaps a simpler
terminology will be developed as statistical agencies pre-
pare to publish social system accounts for general use.

   At the national level, several chapters show how data
embodying behavior setting concepts can be linked, merged,
or fused with official data systems such as those in or
underlying the OECD List and its recommended disaggregations.   Thus, Chapter 3 relates behavior setting concepts
to the OECD List of Social Indicators (published in 1982)
and to the U.S. Bureau of Economic Analysis (BEA) estimates
of stocks of physical capital and consumer durable goods
(published in 1981).

   The OECD indicators are designed to measure trends in
individual well-being.   We make the working assumption
that the well-being of individuals in a society may be
increased by improvements in their behavioral capacities
(health, skills), their environments (the behavior settings
in which they live and work), and their allocations of
time.   We then show that some eight of the 33 indicators
measure changes in attributes of the environment (and hence
of behavior settings); that certain others measure changes
in the behavioral capacities and other attributes of individuals; and that still others measure changes in the allocation of time.   A few indicators measure the results of
interactions between attributes of different categories of
persons and attributes of different categories of behavior
settings (e.g. injury rates for members of a given population subgroup differ as between homes, workplaces, and
trafficways, and injury rates in each category of behavior
settings differ as between population subgroups).

   Chapter 3 also points out that physical capital in the
forms of buildings, other structures, and equipment is a
pervasive feature of most behavior settings.   The contributions of structures and equipment to the performance of
private enterprise settings are well-known;   in a comprehensive system of social accounts we must also recognize
their importance, and that of consumer durable goods, to
the performance of nonmarket settings.

   Chapter 4 shows that data for behavior setting genotypes can be merged with data for SIC (Standard Industrial
Classification) industries. We propose a matrix with a row
for each genotype and a column for each SIC industry such
that the living-time of the U.S. population in a given year
is allocated exhaustively among genotypes and also among

industries, with the latter augmented to include the occupancy times of unpaid persons (e.g. pupils, customers,
spectators, and household members) in addition to gainful
workers.

Chapter 5 identifies paid roles in the programs of
behavior setting genotypes with occupations in the Standard
Occupational Classification (SOC) and the Dictionary of
Occupational Titles (DOT). Three digits in the SOC and DOT
codes are identical;   they refer to the complexity of a
worker's functions in relation to data, people, and things
respectively—the demands that a typical job in a certain
occupation imposes on anyone who tries to fill it. Levels
of job complexity are highly correlated with the levels of
specified worker traits (e.g. general educational development, specific vocational preparation, and general, verbal
and numerical aptitude) required for average performance in
the relevant occupation.

Occupations are also characterized by strength
required or heaviness of work. We note that the three
categories of job complexity plus strength required seem to
correspond roughly to Barker's categories of 'behavior
mechanisms'—thinking, talking and affective behavior,
manipulation (use of the hands), and gross motor activity—
which people use in carrying out their roles in behavior
settings.   Barker rates behavior mechanisms for entire
settings rather than for individual roles. Some developmental research would be required to adapt Barker's rating
scales so that they represented true aggregations or transformations of the SOC-DOT ratings of worker functions for
all persons in the setting.

Chapter 5 also points out that the U.S. Bureau of
Labor Statistics (1981) has published a national industry-
occupation employment matrix with a row for each of 425
occupations and a column for each of 260 industries; all
gainful employment in the U.S. economy is allocated both
among the occupation-rows and the industry-columns. We
suggest that quasi-occupations (student, customer, unpaid
housekeeper, and the like) can be created to describe the
activities of unpaid participants in behavior settings;
many such activities are performed for pay by some persons
and are included in the SOC and DOT systems. The quasi-
occupations plus gainful employment would produce an
exhaustive allocation of living-time among roles (occupations and quasi-occupations) and also, as in Chapter 4,

among industries. Note that <u>private</u> <u>households</u> is one of
the 260 SIC-type industries.

Chapter 6 shows how data on stocks of physical capital
and consumer durable goods in the U.S. (annually from 1929
to 1979) recently published by the U.S. Bureau of Economic
Analysis can be interpreted as the 'circumjacent milieus'
of behavior settings and the durable 'behavior objects'
used in implementing their programs. Several categories of
structures (e.g. religious buildings, educational buildings, hospital and institutional buildings, state and local
government buildings, commercial buildings) are the primary
locations of certain of Barker's <u>action</u> <u>patterns</u> which
embody the purposes for which the various behavior setting
genotypes were created: religion, education, physical
health, government, and business for the types of structures cited. Commercial buildings can be subdivided, with
the help of additional data sources, into food stores and
restaurants (action patterns 'nutrition' as well as 'business'); barber and beauty shops (action pattern 'personal
appearance'); bowling alleys and motion picture theaters
(action pattern 'recreation'); and others. The three remaining action patterns listed by Barker are 'aesthetic',
'professional involvement', and 'social contact'; the last
two are very widely distributed, and the 'aesthetic' action
pattern also appears in a variety of contexts.

Changes in stocks (in constant 1972 dollars) of the
various types of structures during 1929-79 are consistent
with changes in gainful employment in the clusters of industries which use those structures. With additional
effort, it should be possible to allocate these stocks to
specific industries and thence (as suggested in Chapter 4)
to behavior setting genotypes. The same should apply to
stocks of equipment. Changes in stocks of the different
categories of consumer durable goods mirror dramatic
changes in the technology of household production and in
patterns of indoor and outdoor recreation and leisure. In
many cases, the durable good used completely dominates a
particular activity (temporary role) and the time allocated
to it; the stock data should be very helpful in reconstructing uses of time in household settings.

If data on the consumption of services and nondurable
goods were also rearranged to conform to behavior setting
genotypes, along with the corresponding financial flows,
the result of all the procedures outlined would be a rough,

preliminary, but comprehensive system of social accounts at
the national level based on behavior settings.

The matrices and submatrices of this system could be
linked experimentally with existing national models of
various types: large-scale econometric models as conceptu-
alized in Fox (1956) and implemented in the Brookings quarterly econometric model of the United States (Duesenberry
et al., 1965) and its many descendants and counterparts;
the input-output matrices of the U.S. Bureau of Economic
Analysis (1979); demographic models of the type pioneered
by Stone (1971, 1981); simulation models of the type developed by Stone and Brown (1962) and their associates; and
the social accounting matrices (SAMs) developed by Stone,
Pyatt, Roe, Thorbecke and others.

Chapter 7 discusses alternative approaches to comprehensive social accounts for urban-centered regions. The
county data base developed by the U.S. Bureau of Economic
Analysis during the past decade provides an excellent
starting point, as do its more detailed estimates of employment and earnings by industry for Standard Metropolitan
Statistical Areas (SMSAs) and for BEA Economic Areas; the
latter areas partition the U.S. exhaustively into about
183 urban-centered regions, each delineated as a cluster of
contiguous whole counties and each containing an integral
number of home-to-work commuting fields or Functional Economic Areas (FEAs), as proposed by Fox and Kumar (1965).

The 'expected time-allocation matrix (TAM)' approach
described in Chapter 7 could probably be extended upward
successfully from small towns like Midwest, through small
cities (often county seats of 5,000 to 25,000 population
with trade areas approximating counties), to FEA central
cities (usually with 30,000 to 300,000 people) and complete
FEAs (typically with 150,000 to 500,000 residents). BEA
Economic Areas of up to 2,000,000 people could be accounted
for as clusters of FEAs plus some additional industries and
genotypes in the largest city if its population exceeded
300,000.

Alternatively, published data from the U.S. censuses
of population and housing could be used to extend some
elements of a social accounting system from the national
level through BEA Economic Areas, FEAs, and counties down
to townships, villages, and towns in rural areas and to
census tracts, enumeration districts, and blocks within
SMSAs and urbanized areas. These same data are used by
local governments currently, in conjuction with primary

data needed for their various functions. Local governments
could, if they chose, adapt behavior setting accounts to
the analysis of alternative policies in their own departments.

Chapter 8 (by James R. Prescott) proposes an empirically-based dynamic simulation model of the community of
Midwest based on Barker's 1963-64 data. It begins with a
general discussion of modeling strategies and some comments
on the unique nature and promise of Barker's data for
modeling such a community. Successive sections deal with
the theory of manning (the properties of behavior settings
with a shortage or surplus of participants relative to the
number of roles called for by their programs), prototype
behavior settings in each of the five nonhousehold authority systems, and causal relationships among economic, demographic, and other variables affecting the actual performance of behavior settings relative to certain norms.

Chapter 9 discusses some broader implications of behavior settings for the social sciences. It points out the
distinctive features of the behavior setting concept and
some relationships of behavior settings and Barker's proposed 'eco-behavioral science' to established disciplines.
Barker's 1969 article on the need for an eco-behavioral
science independent of psychology is cited, and his mature
views as of 1978 on the scope and content of eco-behavioral
science are quoted at length. The basic units of this
science are behavior settings.

Chapter 9 also suggests that the distinction between
Barker's 'behavior settings' and Lewin's 'life space' may
throw some light on the relationship between objective and
subjective indicators of individual well-being. Sections
9.6 through 9.8 discuss potential uses of behavior setting
concepts by social and economic historians, in social and
economic development planning, and in reconstructing and
reinterpreting earlier community surveys. Section 9.9
describes several recent papers, published and unpublished,
which relate behavior settings to various fields of mathematical social science.

Chapter 10 proposes some next steps in the development
of social system accounts based on behavior settings. The
first step would be the development of time-use accounts
including estimates of person-hours of occupancy time in
each of an exhaustive array of genotypes and for an exhaustive set of population subgroups; the unit of account would
be person-hours. Economic accounts (basic unit, dollars)

and demographic accounts (basic unit, <u>persons</u>) could be
linked with the time-use accounts in specified ways; so
could estimates of the constant-dollar gross values of
stocks of physical capital and consumer durable goods. The
resulting accounts would be completely objective, and the
problems of classification and measurement should be no
more difficult than those dealt with in the economic censuses, the Census of Population and Housing, the Standard
Industrial Classification, and the Standard Occupational
Classification.

The first step would be a major achievement. The
chapter goes on to discuss some possible additional steps
which are less urgent and more speculative. Section 10.5
suggests a number of possibilities for experimentation with
social system accounts and models based on behavior settings by international agencies, by local governments, and
by market and nonmarket organizations. The chapter con-
cludes with a brief appraisal of Roger Barker's contribution to social science.

Appendix 1 presents annotated references to the basic
literature on behavior settings, ecological psychology, and
eco-behavioral science, including seven books by Roger
Barker and his associates. Appendix 2 lists selected publications and unpublished manuscripts by Karl Fox and associates making use of behavior setting concepts.

CHAPTER 2

THE USEFULNESS OF
BEHAVIOR SETTINGS FOR CLASSIFYING
AND DESCRIBING HUMAN ACTIVITIES IN A COMMUNITY

Existing social and economic data systems are most highly
developed at the national level. However, these national
aggregates are based directly or indirectly on data collected from individuals, households, firms, and other
organizations. The aggregates are useful because sociologists and economists have built up extensive bodies of
theory, empirical research, and personal experience con-
cerning the attributes and behaviors of the primary decision-making units.
    Sociologists have also studied the interactions of
primary units in complete communities ranging from small
towns to cities of 50,000 or more people. Human ecologists
have studied metropolitan regions of all sizes. Concepts
and data systems based on these studies have proved useful
to officials, social agencies, and other organizations
concerned with specific communities or urban-centered
regions. Collectively, the activities and experiences of
the residents of these communities and regions (each important for its own sake) add up to corresponding national
aggregates.
    Experimental psychologists have concentrated on inten-
sive studies of individuals and small groups in laboratory
environments. Barker was the first psychologist trained in
this tradition to study the naturally-occurring behavior of
people in their normal environments. Initially his research in Midwest focused on the question "What aspects of
the daily lives of children contribute positively to their
personality development and mental health?" To cover all
aspects would require intensive observation of the waking
activities of selected children throughout the day in home,
neighborhood, school, streets, playgrounds, church, stores,
and other settings. This would be physically and finan-
cially feasible only in a small community which nevertheless provided a fairly wide range of situations and experiences for children. The community should be separated from
its nearest neighbors by several miles of open country so

11

that the children would spend nearly 100 percent of their
time in their own community and have nearly all their
interactions with other members of it. Barker chose such a
community and obtained funding for his research in 1947.
As a matter of empirical fact he found (in 1950-51) that
children under 12 spent 98 percent of their time within the
town limits; the average for all age groups of town
residents combined was 95 percent. The principal 'leakage'
took the form of out-commuting by about 10 percent of the
adult males.

2.1. THE DISCOVERY OF BEHAVIOR SETTINGS

Barker soon found that a child's behavior changed abruptly
when he left one segment of his environment (e.g. a classroom) and entered another (e.g. a playground); a large
proportion of the variance in his behavior was associated
with these transitions. Within each segment the child's
behavior was fairly stable, and so was the pattern of
interactions among all 'inhabitants' of that segment. The
child's ecological environment consisted of a sequence of
such patterned segments. Many of them contained significant adults (teachers, parents), whose ecological environments also consisted of patterned segments. Barker called
these segments 'behavior settings' and concluded that all
or nearly all of the behavior and experiences of the community's residents occurred in them. As an environment for
human behavior, the community was its behavior settings.
His colleague Gump (1971, p. 134) summarized this insight
as follows: "People live out their lives in a sequence of
environmental units; experience in these settings is life.
If the quality of experience is good, life expands; if it
is bad, life diminishes."
    Behavior settings are the basic units of organizations
and communities. From the perspective of an experimental
psychologist, a behavior setting is a marvellously complex
entity. It imposes expectations and demands on each of its
occupants according to his role in its program; minor deviations from the role-norm are countered almost instantly by
pressures from other occupants and major ones lead to his
ejection from the setting. Circumstances may confine a
child to a few settings; if his behavior is appropriate to
them it is not likely to change unless he 'migrates' on a
full-time or part-time basis to other settings which impose

different demands. An adult confined to an institution or
restricted by poverty or physical disability to a few settings will adapt his behavior to them;   he may not be deprived of food, clothing, and shelter but he _is_ deprived of
a normal range of opportunities for social participation--
he subsists but he does not belong to the mainstream of his
society.   An adult in the mainstream will choose to participate in a wider array of behavior settings which collectively define one of the normal, desirable, or accept-
able life styles of his time and place.

2.2.   BEHAVIOR SETTINGS AND THE MEANING OF
       COMPREHENSIVENESS IN SOCIAL SYSTEM ACCOUNTS

The founders of the social indicators movement were interested in social measurement partly for pure science and
partly as a basis for social policy.   Bauer expressed these
two interests succinctly in 1966: "For many of the important topics on which social critics blithely pass judgment,
and on which policies are made, there are no yardsticks by
which to know if things are getting better or worse." Also
in 1966, Gross's article 'The state of the nation: social
systems accounting' expressed the long-term interest of the
movement in comprehensive social system accounts as distinct from a collection of indicators each separately
designed to track a particular problem.   The bill drafted
by leaders of the movement and introduced by Senator Mon-
dale in 1967 was entitled 'The Full Opportunity and Social
Accounting Act of 1967.'
    So far, no one has come forward with an operational
definition of comprehensiveness in social system accounts.
Without such a definition, we are likely to shift problems
around instead of solving them.   Barker's description of a
nearly self-contained community in terms of behavior settings can provide unique insights into the nature and potential usefulness of a comprehensive system.
    To suggest the possibilities, we use (in Section 2.4)
the concept of a 'closed' community of 1000 people which
no residents leave and no nonresidents enter in the course
of a year. At every moment, each resident is in one behavior setting or another.   If an adult loses his job he is
excluded from his workplace and spends an offsetting number
of hours in other settings.   A student who drops out of
school shows up in other settings.   If he gets a job, his

workplace absorbs the hours released by the school; if he doesn't, he shows up as a loafer, onlooker, participant, or TV-watcher in various settings.

2.3.   BEHAVIOR SETTINGS AND THE MEANING OF IMPROVEMENTS IN
        A SELF-CONTAINED COMMUNITY

To increase the well-being of community residents according to the standards of (say) U.S. society it is necessary to improve the quality of their experience in its behavior settings. Some improvements may be accomplished by changes in the physical aspects of the community (buildings, other structures, and equipment, including consumer durable goods); these constitute the circumjacent milieus of behavior settings and some of the behavior objects used in implementing their programs. Other improvements may come through changes in the capacities and value-orientations of individual residents (physical, mental, and emotional health; work-related and other skills; value commitments and character). Still other improvements may be realized through changes in social organization, information flows, decision processes, and leadership within and between behavior settings.

        If these improvements are to be made over a sequence of years in a 'closed' community, they must be produced in the community's existing behavior settings and/or new ones created for such purposes. The activities of some settings concerned with education, training, and health maintenance must be expanded and/or made more efficient; so must the activities of some settings concerned with construction and maintenance of physical facilities; time and effort must be invested in developing management and communications skills in nonmarket as well as market organizations and in activities designed to increase community solidarity. Some residents must reduce their current time allocations and/or performance levels in other settings to participate in these investment-type activities. If the desired improvements are accomplished, they should be observable and measurable in the behavior settings of the community in subsequent years; the increased capacities of individuals should be reflected in their performances in behavior settings. If the improvements have any undesirable side-effects, these should be demonstrable in other settings.

If the processes by which improvements are accomplished can be identified in the behavior settings of a 'closed' community and the improvements themselves can be measured in this framework, the usefulness of corresponding social indicators at the national level will be greatly increased. A comprehensive system of social accounts at the national level based on genotypes (categories of behavior settings) should enable us to predict the consequences of changes in social policies much more reliably than do our present indicators.

2.4. DESCRIBING A HYPOTHETICAL COMMUNITY IN TERMS OF BEHAVIOR SETTINGS: PRELIMINARY CONCEPTUALIZATION

For the moment, assume a town with 1,000 residents containing just the right numbers and kinds of jobs to suit its labor force, and assume that no resident leaves the town and no nonresident enters it during the course of a year. The flow of life whose quality is at risk or might be improved is 1,000 person-years. We pose Roger Barker's question, "What goes on here?", and try to answer it successively at physical, architectural, ecological, and behavioral levels.

2.4.1. Physical

At this level, we might represent the town by a small-scale three dimensional space with South-North and West-East coordinates x_1 and x_2 and altitude coordinates x_3. Each resident would be represented by a particle whose positions at successive moments would trace out a path in the space; if its position were recorded once per second, the resident's 'life-path' over the year would consist of a multivariate time series of 31.536 million observations.
There would be 1,000 such life-paths. If the particles were represented by pins of variable length stuck perpendicularly into the (x_1, x_2) plane and moved whenever necessary, the complete array of 1,000 particles could be photographed with a motion picture camera and the convergences and divergences of the various particles observed. Empirical regularities could be noted in the paths of individual particles--daily, weekly, and perhaps longer recurrent patterns. These might be translated into

probability density functions: What is the probability
that particle i will be found in a specified small volume
of the town-space at time t?   What is the joint probability
that particles i and j will both be found in it at that
time?   And so on.

What we have described is a mathematical space; it
could hardly be called an environment.   We leave open the
question of _why_ the particles move as they do.

2.4.2. Architectural

Architects are designers of the _built_ environment.   Given a
scale model of all buildings, partitions, and fixed equipment, they can state that the physicists' particle i is in
the kitchen at 238 Maple Street and particle j is in Room 1
of the Elementary School.   The arrangement of particles in
Room 1 means that 24 pupils are seated at desks facing the
teacher who is seated at a desk facing them.   Certain lin-
ear segments in the life-paths reflect constraints on
motion imposed by streets, sidewalks, and hallways.

At any given moment, then, the 1,000 residents will be
distributed among various rooms and among outdoor entities
such as streets and playgrounds.   Some rooms have been
designed and equipped for highly specific kinds of behavior: the barber shop, the bowling lanes, the dentist's
office.   What Barker calls 'the circumjacent milieu' (partitions, furnishings, and so on) virtually predetermines
the behavior.   Other rooms are more flexible: the same
meeting room could accommodate wholly unrelated organizations with nonoverlapping memberships on successive
evenings.

2.4.3. Ecological

A closed grocery store is (for the time being) not a human
habitat; an open one is.   If we disregard private households, the town as an environment for human behavior consists, at any moment, of an array of entities which Roger
Barker calls 'behavior settings'.   A grocery store is a
behavior setting when the manager and employees are on duty
and ready to receive customers.   The small town's streets
and sidewalks constitute a behavior setting (trafficways)
which is open 8,760 hours a year.

From the standpoint of a resident, each behavior setting existing at a given moment offers a potential option
for behavior. Hence, the integer N_t, where N is the number
of behavior settings in existence (i.e. 'open') at time t,
is one measure of the extent of the town's environment; N_t
is a step-function varying from hour to hour and day to day
during the year.

A setting that is 'open' 2,000 hours a year evidently
makes a larger addition to the town's environment (ceteris
paribus) than one which is open only 1,000 hours. Hence,
Barker suggests another measure, duration (D) in setting-
hours per year. Mathematically, we could write $dD/dt = N_t$;
then

$$D = \int_{t=0}^{8760} N_t \, dt = N_t t.$$

Finally, a setting that is open on 200 different days
during the year makes a larger contribution to the town's
environment (ceteris paribus) than one which is open on
only 100 days. Barker suggests a third measure, occurrence
(0) in setting-days per year, to represent this factor; we
could write it as $0 = \sum_{k=1}^{365} N_k$, where N_k is the total number
of different settings open at any time on the kth day of
the year.

A summary measure of the extent of the town's (nonhousehold) environment over an entire year might then be
written as

Environment (E) = f (N, 0, D),

where N is the total number of distinct settings occurring
at any time during the year and 0, D are defined as above.
Note that the environment is partitioned exhaustively among
the N behavior settings; as a human habitat, the town is
its behavior settings.

2.4.4. Behavioral

Again, we limit our discussion to the town's nonhousehold
behavior settings; in each setting we pose Barker's question, "What goes on here?"

Barker suggests that each behavior setting may be
viewed as a 'standing wave' or standing behavior pattern.
Each person who enters the setting is analogous to a particle which becomes part of the standing pattern without

losing its particle characteristics. This pattern is gov-
erned by a program which prescribes appropriate behavior
for the occupants of each zone of the setting and deviations are curbed by its single leader (zone 6) or joint
leaders (zone 5); parts of the program may be implemented
by operatives or functionaries (zone 4). The other zones
contain customers, pupils, patients, clients (zone 3) who
interact directly with persons in zones 4, 5, and 6; spectators or audience members (zone 2) who can do little more
than express approval or disapproval of the performers in
zones 4, 5, and 6; and onlookers (zone 1) who have no function in the setting and no power over it.

It should be clearly noted that 'zones' in Barker's
terminology are not spatial entities but identify different
levels of power and different types of functions in the
program of any given genotype. Most programs involve only
two or three zones; some examples are: teacher (zone 6),
pupils (zone 3); dentist (zone 6), assistant (zone 4),
patients (zone 3); law partners (zone 5), secretary (zone
4), clients (zone 3); music director (zone 6), musicians
(zone 4), audience members (zone 2); construction foreman
(zone 6), workers (zone 4), onlookers (zone 1).

We shall defer discussion of other properties of behavior settings and consider here how to measure the behavior output of a setting; the setting itself is part of the
town's environment. Barker and Schoggen (1973) suggest
person-hours of occupancy time (OT) as the most comprehensive output measure. With 1,000 residents, there are
8,760,000 person-hours to be allocated among all settings;
perhaps 20 percent of these would be spent in the nonhousehold settings included in the extent-of-environment measure
$E = f (N, O, D)$.

Probability density functions might then be defined
for each resident over the N nonhousehold settings and the
300 or so homes. Each life-path would then be seen as
linking nonhousehold behavior settings (and homes) in
sequential time-patterns like beads on a string. All trips
would begin and end in nonhousehold behavior settings and
homes. If some settings became more attractive, their
occupancy times would increase. The occupancy times of
other settings would decrease by offsetting amounts.

Finally, the convergences of residents in the same
settings at the same times implies some sharing of common
experiences and opportunities for cooperation and conflict.
If they occupy the same zones in the shared settings, there

are some commonalities in their life styles (for example, pupils in the same class, members of the same church, and so on).

2.5.   DESCRIBING AN ACTUAL COMMUNITY IN TERMS OF BEHAVIOR SETTINGS, I: AUTHORITY SYSTEMS, OCCUPANCY TIMES, AND INHABITANT-SETTING INTERSECTIONS

The next three tables are based on Barker's survey of the nonhousehold behavior settings of Midwest over a twelve month period in 1963-64. Midwest and its trade area (in Northeastern Kansas) had a total population of about 1680, of which 830 resided in the town itself. Of the other residents of the trade area, about three-fifths lived on farms and two-fifths in houses having no current connection with agriculture; both groups were distributed over the countryside within a 5-mile radius of Midwest. Farms were of the Corn Belt type, emphasizing corn, hogs, cattle feeding, and milk production; farm population density was similar to that in Iowa and other major Corn Belt states to the east.

Table 2.1 presents occupancy times by town residents (Town OT), by nonresidents, and by both groups combined (Total OT). Midwest's being a county seat accounts for the relatively large extent of the government authority system, at 16.4 percent of total occupancy time in person-hours. Private enterprise settings absorb the largest block of time, 39.0 percent, but the school settings take up nearly as much (34.6 percent); voluntary association and church settings account for the rest at 6.3 and 3.7 percent respectively.

The total number of nonhousehold behavior settings is 884. Settings with the same program belong to the same genotype; for example, an array of three grocery stores, five eating places, and four gasoline service stations involves only three genotypes. Thus, the number of genotypes may be used to measure the variety of the town's environment.

The zone 6 leader of a behavior setting often carries the title of the genotype: Banker (Genotype 15, Banks); barber (Genotype 16, Barber Shops); and attorney (Genotype 9, Attorneys Offices). In many cases these leaders have received formal training to learn the genotype's program and passed examinations to prove they knew it. Hence, many

Table 2.1.   Person-Hours of Occupancy Time in Behavior Settings, by
       Authority System, Midwest, Kansas, 1963-64

Authority system	Number of settings	Occupancy time: person-hours			Percent by town residents
		Total	By town residents	By non-residents	
Private enterprise	132	734,183	531,555	202,628	72.4
Government	114	308,075	186,896	121,179	60.7
School	233	650,124	310,516	339,608	47.8
Church	193	69,753	33,173	36,580	47.6
Voluntary association	212	118,595	62,994	55,601	53.1
Total	884	1,880,730	1,125,134	755,596	59.8
		Percentages			
Private enterprise	14.9	39.0	47.2	26.8	——
Government	12.9	16.4	16.6	16.0	——
School	26.4	34.6	27.6	44.9	——
Church	21.8	3.7	2.9	4.8	——
Voluntary association	24.0	6.3	5.6	7.4	——
Total	100.0	100.0	100.0	100.0	——

       Source: Compiled and reconstructed from various tables in Roger G.
Barker and Phil Schoggen, Qualities of Community Life, San Francisco,
Jossey-Bass, 1973.

of Barker's genotypes have the built-in stability of the
American occupational structure and translate readily into
categories used in published data systems; this compatibil-
ity is the more impressive for being unpremeditated on
Barker's part.   Barker classified Midwest's 884 behavior
settings into 198 genotypes.

       Barker and Schoggen (1973) also provide some measures
of the extent of participation in the operating and leadership functions (zones 4, 5, and 6) of Midwest's behavior
settings.   If all of the 884 behavior settings were operating at the same moment, a total of 10,220 persons would be
needed to staff all of their zone 4, 5, and 6 positions,
each of which constitutes a habitat-claim for an operative
(see Table 2.2).   If the same habitat-claim were operated
by two or more different persons during the year, it would
give rise to two or more claim-operations, one by each of
the persons involved.

       For the town as a whole, Barker and Schoggen also
provide two other measures: leader acts, which are claim-
operations performed in zones 6 (sole leader) and 5 (joint
leaders) of behavior settings, and inhabitant-setting
intersections (ISI).   An ISI involves an individual's
occupying any zone of a specified behavior setting at least
once during the year.   Claim-operations are a subset of the

Table 2.2. Habitat-Claims and Claim-Operations in Behavior Settings, by
Authority System, Midwest, Kansas, 1963-64

Authority system	Habitat claims for operatives	Claim-operations Total	By town residents	By non- residents	Percent by town residents
Private enterprise	450	694	439	255	63.3
Government	740	1,306	453	853	34.7
School	3,999	5,316	2,149	3,167	40.4
Church	1,682	2,581	1,289	1,292	49.9
Voluntary association	3,349	4,352	2,312	2,040	53.1
Total	10,220	14,249	6,642	7,607	63.3

Source: Compiled and reconstructed from various tables in Roger G.
Barker and Phil Schoggen, Qualities of Community Life, San Francisco,
Jossey-Bass, 1973.

ISI and leader acts are a subset of claim-operations; these
three measures may be summarized as shown in Table 2.3.

On a per capita basis, the town's 830 residents accounted for 61.22 ISIs (50,809/830) consisting of 1.79
leader acts, 6.22 other claim-operations, and 53.21 other
ISIs in zone 3 (customers, pupils), zone 2 (audiences,
spectators), and zone 1 (onlookers). In terms of life-
paths linking successive behavior settings, the average
life-path intersected 61 different nonhousehold settings
during the survey year. This implies a high degree of
selectivity of people for behavior settings and vice versa,
because on the average a resident entered only 100(61/884)
or 6.9 percent of the available settings. Some reasons
are obvious, e.g., a certain school class is restricted to
a certain age group. Other reasons are less so and include customer loyalty, church affiliation, or role expectations. Barker and Schoggen (1973, pp. 385-97) present
measures of various aspects of selectivity in a chapter on
"biases between differential habitats and inhabitant subgroups."

2.6. THE IMPORTANCE OF SCHOOLS, CHURCHES, AND VOLUNTARY
ASSOCIATIONS IN PROVIDING OPPORTUNITIES FOR
LEADERSHIP, SERVICE, AND SOCIAL PARTICIPATION

Assigning weights to the various measures of community
participation and integration is not attempted here. The
schools, churches, and voluntary associations of Midwest
provide a great many opportunities for children, adoles-

Table 2.3. Inhabitant-Setting Intersections, by Zones Within Behavior
      Settings, Midwest, Kansas, 1963-64

| Measure | Inhabitant-setting intersections | | | Percent by town residents |
	Total	By town residents	By non-residents	
Leader acts (zones 5 and 6)	2,104	1,482	622	70.4
Other claim-operations (zone 4)	12,145	5,160	6,985	42.5
Total claim-operations (zones 4, 5, and 6)	14,249	6,642	7,607	46.6
Other inhabitant-setting intersections (zones 3, 2, and 1)	115,831	44,167	71,664	38.1
Total inhabitant-setting intersections, all zones	130,080	50,809	79,271	39.1

     Source: Compiled and reconstructed from various tables in Roger G.
Barker and Phil Schoggen, Qualities of Community Life, San Francisco,
Jossey-Bass, 1973.

cents, and retired people to participate in the leadership
and implementation of behavior settings approved by the
community; these three authority systems accounted for 88.4
percent of all habitat-claims for operatives and 86.0 percent of all claim-operations. A minute percentage of these
claim-operations was performed by paid professionals
(teachers, coaches, ministers) and the rest by amateurs.

     Nonresidents contributed slightly more than half of
the Total OT of schools and churches in Midwest and only
slightly less than half of the Total OT of voluntary associations. Apparently the attendance and membership areas
of these three authority systems were virtually coextensive
and contained about the same number of residents in the
open country as in the town. These same open-country residents likely accounted as customers for about half of the
retail sales and personal services of Midwest's private
enterprises; a large part of the occupancy time of private
enterprises attributed to town residents reflected their
roles as proprietors and employees.

2.7. TOWN AND TRADE AREA AS A COMMUNITY: IMPLICATIONS OF
      RELATIVE COMPLETENESS AND CLOSURE FOR SOCIAL SYSTEM
      ACCOUNTS

As a full convenience trade center (see Chapter 7) with an
elementary school, a high school, three or four churches,

and a number of voluntary associations (not to mention the county courthouse), Midwest and about 50 square miles of the countryside surrounding it formed a relatively complete and self-contained community. If each ISI were viewed as a line on a large map connecting a particular individual to one of the town's behavior settings, the array of settings connected to an open-country resident probably would be nearly identical with the array connected to a town resident of the same age and sex. Beyond a certain radius, very few country residents would be connected with Midwest's behavior settings; rather, they would be connected with similar arrays of settings in other towns ten miles or so from Midwest.

A community with this degree of completeness and closure is the smallest territorial unit for which a complete set of social accounts might be justified. If Midwest lost its high school, over 20 percent of the total occupancy time contributed by nonresidents would be diverted to another location; if it also lost its elementary school, another 20 or 25 percent of nonresident OT would be diverted. The resulting travel patterns of open-country residents to new consolidated schools might also encourage shopping and recreation at a center or centers other than Midwest.

Although Barker did not survey the households of Midwest in detail, he was clear on the points that household activities could also be partitioned into behavior settings and that his approach lent itself to an exhaustive accounting for the living-time of Midwest's residents. Thus, in Barker and Wright (1955, p. 84) he noted that 2030 behavior settings were identified in Midwest during July 1, 1951 – June 30, 1952 and that 1445 of them were located in the homes of the town; the other 585 were found in its more public behavior areas. Further, in Barker and Wright (1955, pp. 97-98) he observed that Midwesterners during the survey year spent 5,130,000 hours in family settings, 1,030,658 hours in community settings, and only 330,620 hours in settings outside the corporate limits of the town. The corporate limits included something less than 500 acres--perhaps two-thirds of a square mile.

2.8. DESCRIBING AN ACTUAL COMMUNITY IN TERMS OF BEHAVIOR
      SETTINGS, II: GENOTYPES, PROGRAMS, ACTION PATTERNS,
      AND BEHAVIOR MECHANISMS.

The figures in Tables 2.1 through 2.3 are extremely heterogeneous aggregates;   the real town of Midwest consists of
individual behavior settings and can be understood clearly
and efficiently in terms of genotypes.

Table 2.4 reproduces the first of seven pages of the
table in which Barker (1968, pp. 110-116) reports some of
his 1963-64 measures for each of the 198 genotypes.   We
defined number (N), occurrence (O), and duration (D) in
Section 2.4;   Barker classifies these as 'resource measures' which describe the extent of each genotype as an
environment for human behavior.   His ecological resource
index (ERI) is a weighted combination of N, O, and D.   We
defined Town OT and Total OT in Section 2.5; Barker classifies them as 'output measures.'

We can illustrate the relationships between these
measures with Genotype 15 (Banks).   There is only one bank
in Midwest (N=1).   It was open on 305 different days (O =
305) for a total of 1750 hours (D = 1750); the average
number of hours per day (D/O = 5.73) reflects a six hour
schedule on weekdays and perhaps four and a half hours on
Saturdays.   The ratio of Total OT to D (36,860/1750 =
21.06) implies that the number of persons in the bank at
any given time averaged about 21.

In Appendix 2, pp. 211-228, Barker (1968) presents a
program for each genotype; the program for Genotype 15
(Banks) is as follows:

"Banks. President (6) manages all operations, makes
loans, gives financial advice, provides credit information; vice-president (4) makes loans, sells insur-
ance;   cashier (4) cashes checks, receives deposits,
provides access to safe deposit, keeps records;
clerks (4) engage in office routines; bank examiners
(4) come at intervals to examine the routines, the
assets and liabilities of the bank in relation to
legal standards; customers (3) deposit and withdraw
money, arrange for or pay back loans, seek advice, use
safe deposit boxes, and converse." (p. 212)

The program includes a president, a vice-president, a cashier, an unspecified number of clerks, customers, and an
occasional bank examiner; like most of Barker's programs,
this one makes no reference to onlookers (children or

Table 2.4. Behavior Setting Genotypes of Midwest, 1963–64. Number (N), Occurrence (O), Duration (D), Ecological Resource Index (ERI), Occupancy Time of Town Residents (Town OT), and Occupancy Time of All Inhabitants (Total OT) of Behavior Settings in Each Genotype

No.	Genotype	Resource measures				Output measures	
		N	O	D	ERI	Town OT	Total OT
1.	Abstract and Title Company Offices	1	305	2,500	0.52	4,054	4,606
2.	Agricultural Advisers Offices	1	250	2,040	0.43	5,206	6,559
4.	Agronomy Classes	2	4	13	0.08	72	341
5.	Animal Feed Mills	1	310	3,344	0.62	8,998	16,881
6.	Animal Feed Stores	1	307	2,736	0.55	5,857	8,127
7.	Animal Husbandry Classes	4	6	20	0.16	23	394
8.	Athletic Equipment Rooms	2	265	180	0.26	284	412
9.	Attorneys Offices	4	1,155	7,250	1.72	20,584	23,347
10.	Auction Sales	2	3	14	0.08	485	1,645
11.	Auditing and Investigating Co. Offices	1	250	2,000	0.47	2,320	2,380
12.	Automobile Washing Services	2	3	18	0.08	113	143
13.	Award Ceremonies	3	3	5	0.12	176	283
14.	Bakery Services, to Order	1	50	200	0.09	242	242
15.	Banks	1	305	1,750	0.43	26,499	36,860
16.	Barbershops	2	450	3,600	0.78	2,760	7,601
17.	Baseball Games	16	71	167	0.67	6,781	13,691
18.	Basketball Games	14	124	272	0.64	14,164	36,058
19.	Beauty Shops	1	305	3,329	0.62	13,099	15,549
20.	Billiard Parlors and Taverns	1	308	4,300	0.73	21,330	39,212
22.	Bowling Games, Ten Pins	25	725	3,204	1.77	23,862	41,214
24.	Building, Construction, Repair Services	6	1,135	9,160	2.00	14,155	19,564

Source: First page (p.110) of Table 5.3 in Roger G. Barker, Ecological Psychology, Stanford, California, Stanford University Press, 1968. © 1968 Stanford University Press

friends accompanying customers), but their time is no doubt included in Total OT. The numbers in parentheses are zones.

The average numbers of persons present in typical settings of certain other genotypes in Table 2.4 are 2.1 for barbershops, 3.2 for attorneys' offices, 5.0 for animal feed mills, 9.1 for billiard parlors and taverns, and 132.6 for basketball games--all calculated as ratios of Total OT to D (duration).

Other attributes of behavior settings to which Barker gives special attention are action patterns and behavior mechanisms. In each setting, each of these attributes is rated from zero (the attribute is not present at all) to a maximum of 10. Table 2.5 lists Barker's ratings for two behavior settings, (1) High School Boys Basketball Game and (2) Household Auction Sale.

The action patterns with high ratings correspond to the purposes the setting is designed to serve; for the basketball game these are recreation (8) and social contact (6); for the auction sale they are buying and selling (7) and gainful employment (6). Other action patterns are present in the basketball game setting but not prominent: a little buying and selling of soft drinks and popcorn and the associated eating and drinking; a little teaching and learning of basketball plays and rules; some appreciation and evaluation of the basketball players as healthy people and of the attractive uniforms of players and cheerleaders; a little gainful employment for the coaches and referees; government marginally represented through a recent fire-safety inspection or perhaps a sales tax on the admission tickets. The auction sale shows a higher-than-expected rating (5) on social contact and a rating of (3) on recreation, but it was held outdoors in a residential neighbor-hood on a nice Saturday afternoon during summer vacation.

Except under unusual circumstances, a setting's maximum rating on any action pattern is 9. This rating would require that the action pattern be involved in at least 81 percent of the setting's Total OT (5 points); that more than half of the occupancy time of the setting be devoted to appreciation or evaluation of the action pattern (2 points); and that more than half of the occupancy time also be devoted to explicit learning and teaching of the action pattern (2 points). The three subscale activities-- participation, appreciation or evaluation, teaching and learning--can go on simultaneously so no inconsistency is to be inferred from the fact that the sum of the three occupancy-time requirements exceeds Total OT. The basket-ball game's rating of 8 on recreation is just one point short of the effective maximum of 9.[1]

Behavior mechanisms are observable activities of people in the setting. A rating of 10 requires that the mechanism be involved in at least 90 percent of the Total OT of the setting (4 points); that its maximal normal tempo when it occurs be near the physiological limit (3 points); and that the maximal normal energy (intensity) with which it is exerted be near the physiological limit (3 points). In the basketball game setting, the spectators account for

Table 2.5. Ratings of Two Behavior Settings on Action Patterns
            and Behavior Mechanisms, Midwest, Kansas, 1963-64

| Behavior setting attributes | Ratings of behavior setting attributes (minimum, zero, maximum, 10): | |
	High school boys basketball game	Household auction sale
Action patterns:		
Aesthetics	0	3
Business		
(buying and selling)	1	7
Education	1	0
Government	1	0
Nutrition	1	2
Personal appearance	2	1
Physical health	2	0
Professional involvement		
(gainful employment)	1	6
Recreation	8	3
Religion	0	0
Social contact	6	5
Behavior mechanisms:		
Affective behavior	9	4
Gross motor activity	7	6
Manipulation		
(use of the hands)	7	3
Talking	9	7
Thinking	4	6

Source: Compiled from Figures 5.1 (p.99) and 5.2 (p.101) of
Roger G. Barker, Ecological Psychology, Stanford, California,
Stanford University Press, 1968.

the great majority of Total OT; they yell and behave emo-
tionally at near-maximum tempo and intensity, giving the
setting ratings of 9 on talking and affective behavior; if
the players and referees behaved like the spectators, these
ratings would rise to 10!

Only the players engage significantly in gross motor
activity (running, jumping, dodging), and this mechanism is
rated on tempo and intensity only while it is being employed. The players are rated 3 on tempo and 3 on intensity,
and these ratings are applied to the setting as a whole;
they account for 6 points of the setting's rating of 7 on
gross motor activity. On the participation subscale, the
players account for a small percentage of total occupancy

time--only enough to give the setting a single point for
participation in gross motor activity. Precisely the same
considerations lead to the setting's rating of 7 on manipulation or use of the hands.

At the auction sale, the auctioneer talks loudly and
fast (talking rated 7); decisions are made quickly (thinking rated 6); and there is a good deal of gross motor activity (rated 6) as purchasers remove household appliances
and pieces of furniture and load them into cars and pickup
trucks.

Table 2.6 throws additional light on action patterns
as expressions of the purposes for which settings are designed. The primary habitat of an action pattern is the
array of settings in which that pattern occurs during more
than 80 percent of the total occupancy time. Basic data on
N, O, D and some derivative measures for these primary
habitats are shown in Table 2.7. In Table 2.6 the percents
of each primary habitat controlled by the various authority
systems are based on 'centiurbs' (weighted combinations of
N, O, and D) but they would not be greatly different if
based on Total OTs.

In 1963-64, churches controlled 98.4 percent of the
primary habitat of 'religion'; private enterprises 90.9
percent of that of 'business'; government officials 74.7
percent of that of 'government'; and the school board 58.8
percent of that of 'education.' Churches are extensively
involved in the action pattern 'education;' the subject
matter is, of course, primarily religious. The county
extension service accounts for most of the government authority systems's involvement in 'education'. The action
pattern 'government' is prominent in several of Midwest's
private enterprises, most notably in the four attorneys'
offices; civics or government courses are taught by the
schools. The primary habitat of 'professional involvement'
roughly parallels that of gainful employment, with 55.6
percent controlled by private enterprises, 26.1 percent by
the school board, 17.0 percent by government units, 0.9
percent by churches, and 0.4 percent by voluntary associations.

Relative to their Total OTs (Table 2.8), churches are
long on 'aesthetics' and voluntary associations are long on
'recreation.' Private enterprises dominate the action
patterns 'personal appearance' and 'nutrition' and schools
the action pattern 'physical health.'

Table 2.6. Primary Habitats of Action Patterns and Behavior Mechanisms in
    Midwest, 1963-64:   Percents Controlled by Each of the Authority Systems

Primary habitat of specified attribute	Percent of primary habitat controlled by:				
	Church	Government	Private enterprise	School	Voluntary association
Action patterns:					
Aesthetics	26.6	7.7	15.6	43.4	6.7
Business					
(buying and selling)	0.0	5.3	90.9	2.9	0.9
Education	26.4	9.5	3.8	58.8	1.6
Government	0.0	74.7	14.5	10.2	0.6
Nutrition	6.1	7.4	64.2	12.6	9.6
Personal appearance	2.8	5.8	78.7	8.5	4.2
Physical health	0.0	1.8	21.3	71.3	5.6
Professional involvement					
(gainful employment)	0.9	17.0	55.6	26.1	0.4
Recreation	7.4	3.3	16.2	28.2	44.9
Religion	98.4	0.0	0.0	1.1	0.5
Social contact	n.a.	n.a.	n.a.	n.a.	n.a.
Behavior mechanisms:					
Affective behavior	16.3	13.6	5.3	48.1	16.7
Gross motor activity	2.4	7.6	60.0	21.0	9.0
Manipulation					
(use of the hands)	1.3	7.6	74.8	12.9	3.3
Talking	15.9	3.4	13.4	44.1	23.3

    Source: Compiled and reconstructed from various tables in Roger G. Barker
and Phil Schoggen, Qualities of Community Life, San Francisco, Jossey-Bass,
1973.

     Less need be said about the primary habitats of behav-
ior mechanisms. The private enterprises of Midwest are
long on gross motor activity and use of the hands, and
short on talking and affective behavior; churches, voluntary associations, and schools are just the opposite.
Midwest's high school sponsored athletic competitions and
cultural programs which attracted hundreds of spectators;
the high school and elementary school together controlled
28.2 and 43.4 percent of the respective primary habitats of
'recreation' and 'aesthetics' and a great deal of affective
behavior and talking was associated with those action patterns.

2.9.   THE SIGNIFICANCE OF TIME-ALLOCATIONS AMONG BEHAVIOR SETTINGS AND SOME COMMENTS ON BARKER'S TERMINOLOGY

The immediate object of economic data systems and economic
accounts is description. The same is true of social data
systems and time-use accounts based on behavior settings.

Table 2.7. Primary Habitats of Action Patterns and Behavior Mechanisms in Midwest, 1963-64: Basic Data on Number, Occurrence, and Duration of Behavior Settings

Primary habitat of specified attribute	Number of settings N	Setting-Days (occurrences) O	Setting-hours (duration) D	Occurrences per setting, days per year O/N	Duration per setting, hours per year D/N	Duration per occurrence, hours per day D/O
Action patterns:						
Aesthetics	75	2,123	3,514	28.3	46.8	1.66
Business	63	10,028	82,570	159.2	1,310.6	8.23
Education	144	10,687	27,230	74.2	189.1	2.55
Government	69	8,638	59,731	215.1	865.7	6.92
Nutrition	52	3,184	26,352	61.2	506.8	8.28
Personal appearance	23	1,610	13,176	70.0	572.9	8.18
Physical health	20	2,342	3,514	117.1	175.7	1.50
Professional involvement	297	43,920	263,520	147.9	887.3	6.00
Recreation	207	3,989	17,568	19.3	84.9	4.40
Religion	137	3,221	3,514	23.5	25.6	1.09
Social contact	754	28,987	120,341	38.4	159.6	4.15
Behavior mechanisms:						
Affective behavior	184	6,625	13,176	36.0	71.6	1.99
Gross motor activity	181	17,458	93,110	96.4	514.4	5.33
Manipulation	164	17,934	115,949	109.4	707.0	6.46
Talking	181	4,648	12,298	25.7	67.9	2.65

Source: Compiled and reconstructed from various tables in Roger G. Barker and Phil Schoggen, Qualities of Community Life, San Francisco, Jossey-Bass, 1973.

Table 2.8. Person-Hours of Behavior Output of the Primary Habitats of Action Patterns, Behavior Mechanisms, and Authority Systems, Midwest, 1963-64: Output via All Inhabitants and Town Inhabitants, Total and Per Behavior Setting

Primary habitat of specified attribute	Person-hours of behavior output via:		Person-hours per behavior setting via:		Person-hours as percent of town total via:	
	All inhab-itants (GBP) = Total OT	Town inhab-itants (TBP) = Town OT	All inhab-itants, Total OT/N	Town in-habitants, Town OT/N	All inhabitants = 100GBP/1880730	Town inhabitants = 100TBP/1125134
Action patterns:						
Aesthetics	71,696	38,806	956	517	3.8	3.4
Business	406,625	298,411	6,454	4,737	21.6	26.5
Education	443,673	211,174	3,081	1,466	23.6	18.8
Government	218,643	122,524	3,169	1,776	11.6	10.9
Nutrition	229,644	176,492	4,416	3,394	12.2	15.7
Personal appearance	52,982	35,895	2,304	1,561	2.8	3.2
Physical health	45,298	19,720	2,265	986	2.4	1.7
Professional involvement	1,566,686	967,858	5,275	3,259	83.3	86.0
Recreation	262,147	138,586	1,266	700	13.9	12.3
Religion	54,801	26,839	400	196	2.9	2.4
Social contact	1,271,494	706,402	1,686	937	67.6	62.8
Behavior mechanisms:						
Affective behavior	265,241	120,236	1,442	653	14.1	10.7
Gross motor activity	543,710	330,440	3,004	1,826	28.9	29.4
Manipulation	630,136	443,757	3,842	2,645	33.5	38.5
Talking	263,220	128,253	1,454	709	14.0	11.4
Authority systems:						
Church	69,753	33,173	361	361	3.7	2.9
Government	308,075	186,896	2,702	1,639	16.4	16.6
Private enterprise	734,183	531,555	5,562	4,027	39.0	47.2
School	650,124	310,516	2,790	1,333	34.6	27.6
Voluntary association	118,595	62,994	559	297	6.3	5.6
Town (Total, 5 authority systems):	1,880,730	1,125,134	2,128	1,273	100.0	100.0

Source: Compiled and calculated from various tables in Roger G. Barker and Phil Schoggen, Qualities of Community Life, San Francisco, Jossey-Bass, 1973.

Once developed, economic data systems and accounts found many uses, some suggested by formal theories, some by empirical relationships, and some by both. We believe the same will be true of the social data systems and accounts we are recommending.

In working out the methodology of behavior setting surveys Barker had to develop many new concepts, and the new concepts required new names. He was very much aware of the community studies that had been made by sociologists and anthropologists, but they had been looking for phenomena they regarded as important within the conceptual frameworks of their own disciplines.

Barker had done brilliant work in experimental psychology in association with Kurt Lewin. His own objective in studying Midwest was to add an ecological dimension to psychology--that is, to observe under 'field conditions', in the everyday lives of normal people, the phenomena he and many other experimental psychologists had studied under carefully controlled laboratory conditions. The office of his research group in Midwest was called the Midwest Psychological Field Station. The subtitle of his (and Herbert F. Wright's) 1955 book, Midwest and Its Children, was "the psychological ecology of an American town." At least until 1968, Barker called his field of study 'ecological psychology' and addressed his books and articles to his fellow psychologists.

In his 1969 article 'Wanted: An Eco-Behavioral Science', Barker recognized the need for "an eco-behavioral science, independent of psychology" which would make field studies of a wider range of phenomena and adapt methods from other social and ecological sciences. Our present book is in the spirit of eco-behavioral science, but some of the terminology and rating scales we have perforce reported in Chapter 2, based on Barker's 1963-64 survey, may be more appropriate to his earlier conception of his work as a branch of psychology.

In our remaining chapters, we will be relating Barker's concepts to various official data systems and in most cases using the terms familiar to users of those systems. However, the development of a simple, clear, and widely accepted terminology will be of some importance in extending the usefulness of social system accounts.

NOTE

1.   A restaurant in which at least 81 percent of Total OT was devoted to serving and eating food within the setting and at least 1 percent was spent preparing food for custom- ers to take home would get the maximum rating of 5 points for participating in 'nutrition' and one point for supply- ing 'nutrition' to other settings.   If the restaurant also scored 2 points each on appreciation or evaluation and teaching and learning, it would get an overall rating of 10 on the action pattern 'nutrition.'   Conversely, a grocery store could get the maximum rating of 5 points for supply- ing 'nutrition' to other settings and one point for partic- ipating in 'nutrition' if at least 1 percent of Total OT was spent in eating food on the premises.   But the sum of the ratings on participating and supplying can never exceed 6.

CHAPTER 3

BEHAVIOR SETTINGS
AND OBJECTIVE SOCIAL INDICATORS

Chapter 2 defined many behavior setting concepts and used
them to describe a wide range of human activities in the
town of Midwest. In doing so, it presented eight tables of
empirical results from an actual survey of the behavior
settings of Midwest during a twelve-month period in 1963-
64.

The present chapter relates behavior setting concepts
in a preliminary way to the OECD List of Social Indicators
(published in 1982) and to the U.S. Bureau of Economic
Analysis (BEA) estimates of stocks of physical capital and
consumer durable goods (published in 1981). The OECD list
will shape the development of objective social indicators
in many countries during the decade ahead; most of these
indicators are now, or will soon become, components of the
official data systems of OECD countries. The BEA series
relate only to the United States and result from the research efforts (often interrupted) of successive economists
over a period of decades. Their development was wholly
independent of the social indicators movement, but the BEA
estimates are potentially of great importance for a system
of social accounts based on behavior settings.

Our discussion in Chapter 3 will be verbal and conceptual. Several tables based on the BEA series will be presented and discussed in Chapter 6.

Official data systems are oriented to social concerns.
Their scope has been extended as new concerns have emerged
and as citizens have come to believe that their governments
could and should deal with them. In the United States, the
catastrophic depression of 1929-33 caused government to
accept some responsibility for the aggregative performance
of the economy and for providing a minimum level of social
security for the aged, the disabled, and other disadvan-
taged groups. Economic data systems were rapidly extended
and improved; Keynes' (1936) macroeconomic theory, Kuznets'
(1937) national income and product accounts, Tinbergen's
(1939) national econometric models, and Leontief's (1936)

national input-output matrices all reinforced the view that the economy was indeed a system. Since World War II economic data systems and models have been further expanded and integrated.

As a discipline, economics was fortified by theories of the behaviors of profit-maximizing firms and utility-maximizing consumers and of the general equilibrium to which such behaviors could lead in a hypothetical economy. The variables called for by these theories—prices and quantities of commodities, money incomes of consumers, revenues and costs of firms—were observable in principle and increasingly so in fact as data systems developed.

Sociology had its share of great theorists and it could claim comprehensiveness for its view of human societies, something economics could not. However, its very comprehensiveness was for long an insuperable obstacle to the specification of its data needs and the establishment of official data systems to meet them.

In the United States, this situation changed dramatically in the 1960s as government assumed broader responsibilities for health maintenance, medical care, education, the rights of women and minorities, urban renewal, community development, and the attempted elimination of poverty-—in brief, for a 'Great Society'. The founders of the social indicators movement in the U.S. were quick to see the implications of these commitments for official data systems. Their objectives, as stated in the proposed 'Full Opportunity and Social Accounting Act of 1967', included an annual social report of the president, a council of social advisers to aid in preparing the report, and a joint committee (of Congress) on the social report. If created, these institutions would have encountered many data problems and might have enlisted the best efforts of government and university statisticians in developing solutions for them.

The Act was not passed and improvements came more slowly. A good deal of the published work done in the name of 'social indicators' during the late 1960s and early 1970s was undisciplined and eclectic. Sophisticated social scientists and government statisticians avoided publicity during these years and concentrated on the development of data systems which would address the new social concerns while maintaining high standards of statistical quality. In particular, the OECD sponsored a Social Indicators Program which began in 1970 and published a List of Social

Concerns Common to Most OECD Countries in 1973. Several
years of complex developmental work ensued on designing
indicators to measure these concerns. The OECD List of
Social Indicators (1982) is the result.

3.1. THE OECD LIST OF SOCIAL INDICATORS

The OECD List of Social Indicators is reproduced in Table
3.1. It includes 33 specific indicators grouped under
eight major headings: health; education and learning;
employment and quality of working life; time and leisure;
command over goods and services; physical environment;
social environment; and personal safety. We believe all
the objective indicators in the OECD List can be picked up
and/or incorporated in social accounts based on behavior
settings.
    The 1982 OECD report recommends that five standard
disaggregations be used in presenting nearly all indicators: age, sex, household type, socioeconomic status, and
community size. It suggests optional 'standard' disaggregations by ethnic group and citizenship in countries where
these distinctions are relevant and also by region (i.e. by
geographical location within a country) according to the
classifications customary in each country.
    The OECD report lists other disaggregations applicable
to several indicators: branch of economic activity, occupation, type of activity, working hours, level of education, tenure status (home owner versus tenant), and age of
dwelling. It states that the breakdown of branch of economic activity should be based on the International Standard Industrial Classification (ISIC) codes at the two digit
level; that of occupation should follow the International
Standard Classification of Occupations (ISCO) at the two
digit level, with three digits used where possible in
coding occupational groups with a wide range of occupations
such as managers; and that of levels of education should
follow the International Standard Classification of Education (ISCED) which defines seven levels of education plus a
residual category. The corresponding classifications used
in the United States are closely comparable to the international ones cited.
    The OECD List of Social Indicators is still, quite
properly and explicitly, in the tradition of social indicators rather than social accounts. Each of its 33

Table 3.1. The OECD List of Social Indicators

Social concern	Indicator
HEALTH	
Length of Life	– Life Expectancy
	– Perinatal Mortality Rate
Healthfulness of Life	– Short-term Disability
	– Long-term Disability
EDUCATION AND LEARNING	
Use of Educational Facilities	– Regular Education Experience
	– Adult Education
Learning	– Literacy Rate
EMPLOYMENT AND QUALITY OF	
WORKING LIFE	
Availability of Employment	– Unemployment Rate
	– Involuntary Part-time Work
	– Discouraged Workers
Quality of Working Life	– Average Working Hours
	– Travel Time to Work
	– Paid Annual Leave
	– Atypical Work Schedule
	– Distribution of Earnings
	– Fatal Occupational Injuries
	– Work Environment Nuisances
TIME AND LEISURE	
Use of Time	– Free Time
	– Free Time Activities
COMMAND OVER GOODS AND SERVICES	
Income	– Distribution of Income
	– Low Income
	– Material Deprivation
Wealth	– Distribution of Wealth
PHYSICAL ENVIRONMENT	
Housing Conditions	– Indoor Dwelling Space
	– Access to Outdoor Space
	– Basic Amenities
Accessibility to Services	– Proximity of Selected Services
Environmental Nuisances	– Exposure to Air Pollutants
	– Exposure to Noise
SOCIAL ENVIRONMENT	
Social Attachment	– Suicide Rate
PERSONAL SAFETY	
Exposure to Risk	– Fatal Injuries
	– Serious Injuries
Perceived Threat	– Fear for Personal Safety

Source: Organization for Economic Cooperation and
Development, 1982, The OECD List of Social Indicators (Paris:
OECD), p. 13.

indicators is treated as a distinct entity. Even within
groups (e.g. health), the various indicators involve different units of measure and there is no obvious way to
assign 'relative importance' weights to these units.
Similarly, there is no obvious way to weight the relative
importances of the eight major groups or social concerns.
   The OECD List, recommended for implementation by OECD
member countries as their circumstances permit, includes
"systematically selected statistical measures of individual
well-being which can be influenced by social policies and
community actions. Over time they provide a picture of
some of the significant ways in which the societies of
Member countries are changing." (p. 12).
   The list is intended to be comprehensive in coverage.
It includes very few perceptual or subjective indicators;
the majority are objective measures verifiable in fact or
in principle by trained observers and collected or collect-
ible in official reporting systems, censuses, and sample
surveys. The one clearly subjective indicator 'perceived
threat, or fear for personal safety' could also be collected and interpreted in terms of the time-and-place settings
in which the threat is perceived to be concentrated.

3.2. A FRAMEWORK FOR DISCUSSING THE RELATIONSHIP OF
     INDIVIDUAL WELL-BEING TO BEHAVIOR SETTINGS, STOCKS OF
     PHYSICAL CAPITAL, AND OBJECTIVE SOCIAL INDICATORS

We assume for purposes of classification that an individual's well-being can be increased (a) by improving his
behavioral capacities (e.g., health, skills); (b) by improving some of the behavior settings in which he partici-
pates so that he receives greater rewards per hour of occupancy time in those settings; and (c) by improving his
allocation of time among behavior settings in favor of
those which are more rewarding per hour of occupancy time.
By 'improving' we mean changes which would generally be so
regarded in OECD countries and in applications of the OECD
list of indicators.
   We assume further that the three types of improvements
can be associated with different components of the Fox-van
Moeseke (1973) model. In this model, an individual tries
to choose an optimal life style for the coming year within
the limits of the array of behavior settings available and
of his personal resources (time, health, skills, income

from property and transfer payments, and others). In mathematical programming terms, his problem is to:

$$\text{Maximize } \underline{u}(\underline{x}), \text{ subject to } \underline{Ax} \leq \underline{b}, \ \underline{x} \geq \underline{0}$$

where $\underline{u}(\underline{x})$, the individual's utility function, measures the level of satisfaction he attains; $\underline{x}$ is a vector consisting of the amounts of his time he spends in each of the $\underline{n}$ available settings; $\underline{b}$ is a vector of the maximum amounts of $\underline{m}$ personal resources he can expend in behavior settings during the year; and $\underline{A}$ is a matrix with one column for each of the $\underline{n}$ settings and one row for each of the $\underline{m}$ resources-- its typical element, $\underline{a}_{ij}$, is the amount of his $\underline{i}$th resource absorbed per unit of time spent in the $\underline{j}$th setting. We said, perhaps too succinctly, that "the matrices $\underline{x}$, $\underline{A}$, $\underline{b}$ express the individual's life style, environment, and endowment, respectively" (p. 26).

The original statement of the Fox-van Moeseke model was mathematically rigorous, but it involved some assumptions which are too specialized and technical for our present purpose. In the ensuing discussion, we will assume that $\underline{b}$ is simply a logical category containing all relevant attributes of individuals and that $\underline{A}$ is simply a logical category containing all relevant attributes of the environments in which they live and work; $\underline{x}$ is simply a set of time segments adding up to 8760 hours a year for any person. We will no longer treat $\underline{b}$, $\underline{A}$, and $\underline{x}$ as connected by formal mathematical relationships.

3.3. THE RELEVANCE OF STOCKS OF PHYSICAL CAPITAL TO BEHAVIOR SETTINGS AND INDIVIDUAL WELL-BEING

Our extended concept of the environment $\underline{A}$ permits us to take explicit account of the physical aspects of behavior settings (buildings, partitions, furnishings, machines, appliances, utensils, and the like) which are needed to implement their programs. Differences in output per worker in private enterprise settings often depend on the types of equipment used; good lighting, acoustics, and air conditioning increase worker satisfaction (a legitimate social system output) even when they do not demonstrably increase economic outputs. Similar considerations apply to settings in the nonmarket authority systems: households, schools, churches, voluntary associations, and governments.

Standards of comfort and aesthetic design achieved in
the majority of private homes in a community tend to be
replicated in its schools and churches, in the offices of
white-collar workers in private enterprises and government
agencies, and in the sales or reception areas of retail
stores and service establishments. The same households
that bought goods and services for current consumption also
bought the houses, kitchen appliances, and furnishings that
are included in stocks of residential capital and consumer
durables. As customers, their patronage encouraged retailers to introduce carpeting and air conditioning (indirectly
paid for by customers); as taxpayers, they paid for similar amenities in schools and government offices.

For such reasons, estimates of the constant-dollar
values of physical capital embodied in the circumjacent
milieus and durable behavior objects of behavior settings
should be included in social accounts. The value of physical capital in the forms of streets and sidewalks, public
water supply and sanitary systems, gas and electric utilities, and telephone networks should also be included, as
these are essential to the functioning of most behavior
settings in a modern community. At the national level,
physical capital in the forms of highways, railroads, air-
ports, and associated transportation equipment also belongs
in the accounts.

3.4. THE BUREAU OF ECONOMIC ANALYSIS (BEA) ESTIMATES OF
     STOCKS OF PHYSICAL CAPITAL AND CONSUMER DURABLE GOODS
     IN THE UNITED STATES, 1929-1979

Recently published BEA estimates of stocks of physical
capital in the United States, annually from 1925 through
1979, have been integrated with corresponding items in the
national income and product accounts (NIPA): gross private
domestic fixed investment, by types of buildings, other
structures, and durable equipment; consumer expenditures
for durable goods subdivided into ten categories; and government purchases of structures and equipment, by types of
structures, by level of government (state and local versus
federal), and, at the federal level, by nondefense versus
defense purposes. The stock estimates have been developed
over a period of several decades. Now that they are published, exploratory efforts should be made to relate them
to categories of behavior settings and to disaggregate them

to smaller areas (communities, counties, census tracts, and metropolitan regions) which constitute or contain the ecological environments of their residents. City managers and planners could relate these small-area estimates to still more detailed inventories of structures and behavior settings, the socioeconomic characteristics of neighborhoods, and the prevalence and incidence of health problems, crime rates, and environmental pollution.

Improvements in physical capital are improvements in physical aspects of the environment $\underline{A}$. They increase the flows of rewards received per unit of time spent in certain settings, reduce the flows of contributions required, or reduce the amounts of time that must be spent in bland settings (e.g. streets and sidewalks) while in transit between highly valued ones (e.g. homes, shopping centers, and recreational facilities).

3.5. OECD INDICATORS RELATING ASPECTS OF THE PHYSICAL ENVIRONMENT TO INDIVIDUAL WELL-BEING.

In this section and the two following ones the reader should refer frequently to Table 3.1 and the accompanying text.

Three of the OECD indicators relate to housing conditions: indoor dwelling space (number of persons per room); basic amenities (private kitchens, bathrooms, flush toilets and other features); and access to outdoor space (private or shared gardens, roof gardens, terraces, balconies, nearby parks or plazas). A fourth is based on the proximity of residents, in minutes, to medical emergency services, stores satisfying daily needs, a pre-primary school, a primary school, a sports center where pupils can participate, a post office, and a public transport stop. All these services involve physical capital--structures and equipment.

Two other indicators, exposure to air pollutants and exposure to noise, are to be measured outdoors in residential areas. The equivalent behavior settings in Midwest would be Trafficways (streets and sidewalks) and Home Outdoors. The noise and pollutants are attributes of the physical environments of these settings and hence of the environment $\underline{A}$.

All six of the OECD indicators so far discussed are measurable attributes of the physical environments in which

people live; their levels can be improved only through
operations in and on these environments. A seventh, travel
time to work, is also a fact of the physical environment.
An eighth, work environment nuisances, also involves buildings, equipment, vibration, heat, cold, dust, noise--all
attributes of the physical environment and hence of $\underline{A}$.

3.6. STANDARD DISAGGREGATIONS OF THE OECD INDICATORS AS ATTRIBUTES OF INDIVIDUALS AND ATTRIBUTES OF THE ENVIRONMENT

The standard set of disaggregations recommended by the OECD
includes age, sex, household type, socioeconomic status,
and community size. The first two of these are clearly
part of the individual's endowment--elements of $\underline{b}$. Socioeconomic status and household type may be viewed as $\underline{b}$-ele-
ments shared with other household members, if any; community size should probably be treated as a shared attribute
of some or all behavior settings in communities of that
size, and hence of the environments $\underline{A}$ of those communities.

3.7. COMMENTS ON THE REMAINING OECD INDICATORS

Our comments on OECD indicators other than the eight already mentioned will be suggestive rather than rigorous;
we try to relate them to the logical categories $\underline{b}$ and $\underline{A}$ and
to the time-allocation vectors $\underline{x}$.

3.7.1. Health

Life expectancy would be a $\underline{b}$-element, the same stated number of years expected for all persons identically situated
as to age, sex, and perhaps color or socioeconomic status
if supported by a country's actuarial data. The perinatal
mortality rate might be represented as an attribute ($\underline{b}$-
element) of expectant mothers--a probability, differentiated perhaps by the mothers' ages and socioeconomic statuses, that the pregnancy will result in a stillbirth or
early neonatal death.

Short-term disability is measured by "disability days
per person per year by level of restriction." A disability

day is "any day for which an individual has to cut down on
the things he usually does because of illness or injury."
The effect of the disability is measured by changes in the
person's allocation of time among behavior settings--the
vector x; its cause is a temporary impairment of certain
behavioral capacities in his endowment b. The same comments apply to long-term disability, but the impairment of
capacities and distortion of time-use (life style) are more
persistent.

3.7.2. Education and Learning

Regular education experience is the number of years of
schooling completed by an individual; a b-element, it will
not change unless the individual takes an additional year
or more of formal education. For an individual, the literacy rate is a zero-one element or attribute of b: he has
either achieved "an adequate level of functional literacy"
or he has not. Adult education would be measured by the
amount of time an individual (over a certain age and not in
regular school) spent during the previous year in "organized programs of education;" this would be an element in
his x-vector for the year just past.

3.7.3. Employment and Quality of Working Life

Three of the OECD indicators relate to the availability of
employment. If a worker is unemployed and seeking work, or
is discouraged (wants work but has stopped looking because
he considers that no employment is available to him), or
has only part-time work but is seeking a full-time job, he
is sustaining a major disruption in his life style vector
x with (initially, at least) no impairment in his occupational skills or other behavioral capacities.

Seven indicators relate to quality of working life;
two of these (travel time to work and work environment
nuisances) have already been mentioned. All seven are to
be disaggregated by occupation and industry (i.e. by roles
in work-related behavior settings); the same applies to
workers involuntarily on part-time and to the previous jobs
of currently unemployed or discouraged workers. Occupational skills are, of course, attributes (b-elements) of
persons.

Average working hours (number of hours worked per
week) partitions a person's x-vector between gainful employment and all other activities. An atypical work schedule means that the worker may not be able to participate in
some customary activities (when he is free, the settings
are closed) or to synchronize his participation with that
of family members and friends; his x-vector is 'out-of-
joint.' Paid annual leave means an increase in leisure
time with no reduction in money income. For an individual
worker, earnings (his share of the 'distribution of earnings') are a reward received for, and presumably produced
by, his contributions to the behavior setting or settings
in which he works.

Fatal occupational injuries is a rate per year per
100,000 persons employed. The rates vary over occupations
and industries and are attributes of the work environment
(i.e. attributes of particular kinds of 'habitat-claims' in
particular genotypes of behavior settings) and hence of
A.

3.7.4. Time and Leisure

Free time is the "time left in 24 hours after subtraction
of the other three types of time." These are necessary
time (sleep, meals, personal hygiene and care); contracted
time (paid work, work of family helpers, regular schooling
and occupational training--including associated travel
time); and committed time (house care, care of children,
shopping, care and maintenance of possessions, etc.--in-
cluding associated travel time). On a yearly basis, free
time is simply a certain total number of hours available
for voluntary allocation. Free time activities are the
actual role-and-behavior setting combinations among which
that number of hours is allocated. Illustrative categories
of free time activity which require the active participation of the individual are "activities involving physical
effort (all sports, exercises, promenades, etc.); creative
or artistic activities involving self-expression (art,
drama, etc.); cultural and educational activities; and
organizational activities (including local/civic responsibilities and active participation in religious events,
clubs and associations)." (p. 34).

3.7.5. Command Over Goods and Services

Three indicators are based on income. The income concept
is "disposable income, i.e. post-tax, post-transfer income
from all sources." Rights to income from property and
transfer payments are positive elements in the endowments
b of persons; obligations to pay taxes may be regarded as
negative elements in b. The indicators themselves are
based on the distribution of income among households, but
this goes beyond our present expository purpose. The earnings component of a person's disposable income has already
been described as a reward for his contributions to the
setting in which he is employed.

The wealth concept used in the distribution-of-wealth
indicator is personal net worth; the wealth-holding unit is
the household. The household's wealth includes marketable
assets (financial assets, consumer durables, real estate,
capital of the self-employed members, if any) plus the
capitalized value of pension rights. Wealth, prorated
among the members of the household where appropriate, is
part of their endowments b. (Human capital is excluded
from the OECD wealth concept).

3.7.6. Social Environment

Social attachment is measured by the suicide rate per
100,000 population. Presumably, a specified probability of
self-destruction, actuarially based, would be ascribed (as
a b-element) to all persons identically classified as to
age, sex, household type, and socioeconomic status; if a
person's household type or socioeconomic status changed,
the ascribed probability would change. Suicide rates also
vary by community size; the deviations from national average rates should evidently be attributed to community size
as an aspect of the environment A.

3.7.7. Personal Safety

Fatal injuries (per year per 100,000 persons) are classified by the most important causes: for example, traffic
deaths, fatal occupational injuries, fatal injuries in the
home, homicides, and others. The first three causes imply
that the rates are different in different categories of

behavior settings--trafficways, workplaces, and homes--and
to that extent are attributes of the environment. However,
the rates also differ by age, sex, color, and socioeconomic
status and to that extent are attributes of individuals.
The joint causation would become clearer if the death rate
of each population subgroup from each cause were expressed
as a rate per million hours of occupancy time by that subgroup in settings where that cause was operative. The same
considerations apply to the associated indicator, serious
(but nonfatal) injuries.

The final indicator, fear for personal safety, would
be represented by a person's statement that he or she was
either (1) not afraid, (2) afraid, or (3) very afraid to
walk alone in his or her neighborhood at night. This is a
subjective indicator. Its objective counterpart would
presumably be a set of victimization rates experienced by
persons' of specified age, sex, color, and socioeconomic
status categories while walking alone at night in the
streets of this or similar neighborhoods--per million hours
spent in these circumstances by members of each population
category. But fear would have distorted the actual time-
allocations or life styles ($\underline{x}$-vectors) of many residents
who would enjoy an evening stroll if they perceived the
neighborhood as safe.

3.8. CONCLUDING REMARKS

The well-being of individuals in a society may be increased
by improvements in their behavioral capacities, their environments, and their allocations of time. In Chapter 2 we
pointed out that, in a self-contained community, additions
to behavioral capacities (health, skills, and others) require increases in the levels of activity in the behavior
settings in which these additions are produced; improvements in the environment may require additions to stocks of
physical capital and hence increased levels of activity at
construction sites and in durable goods factories. The
increase in investment-type activities implies changing
allocations of time.

In future years the OECD indicators will no doubt be
incorporated into formal models based on theories derived
from sociology, economics, and perhaps other disciplines.
However, our present concern is to establish firm linkages
between behavior setting concepts and official data

systems.   We consider such linkages with the Standard
Industrial Classification (SIC) system in Chapter 4.

CHAPTER 4

THE CLASSIFICATION OF BEHAVIOR
SETTINGS IN SOCIAL SYSTEM ACCOUNTS

Chapters 4 through 7 deal with problems of classification
in social system accounts. We maintain, with Barker, that
all human behavior occurs in behavior settings and (hence)
that all the living-time of all members of a given society
is spent in them.[1]

A behavior setting is a standing behavior pattern that
is recognized by most members of the society and can be
identified by a name and a descriptive program: grocery
store, bank, high school English class, or whatever. All
settings with the same program belong to the same genotype;
every setting belongs to some genotype. Therefore, the
living-time of all members of the society in a given year
is, in fact or by definition, allocated exhaustively among
genotypes. Chapter 4 is concerned with problems of defining genotypes and of reconciling them with the Standard
Industrial Classification and other familiar systems.

The program of each genotype specifies the roles and
zones (degrees of power) of all types of occupants normally
found in its settings, even including onlookers. The paid
roles, if any, are occupations. People use their behavioral capacities to perform roles in behavior settings; all
living-time is allocated exhaustively among roles. Chapter
5 discusses problems of defining roles and reconciling them
with the Standard Occupational Classification and other
systems.

Each behavior setting has a circumjacent milieu that
marks it off from other settings. Quite commonly, the
circumjacent milieu consists of a physical structure (for
example, walls and an arrangement of furniture and other
objects) designed to enclose and facilitate the behavior.
Each setting also contains some behavior objects (tools,
typewriters, sports equipment, eating utensils, or whatever) which are also required in order to perform the roles
and maintain the standing behavior pattern. Chapter 6
deals with the classification of stocks of physical capital
and consumer durables and possible disaggregations of

48

existing data to correspond with behavior setting genotypes.

Over time, programs, roles, structures, and behavior
objects all evolve and change, some gradually, some
rapidly. New genotypes may be introduced and old ones may
disappear. Units of some genotypes may disappear from
villages and towns while other and larger units flourish in
cities. Chapter 7 considers problems of classifying and
delineating communities and regions in a system of social
accounts based on behavior settings.

The measurement of social change and trends in individual well-being will require simultaneous and continuing
attention to the classification of settings, roles, physical capital, and consumer durables and to the delineation
of communities and regions.

4.1. INTERRELATIONS BETWEEN BEHAVIOR SETTING GENOTYPES AND SOME OTHER PRINCIPLES OF CLASSIFICATION

A classification of human behavior according to genotype
settings will overlap other logical or customary schemes.
We will briefly consider three of these.

4.1.1. Genotypes and Barker's Authority Systems

Table 2.1 shows that the total occupancy time (Total OT) of
Midwest's 884 behavior settings in 1963-64, namely
1,880,730 person-hours, can be allocated exhaustively among
Barker's five nonhousehold authority systems: private
enterprise, government, school, church, and voluntary association. Table 2.4 reproduces the first of seven pages
from Barker's (1968, pp. 110-116) Table 5.3. The complete
table shows the Total OT's of Midwest's 198 genotypes;
these also add up to 1,880,730 person-hours.

It would be convenient for social accounting purposes
if each genotype could be assigned to a single authority
system. This is true (in some cases trivially so) of all
genotypes which, in Midwest, contain only one setting--
since each individual setting belongs unequivocally to one
authority system or another. It is true also that all four
of Midwest's service stations (Genotype 177) belong to the
private enterprise authority system and that all 42 of its
religion classes (Genotype 157) are sponsored by churches.
However, the 103 settings of Genotype 117 (meetings,

business), all conducted in general accordance with
Roberts' Rules of Order, are distributed among all five
authority systems; the 15 settings of Genotype 162 (restaurants and organization dinners for the public) are distributed among four. The elementary school, voluntary associations, and the town of Midwest as a government entity all
sponsor settings of Genotype 17 (baseball games).

This inconvenience is not a serious one. Table 2.1
shows that the 884 individual settings are allocated exhaustively among the authority systems as follows: private
enterprise, 132; government, 114; school, 233; church,
193; and voluntary association, 212. Each setting could be
assigned to the proper element of a matrix with 198 rows
for genotypes and five columns for authority systems.

Barker never collected detailed data for genotypes in
the household authority system. In Barker and Wright
(1955, p. 84), he states that "common varieties of family
behavior settings are Home Meals, Home Indoors, Home Outdoors, Home Bathroom, and Home Festive Occasions." The
time was 1951-52 and the place, of course, Midwest, a town
of single-family dwellings each on its own lot of about
0.25 acres.

If Barker had surveyed households in 1963-64, he presumably would have listed (and written programs for) a few
additional genotypes beyond the 198, and we would need a
sixth column in our assignment matrix to cover the household authority system. It is possible that some settings
in private homes (for example, card parties and dinner
parties not announced in Midwest's weekly newspaper) would
have been assigned to genotypes already included in the
nonhousehold list.

4.1.2. Genotypes and the OECD Categories of Time Use

In Chapter 3, we cited categories of time use mentioned on
page 34 of The OECD List of Social Indicators (1982).
These reflect a growing amount of experience in several
countries with sample surveys of time use in which each
respondent makes a detailed report of his or her activities
during the 24 hours preceding an interview.

OECD (1982, p. 34) distinguishes four broad types of
time use, which we may first try to relate to Barker's
authority systems.

Necessary time includes sleep, meals, personal hygiene and care. Except for meals eaten away from home, these activities belong almost exclusively to the household authority system.

Contracted time includes paid work, work of family helpers, regular schooling and occupational training (including associated travel time). Almost all of these activities are conducted outside the home: gainful employment mainly in private enterprise, government, and school authority systems; educational and occupational training in the school authority system broadly defined.

Committed time includes house care, care of children, shopping, care and maintenance of possessions, etc., along with associated travel time. House care (i.e. housework) is exclusively in the household authority system, along with some of the child care and some of the care and maintenance of possessions. Shopping takes household members as customers (and sometimes as onlookers) into a wide array of private enterprises; the term 'shopping' is often extended to include visits to banks, post offices, and local government offices where various fees or bills are paid and licenses acquired. Care and maintenance of possessions also brings household members into garages, service stations, appliance repair shops, and the like--all or nearly all in the private enterprise authority system.

Free time is what is left of a 24-hour day after subtracting necessary, contracted, and committed time. One categorization of free time activities (not specifically by OECD) consists of passive leisure, active leisure, recreation, and religious and other organizations' activities. The OECD (1982, p. 34) gives illustrative examples of all these types except passive leisure. Nearly all of the behavior settings sponsored by Midwest's churches and voluntary associations would evidently be classed as free time activities.

Passive leisure in the U.S. includes an enormous amount of television viewing, plus much smaller time allocations to reading and listening to radios and record players; passive leisure is nearly all spent at home. Active leisure involves physical activity and/or creative effort: the individual is in zone 4, 5 or 6 of the relevant setting. If these zones are conceded to active leisure, then 'recreation' may be reserved for settings in which the individual is a zone 2 spectator or audience member.

Settings for particular types of active leisure (e.g. swimming, tennis, bowling) may be sponsored by private enterprises, local governments, schools, voluntary associations, and, in some cases, households; the same applies to particular types of recreation.

A time-use diary may be viewed as recording the life-path of an individual during a 24-hour period. He or she intersects a number of different settings belonging to different genotypes and performs a single role in the program of each setting for a certain number of minutes or hours. A random sample of life-paths will tell us a great deal about the experiences of individuals but it may tell us very little about the structures and performance levels of behavior settings.

Conversely, a random sample of behavior settings, each observed and described by Barker's methods, would tell us a great deal about the sizes, programs, and performance levels of settings but very little about the success of individuals in achieving full and rewarding lives. So, the two approaches complement each other and both must be used in creating and maintaining social system accounts.

4.1.3. Genotypes and Industries

The most elaborate framework for classifying human activities in a major sector of the U.S. social system is the Standard Industrial Classification. We will discuss it at some length in Section 4.6. But first we must give some attention to Barker's methods for partitioning the environment of human behavior into genotypes. As a prelude, we consider some possible alternatives to genotypes within Barker's own conceptual framework.

4.2. SHOULD BEHAVIOR SETTINGS BE CLASSIFIED ACCORDING TO THEIR PROFILES OF RATINGS ON ACTION PATTERNS AND BEHAVIOR MECHANISMS?

In Table 2.5 and the adjacent text, we described the profile of ratings for the setting High School Boys Basketball Game on action patterns and behavior mechanisms. Given Barker's method of weighting the participation subscales of players and spectators by (approximately) their proportions of total occupancy time, the ratings on affective behavior, talking, gross motor activity, and manipulation (use of the hands) could not have been higher! The rating on recreation was also at its effective maximum, at least for the spectators, and it is hard to see how the rating on social contact (6) could have been higher unless the spectators had turned their backs on the players and concentrated on talking with each other.

Barker and Schoggen (1973) define the primary habitat of an action pattern as the array of behavior settings in which that pattern occurs during more than 80 percent of Total OT. In all or nearly all cases, this implies a rating of 6 or higher. The same standard is used to define the primary habitat of a behavior mechanism. Patterns and mechanisms with ratings of 6 or more in a setting are called prominent and those with ratings of 1 to 5 secondary; those with ratings of zero are absent.

During 1976-78, Fox took the further step of coding Barker's 1951-52 ratings as '1' for prominent and '0' for not prominent. James R. Prescott then applied cluster analysis techniques to classify the 585 settings into groups which were relatively homogeneous internally and relatively 'distant' from one another; action patterns and behavior mechanisms were used simultaneously in the clustering process.

The resulting groups were difficult to rationalize on a common sense basis. A closer reading of Barker reveals at least one major flaw in our work. Barker says that action patterns are goal-directed: toward education, religion, recreation, social contact, physical health or other objectives. In contrast, behavior mechanisms have no obvious relation to the goal-directedness of settings; gross motor activity is prominent at construction sites and also in basketball games. At best, the behavior mechanisms are means to ends.

An attempt to classify Midwest's behavior settings on the basis only of their prominent action patterns should be more fruitful. Most settings with prominent ratings on 'religion' would belong to the church authority system. A combination of prominent ratings on 'religion' and 'aesthetics' would identify church worship services (Genotype 161) or, on rare occasions, church weddings or funerals. A combination of prominent ratings on 'religion' and 'education' would identify religion classes (Genotype 157) or religion study groups (Genotype 158).

However, Barker's criteria for classifying behavior settings into genotypes are more flexible and sophisticated than those reflected only in prominent action patterns. Barker's genotypes are closely related to occupations and industries and are recognized in the everyday speech and activities of community residents.

4.3.   SHOULD BEHAVIOR SETTINGS BE CLASSIFIED ACCORDING TO THE AGE GROUPS FOR WHICH THEY ARE DESIGNED, THE EXTENT TO WHICH THEIR PERFORMERS ARE PAID PROFESSION-ALS, AND/OR THE DEGREE TO WHICH THEIR AMATEUR PER-FORMERS APPROACH PROFESSIONAL STANDARDS?

Because economic data systems include only gainfully employed persons, the designers of those systems have not had to classify the activities of children and retired persons or to recognize different levels of proficiency among amateur performers. A comprehensive system of social accounts must deal with these things.

Barker's surveys of Midwest are particularly rich in information about the activities of children. In every setting, the occupants are classified into seven age groups: infants (0-1 years), preschool (2-5), younger school (6-8), older school (9-11), adolescents (12-17), adults (18-64) and aged (65 and over). The occupants are also classified by sex and by socioeconomic status. More-over, in each setting, the most central zone penetrated by the members of each of these subgroups is recorded.

Barker's complete data sheet for the high school boys basketball game (Barker 1968, p. 99) is reproduced as Figure 4.1. The maximum penetration ratings show infants only in zone 1 (onlookers); the preschool, younger school, and aged occupants reached zone 2 (spectators); the older school and adolescent groups reached zone 4 (performers, functionaries); and adults reached zone 5 (joint leaders). Females reached zone 4 and males zone 5. The coaches (zone 5) were judged to belong to Barker's Socioeconomic Class II, corresponding to W. L. Warner's (1949) Lower Middle Class. All three of Barker's classes (with Classes I and III corresponding to Warner's Upper Middle and Upper Lower Classes respectively) were represented among the perform-ers.

Many settings in Midwest were designed for specific age groups: a baseball game (league) for boys 8-11,

Name: *High School Boys Basketball Game*		
Genotype # 1-3: 0·1·8 Genotype Commonality # 8: 9		Locus 16: 1
BS # 4-6: 0·0·5 Authority System 13-14: 0·1		No. of Occurr. 17-19: 0·0·8
Genotype Date 7: 3 Class of Authority Systems 15: 4		Survey # 20: 5

Occupancy Time of Town Subgroups				Max. Penetration of Subgroups		ACTION PATTERN RATINGS	
Group	No. P	Hours	OT Code	Group			
Inf	3	24	21-22: 0·4	Inf	21: 1	Aes:	53: 0
Presch	12	54	23-24: 0·5	Presch	22: 2	Bus	54: 1
Y S	10	87	25-26: 0·6	Y S	23: 2	Prof	55: 1
O S	18	258	27-28: 0·9	O S	24: 4	Educ	56: 1
Town Child	43	423	29-30: 1·1			Govt	57: 1
Adol	63	1720	31-32: 1·7	Adol	25: 4	Nutr	58: 1
Adult	72	1676	33-34: 1·7	Adult	26: 5		
Aged	7	81	35-36: 0·6	Aged	27: 2	PersAp	60: 2
Town Total	185	3900	37-38: 2·3	Grand Max	28: 5		
Males	97	2264	39-40: 1·9	Males	29: 5	PhysH	62: 2
Female	88	1636	41-42: 1·7	Females	30: 4	Rec	63: 8
I	35	600	43-44: 1·2	I	31: 4	Rel	64: 0
II	105	2236	45-46: 1·9	II	32: 5	Soc	65: 6
III	42	1014	47-48: 1·4	III	33: 4	MECHANISM RATINGS AffB	66: 9
N-G	3	50	49-50: 0·5	N-G	34: 4	GroMot	67: 7

POPULATION (number)		PERFORMERS (number)		Manip	68: 7
Town Child	51-53: 0·4·3	Town Child	35-36: 0·1	Talk	69: 9
Out Child	54-56: 1·8·7	Out Child	37-38: 0·0	Think	70: 4
Total Child	57-59: 2·3·0	Total Child	39-40: 0·1	GEN RICH	71-72: 23
Town Total	60-62: 1·8·5	Town Total	41-42: 5·3		
Out Total	63-65: 9·3·7	Out Total	43-45: 2·4·9	PRESSURE RATING Children	73: 4
Grand Total	66-69: 1·1·2·2	Grand Total	46-48: 3·0·2	Adolesc	74: 2
Grand O.T. (code) 71-73: 0·3·1	70: blank	Perf/Pop	49-50: 2·7	WELFARE RATING Children	75: 0
Total Duration	74-77: 0·0·2·4	Aver. No.	51-52: 8·4	Adolesc	76: 3
Average Attendance 78-80: 3·6·3				AUTONOMY RATING wtd	79: 7

Figure 4.1. Data sheet for behavior setting 18.5: High school boys' basketball game. (Source: Figure 5.1, p. 99, Roger G. Barker, Ecological Psychology, Stanford, California, Stanford University Press, 1968). © 1968 Stanford University Press

another for boys 12-14, and a third for boys 15-17; school
classes for each year of age or, at most, two adjacent
years of age; religion classes for age groups such as 4-5,
6-8, and 9-11. The concept of 'curricula' in which topics
of increasing difficulty are taken up in sequence is
explicit in the schools and at least implicit in the age-
graded Sunday School classes, athletic teams, and youth
organizations.

With Barker's data, time-allocation vectors (TAVs)
covering the 884 behavior settings could be computed separately for each of the seven age groups, the two sexes,
whites of three socioeconomic statuses, and blacks; some
indication of the possibilities are given in Tables 4.1,
4.2, and 4.3. His basic data might or might not permit the
computation of time-allocation vectors for the 14 age-and-
sex or the 56 age-sex-socioeconomic status or color combinations, but such possibilities could be designed into
future surveys. Reasonable approximations might be reconstructed from the 1963-64 data by multiple regression techniques or other methods.

Barker's colleague Herbert F. Wright designed and
implemented extremely detailed day-long records of the
activities of a few selected children with the approval and
cooperation of their parents and teachers. It should be
possible to extend time-use surveys to cover the household
activities of children, partly by parental report and partly by self-report. Children learn their behavior in behavior settings, and complete time-allocation vectors (estimated breakdowns of 8760 hours per year) should throw considerable light on the relative contributions of home,
neighborhood, school, and other settings to the development
of children's skills, knowledge, attitudes, and behavior.
Time series would show how the life-experience vectors of a
particular cohort of children changed as they grew older
and also how their vectors differed from those of earlier
cohorts at each specific age.

As we have seen, Barker rates behavior mechanisms on
tempo and intensity, with ratings of 3 on each denoting a
near approach to the physiological limits. In absolute
terms, these limits increase as children grow older and no
confusion should arise if a preschooler is rated 3 on gross
motor activity for running as fast as he can.

For Barker, all of Midwest's settings involving
basketball belong to the same genotype; the youngest team
consists of boys 11-13 and the oldest of boys and girls

Table 4.1. Estimates of Occupancy Times by Town Residents in Behavior Settings Controlled by Specified Authority Systems, Midwest, 1963-64: Differentiated by Age, Sex, and Socioeconomic Group

Inhabitant subgroup	Number of persons	Town OT per person (hours)	Authority system					Town: total, 5 authority systems
			Church	Government	Private enterprise	School	Voluntary association	
			Person-hours of Town OT					
Infants	13	420	117	871	3,874	273	429	5,564
Preschool	53	393	1,749	5,936	9,063	742	3,657	21,147
Younger school	46	1,614	2,254	6,302	6,992	55,522	3,220	74,290
Older school	47	1,926	2,585	7,191	9,823	65,142	6,204	90,945
Adolescents	84	2,251	3,108	12,264	34,860	127,764	11,424	189,420
Adults	411	1,600	14,385	129,054	425,385	56,307	30,414	655,545
Aged	176	475	8,800	25,696	39,776	1,232	7,216	82,720
Town	830	1,356	33,200	186,750	531,200	320,420	63,080	1,124,650
Males	415	1,451	11,620	104,995	275,560	156,455	34,445	583,075
Females	415	1,261	21,995	84,245	244,850	157,285	29,050	537,425
Whites:								
Social class I	73	2,102	7,008	21,973	76,723	38,909	9,417	154,030
Social class II	438	1,410	18,396	100,302	274,188	187,026	41,172	621,084
Social class III	293	1,153	5,860	61,823	171,991	84,677	12,306	336,657
Blacks	26	664	1,144	4,394	5,954	4,966	1,066	17,524

Source: Compiled and calculated by Karl A. Fox and Shu Y. Huang from various tables in Roger G. Barker and Phil Schoggen, Qualities of Community Life, San Francisco, Jossey-Bass, 1973. Since published index numbers ranging from 1 to 389, all rounded to the nearest whole number, were used in the calculations, rounding errors should average less than 1 percent but may run from 2 to 10 percent in some cases.

Table 4.2. Estimates of Occupancy Times by Town Residents in the Primary Habitats of Specified Action Patterns, Midwest, 1963-64: Differentiated by Age, Sex, and Socioeconomic Group

Inhabitant subgroup	Number of Persons	Town OT per person (hours)	Aes- thetics	Busi- ness	Educa- tion	Govern- ment
Infants	13	420	65	1,027	13	195
Preschool	53	393	636	3,233	2,968	318
Younger school	46	1,614	4,692	3,726	38,640	322
Older school	47	1,926	6,063	5,076	45,590	470
Adolescents	84	2,251	12,096	18,564	88,956	2,268
Adults	411	1,600	10,686	249,888	27,948	104,805
Aged	176	475	4,048	19,008	1,408	16,368
Town	830	1,356	39,010	298,800	210,820	122,840
Males	415	1,451	17,430	164,755	101,675	72,625
Females	415	1,261	21,165	120,765	109,560	57,685
Whites:						
Social class I	73	2,102	5,986	53,728	26,134	30,806
Social class II	438	1,410	24,090	167,316	122,640	60,006
Social class III	293	1,153	7,032	74,422	58,307	32,230
Blacks	26	664	988	4,082	3,692	3,302

Source: Compiled and calculated by Karl A. Fox and Shu Y. Huang from various tables in Roger G. Barker and Phil Schoggen, Qualities of Community Life, San Francisco, Jossey-Bass, 1973. Since published index numbers ranging from 1 to 389, all rounded to the nearest whole number, were used in the calculations, rounding errors should average less than 1 percent but may run from 2 to 10 percent in some cases.

(separate teams) 15-17. At the national level, would Barker have added university and professional basketball games to the genotype already established for Midwest?

In U.S. occupational statistics, college and university teachers are distinguished from primary and secondary school teachers. Probably Barker's criterion of interchangeability (see section 4.4) would support the judgment that settings controlled by university teachers belong to different genotypes (subject for subject) than those controlled by high school teachers. In general, it would take a high school teacher at least two years to get a Ph.D. (compared with the four or five years spent by the university teacher in going from the B.S. level to the Ph.D.) and it might take the university teacher at least half as long to obtain a high school teaching credential as it took the high school teacher starting from his B.S. degree. Barker would place high school and university settings in the same

Table 4.2. Continued

Person-Hours of Town OT in Primary Habitats of:

Nutri-tion	Personal appearance	Physical health	Professional involvement	Recre-ation	Religion	Social contact
650	143	13	4,745	598	39	4,082
2,067	689	0	17,225	1,961	1,484	11,872
6,164	690	2,760	65,734	10,258	2,978	65,182
5,405	799	6,063	77,832	16,356	2,021	78,349
16,044	1,680	8,484	168,168	33,768	2,352	147,084
138,096	26,715	2,466	593,484	62,883	12,330	358,803
10,560	4,752	176	64,592	10,912	6,160	36,080
176,790	35,690	19,920	967,780	138,610	26,560	706,330
86,320	8,300	9,960	522,900	83,000	9,960	355,240
93,790	29,050	11,205	445,295	54,780	16,600	351,505
21,754	6,570	2,117	129,356	13,797	5,548	103,076
95,922	15,768	11,826	520,782	64,824	14,454	391,572
55,670	12,306	6,153	304,720	54,791	4,688	203,342
2,340	78	312	13,806	2,444	962	9,334

genotype only if high school teachers could get Ph.D.s
within a year and if university teachers could get high
school teaching credentials in less than (say) six months.

So, it may be that larger, more sophisticated, and
more nearly professional (or literally professional) settings with the same names as those settings found in
Midwest will, on Barker's criteria or others yet to be
developed, be assigned to additional genotypes over and
above Midwest's 198.

4.4.   BARKER'S CRITERIA FOR DECIDING WHETHER OR NOT TWO
       BEHAVIOR SETTINGS BELONG TO THE SAME GENOTYPE.

Barker (1968, p. 110) indicates that Midwest in 1963-64 had
14 settings of Genotype 18 (basketball games); there were
124 occurrences, or an average of about 9 per setting.

Table 4.3. Estimates of Occupancy Times by Town Residents in the Primary
   Habitats of Specified Behavior Mechanisms, Midwest, 1963-64:
   Differentiated by Age, Sex, and Socioeconomic Group

Inhabitant subgroup	Number of persons	Town OT per person (hours)	Affective behavior	Gross motor activity	Manip- ulation	Talking
			Person-hours of Town OT in primary habitats of:			
Infants	13	420	2,275	2,756	1,248	260
Preschool	53	393	5,936	5,141	3,286	1,219
Younger school	46	1,614	18,170	15,732	9,154	15,456
Older school	47	1,926	23,688	27,636	19,223	19,975
Adolescents	84	2,251	32,340	53,844	51,744	34,272
Adults	411	1,600	34,524	208,377	327,156	50,964
Aged	176	475	3,168	14,784	25,268	6,160
Town	830	1,356	120,350	330,340	434,096	128,650
Males	415	1,451	63,080	197,955	255,225	58,930
Females	415	1,261	56,100	113,710	165,585	70,965
Whites:						
Social class I	73	2,102	13,578	31,536	54,458	13,359
Social class II	438	1,410	67,890	192,282	242,652	64,386
Social class III	293	1,153	35,746	101,964	126,283	46,294
Blacks	26	664	2,470	6,942	8,138	2,730

   Source: Compiled and calculated by Karl A. Fox and Shu Y. Huang from
various tables in Roger G. Barker and Phil Schoggen, Qualities of
Community Life, San Francisco, Jossey-Bass, 1973. Since published index
numbers ranging from 1 to 389, all rounded to the nearest whole number,
were used in the calculations, rounding errors should average less than 1
percent but may run from 2 to 10 percent in some cases.

Barker and Schoggen (1973, p. 452) identify the 14 individual settings. Three of them involve the high school boy's
basketball team:
      5. High School Boys Basketball Game (presumably games
          played in Midwest)
      6. High School Boys Basketball Game out of town
          including Tournament at Patton
      7. High School Boys Basketball Practice
      All of our discussion has been devoted to setting 5;
presumably it would apply equally to setting 6, with the
same profile of shouting spectators and straining players
occurring in other towns. Setting 7 is different: absent
are spectators, cheerleaders, and band; present is repetitive practice of particular plays and skills.
      Why are exciting games and dull practice sessions
placed in the same genotype? They are so placed because

their zone 5 or 6 leaders, if interchanged between the two
settings, could "receive and process the same inputs as
formerly, in the same way and without delay" (Barker, 1968,
p. 83).   In the particular case of settings 5 and 7, the
same coaches may control the programs of both; both require
a detailed knowledge of the game of basketball.

Of the other 11 settings in Genotype 18, four involve
the Upper Elementary School team (boys aged 11 to 13);
others involve the High School Girls team, the Freshman
Boys team, the Sophomore Girls team, and the Midwest Town
team.   No doubt several different coaches are used; the key
to control of each setting is knowledge of the game of
basketball.   The presumption is, as in most occupational
statistics, that each of the persons currently coaching
basketball teams in Midwest is qualified for that occupation and could function adequately in any of the 14 basketball settings.

Barker qualifies the phrase "without delay" essentially as follows: If it takes a previously untrained person X
years to become a skilled zone 6 leader of setting A or Y
years to become a skilled zone leader of setting B;   if,
further, a skilled leader of setting A could learn to be a
skilled leader of setting B in less than 0.25 Y years and
also a skilled leader of setting B could learn to be a
skilled leader of setting A in less than 0.25 X years; then
setting A and setting B belong to the same genotype.

While Barker's method may seem unduly formal, he was
properly insistent that his methods and ratings be reproducible by other investigators.   For example, Kansas law
prescribed nine months of training to become a licensed
barber and three years to become a dentist.   Thus, unless
Midwest's dentist could become a licensed barber in less
than 2 1/4 months and Midwest's barbers could become certi-
fied dentists in less than 9 months, the dentist's office
and the barbershops were in different genotypes.   A more
detailed statement of Barker's method of classifying behavior settings into genotypes is given in Barker (1968, pp.
80-89).

Not all the 'separation' problems were this simple;
some of them will be mentioned in section 4.5.

It may appear that Barker's genotypes are classified
on the basis of occupations.   If this were true, the occupations would be those of proprietors, managers, administrators, self-employed professionals, teachers, shop fore-
men, and others who control the programs of entire

settings. The scope of the setting as a whole is the basic reality. Barker first identifies the setting and then identifies its single leader (zone 6) or joint leader (zone 5). A drugstore might be controlled by a pharmacist (zone 6) who employs others (zone 4) to handle the variety department and fountain; alternatively, it might be controlled by a proprietor (zone 6) who handles the variety department and fountain himself and hires a pharmacist (zone 4) to fill prescriptions. In Midwest's drugstore the pharmacist and the manager were partners, joint leaders (zone 5) of the drugstore setting.

4.5. BARKER'S CRITERIA FOR DECIDING WHETHER OR NOT TWO ENTITIES ARE COMPONENTS OF A SINGLE BEHAVIOR SETTING

It may seem obvious that the pharmacy, the fountain, and the variety department of Midwest's drugstore are components of a single behavior setting. However, Barker uses an index of interdependence, K, ranging from 7 to 49 and composed of seven subscales each ranging from 1 to 7, to decide such questions in a formal, reproducible way for each pair of entities which are candidates for separate behavior setting status.

If K = 7 (a score that could hardly arise in practice), the two entities must be identical, occupying the same space at the time, using literally the same behavior objects and the same array of behavior mechanisms, having the same performers in zones 4, 5 and/or 6 and a 95 to 100 percent overlap among all individuals present, and so related functionally that at least 95 percent of the behavior in entity A terminates or has physical consequences in entity B.

If successive pairs of entities being compared are increasingly separated in time and space, increasingly differentiated in terms of behavior objects and mechanisms, and increasingly independent in terms of leadership, other occupants, and physical contacts, the values of K increase. As an empirical matter, Barker uses K = 21 as a cutting point: if K is equal to or greater than 21, the two entities are separate behavior settings; if K = 20 or less, they are components of a single setting. Barker sometimes refers to the resulting behavior settings as K-21 behavior settings.

In practice, Barker chose the K-21 cutting point because it partitioned Midwest's ecological environment into units which 'made sense' in terms of the everyday language, perceptions, and behavior of Midwest's residents. He noted explicitly (Barker 1968, pp. 20-23 and pp. 45-46) that a lower value of K would partition Midwest into a larger number of entities, each having a higher degree of internal interdependence.

Thus, a cutting point of K=14 would separate the fountain, pharmacy, and variety departments of Midwest's drugstore into three distinct units. Presumably, if Midwest's residents perceived its environment as partitioned at the K-14 level, they would rarely speak of "going to the drugstore" but rather of "going to the pharmacy" or "going to the soda fountain"; the fact that the fountain and the pharmacy were located in the same structure, if noted at all, might be regarded as a coincidence.

A critical value of K greater than 21 would partition Midwest into a smaller number of entities, each with a lower degree of internal interdependence. A cutting point between 30 and 31 would place all of Midwest's garages and service stations in a single unit; the grocery stores would form another unit; and so on. A motorist driving through Midwest may be thinking of service stations as a genotype, but as a concrete, behavioral matter he will drive into a particular behavior setting of that genotype. Life is lived in behavior settings, not genotypes.

Other examples cited by Barker (1968, p. 46) related to the elementary school. The K-values (always pairwise) for the Third Grade reading class, the Third Grade writing class, and the Third Grade arithmetic class range from 14 to 16; therefore they belong to a single behavior setting, Third Grade Academic Subjects. In contrast, the K-values between Third Grade Academic Subjects, Fourth Grade Academic Subjects and Fifth Grade Academic Subjects range from 28 to 30; they are indeed three separate behavior settings.

It is quite possible that a very large drugstore, with several employees in each of the three departments, will be found to have K-values of 21 or more between departments; according to Barker's criterion, each department is a separate behavior setting. The increase in drugstore size has implications for the organization of its work force, its patterns of communication and authority, and presumably for

the quality of interactions between employees and customers.

4.6. RELATIONSHPS BETWEEN BARKER'S CATEGORIES AND THE
      STANDARD INDUSTRIAL CLASSIFICATION

The Standard Industrial Classification (1978) Is so widely
known that few descriptive comments are needed here. A
succinct statement of its principles is contained in
Appendix D, pp. 645-649 of the document cited.
    The SIC was developed for use in classifying estab-
lishments. An operating establishment is an economic unit
which produces goods or services--for example, a farm, a
mine, a factory, a store. In most instances, the establishment is at a single physical location; and it is
engaged in one, or predominantly one, economic activity for
which an SIC industry code is applicable.
    In Barker's terms, an SIC establishment (when open and
operating) is either a single behavior setting or a cluster
of several or many behavior settings. Small retail stores
and service establishments, like those in Midwest, often
consist of a single behavior setting.
    Larger establishments may consist of two or more set-
tings. For example, Midwest had a small establishment
code-named the Eggleston and Dean Window and Door Company
which consisted of two settings, each belonging to a different genotype.
    The company office belonged to Genotype 38 (commercial
company offices). It contained a secretary, a bookkeeper,
and the two proprietors, plus customers interested in
buying windows and doors. The other setting was an assembly shop, in which the foreman directed nine or ten workers
in assembling aluminum and glass components into
doors and windows. This setting belonged to Genotype 64
(factory assembly shops).
    The assembly shop program implies that only gainfully
employed persons enter the shop: workers (zone 4), the
foreman (zone 5), and the proprietors (zone 5). The company office program explicitly includes customers (zone 3)-
-without whom both shop and office would have to close
down.
    The difference between the two programs has an impor-
tant implication for data sources: all roles in the assembly shop are occupations; all occupancy time is included in

statistics on hours worked; all time is compensated by earnings (and fringe benefits) which are included in the national income and product accounts. In contrast, the time spent by customers in the company office is not noted in the company's accounts or in any other data system.

Barker had no opportunity or need to classify behavior settings in large factories or other large private enterprises. However, he did classify Midwest's schools into 233 behavior settings belonging to a rather large number of genotypes. His data imply that the elementary school had 286 pupils and the high school 97; in addition, there were perhaps 40 teachers and other school employees. Moreover, the high school's athletic and cultural events attracted hundreds of spectators. The Total OT of the school authority system was 650,124 person-hours. The 'factory equivalent' would be 325 workers averaging 2000 hours a year. So, Barker's approach has indeed been tested in large and complex organizations. In fact, Barker and Gump (1964) surveyed city high schools with as many as 2,200 students each and consisting of nearly 500 behavior settings.

Perhaps even more to the point, only about 10 percent of the person-hours spent in Midwest's school authority system entered the economic data systems as gainful employment. The percentage of gainful employment was no higher within the 69,753 hours of OT spent in church settings and no doubt a great deal lower within the 118,595 hours devoted to voluntary associations.

There will be enormous advantages in integrating social accounts based on behavior settings and genotypes with economic accounts and models based on SIC establishments and industries.

4.7. SOME EXAMPLES OF SIC ESTABLISHMENTS PICKED UP IN BARKER'S SURVEY OF MIDWEST AND IN ECONOMIC CENSUSES FOR THE DES MOINES SMSA

Table 7.1 (page 114) presents data for 18 of Midwest's more important private enterprise genotypes, all of which correspond to SIC industries involved in retail trade and personal services. (Where a genotype includes some settings from other authority systems, our estimate includes only the private enterprise settings.) The first nine genotypes qualify Midwest as a 'minimum convenience retail trade center' according to the criteria used by Borchert and

Adams (1963) and discussed in Chapter 7. They include
gasoline service stations, grocery stores, drug stores,
hardware stores, banks, eating places, garages, farm implement agencies, and variety stores.

These nine genotypes account for nearly 373,680
person-hours of occupancy time, an average of nearly 42,000
per genotype. Nine more genotypes establish Midwest as a
'full convenience retail trade center'; these nine account
for 87,262 person-hours of Total OT, or about 9,700 per
genotype.

Table 4.4 presents Midwest data for 23 more private
enterprise genotypes, each accounting for at least 2,000
hours of occupancy time. Their Total OT amounts to 253,577
person-hours, an average of 11,000 per genotype.

Thus, 41 private enterprise genotypes account for
715,812 person-hours of OT, or more than 95 percent of the
private enterprise total. While it is clear that Midwest
residents had to visit other places to buy automobiles and
to find a wider selection of 'specialty' goods (see Figure
7.1) purchased infrequently, the Midwest stores must have
absorbed the great majority of their shopping time and
personal consumption expenditures.

In brief, if Barker's data for the stores of Midwest
could be integrated successfully with that for similar SIC
establishments, no intractable problems should be encountered in accomplishing similar linkages for types and sizes
of stores not found in Midwest.

The prevalence of small establishments even in cities
of 250,000 or more people is indicated by some 1967 figures
for the Des Moines metropolitan area (SMSA population about
300,000).

The SMSA had 2,051 service establishments, 947 with
payroll and 1,104 without. The establishments without
payroll were no doubt single behavior settings in nearly
all cases, and most of those with payroll were also of
modest size. Thus, the total labor forces of barber and
beauty shops with payroll averaged 2.9 and 5.7 persons
respectively. All but one of the other major categories of
service establishments had labor forces averaging from 5.6
to 12.7 persons; the hotel, motel, and tourist court group
averaged 31.2.

Of the SMSA's 2,348 retail stores, 713 were without
payroll. The total labor forces of all stores with payroll
averaged 12.6 persons, only moderately larger than some of
the stores in Midwest. Des Moines' drug stores, eating

Table 4.4. Additional Genotypes in the Private Enterprise Authority
System Each Accounting for More than 2,000 Person-Hours of Occupancy
Time (Total OT), Midwest, 1963-64*

No.	Genotype	Number of settings, N	Total = Total OT	Per setting = Total OT/N	Centi-urbs
1.	Abstract and Title Companies	1	4,606	4,606	0.51
5.	Animal Feed Mills	1	16,881	16,881	0.61
6.	Animal Feed Stores	1	8,127	8,127	0.54
9.	Attorneys Offices	4	23,347	5,837	1.70
11.	Auditing and Investigating Companies	1	2,380	2,380	0.46
16.	Barbershops	2	7,601	3,800	0.77
19.	Beauty Shops	1	15,549	15,549	0.60
20.	Billiard Parlors and Taverns	1	39,212	39,212	0.77
24.	Building, Construction, Repair Services	6	19,564	3,261	2.00
38.	Commercial Company Offices	1	7,200	7,200	0.43
47.	Day Care Homes and Nurseries (commercial only)	1	[20,000]	[20,000]	[0.46]
48.	Delivery and Collection Routes	6	7,436	1,239	1.36
49.	Dentists' Offices	1	[4,600]	[4,600]	[0.35]
62.	Excavating Contracting Services	3	2,298	766	0.51
64.	Factory Assembly Shops	1	18,288	18,288	0.51
97.	Insurance Offices and Sales Routes	2	5,418	2,709	0.78
98.	Ironing Services	5	2,460	492	0.72
128.	Newspaper and Printing Plants	1	10,920	10,920	0.51
129.	Nursing Homes	1	6,805	6,805	0.68
145.	Plumbing, Heating, and Electrical Companies	2	7,691	3,846	0.79
180.	Sewing Services	2	2,674	1,337	0.61
194.	Taverns	1	18,288	18,288	0.73
205.	TV and Radio Repair Shops	1	2,232	2,232	0.45
23	Totals	46	253,577	5,513	16.85
	Plus totals for 18 genotypes in Table 7.1:				
18		31	460,942	14,869	16.57
41	Cumulative Totals	77	714,519	9,279	33.42
70	Barker and Schoggen Totals	132	734,183	5,562	41.00
29	Apparent Remainders	55	19,664	358	7.58

*Additional to the 18 genotypes listed in Table 7.1.

places, and apparel and accessory stores averaged between
10.4 and 12.8 workers. The giants among Des Moines' retail
establishments were in the general merchandise group; its
54 stores had an average of 88 workers, and a few of the
downtown department stores had more than 250.

4.8.   FURTHER OBSERVATIONS ON BEHAVIOR SETTINGS AND THE
        STANDARD INDUSTRIAL CLASSIFICATION

Most of Barker's behavior setting genotypes in the private
enterprise authority system are identical with industries
in the Standard Industrial Classification (SIC). The SIC
is used in the economic censuses and underlies the national
income and product accounts, the input-output or interindustry relations matrices, and other major economic data
systems in the United States. It is also used in the various large-scale econometric models of the United States.
    For any genotype which is identical with an SIC indus-
try, it should be possible to merge data on behavior settings (action patterns, behavior mechanisms, programs,
zones and others) with data available for the SIC industry.
Barker did not collect data on flows of money and commodities, as they do not 'behave'; the economic censuses give
primary attention to goods and money. As a starting point,
SIC data for an industry (e.g. Banks) could be used to
approximate the receipts and expenditures of a bank with
the same staffing pattern, staff size, and number of customers as the bank surveyed by Barker in Midwest in 1963-
64. SIC data for other industries (drug stores, grocery
stores, garages, service stations, animal feed mills,
window and door assembly shops, and so on) could also be
adapted to the sizes of specific settings surveyed by
Barker.
    The challenge would then be to determine whether the
two sets of data (eco-behavioral and economic) supplement
one another in useful ways. What effects would changes in
prices, costs, and levels of output in each setting have
upon the variables measured by Barker? What effects would
a change in zone 3 occupancy time (time spent in a setting
by customers) have upon prices, costs and output? How
would a 10 percent increase or decrease in town and trade
area population affect (a) the economic variables and (b)
the eco-behavioral variables in the 20 most important
private enterprise genotypes in a community like Midwest?

Many of the economic variables can be classed as inputs or outputs. Can the eco-behavioral variables also be classified in this way? Belcher (1974) organizes his book on Compensation Administration around the concepts of 'contributions' made by workers to an organization and 'rewards' received by them. He lists 170 kinds of nonfinancial rewards; while some of these can be given an economic interpretation (e.g. job security, retirement policies, promotion policies) a great many cannot. He also lists several major categories of contributions, some of which are usually not compensated with money. Contributions are made in (to) the behavior settings which constitute the employing organization; rewards are received in (from) these behavior settings. Can these contributions and rewards be recognized in Barker's private enterprise behavior settings? Can they be translated into his particular eco-behavioral variables?

The Standard Industrial Classification is not limited to private enterprises; it also includes schools, government agencies, voluntary associations, churches, and households. It includes these nonmarket categories only to the extent that they engage in economic transactions (purchase goods and services, employ workers, charge tuition fees and the like); these are needed to complete the national income and product accounts and employment statistics.

All gainfully employed persons are in zones 4, 5, or 6 of the relevant behavior settings. Many behavior settings in mines, factories, and other establishments contain only such persons, all of whom are included in employment and earnings statistics. These are the kinds of workplaces Belcher generally had in mind; they provide a challenge to identify and measure noneconomic inputs and outputs which can only be attributed to employed persons. In retail stores and service establishments, customers (zone 3) may supply as much occupancy time as employees. The economic data systems pay no attention to customers, so data about their occupancy times, rewards, and contributions (other than money paid for goods and services) must be pieced together from other sources. These settings may provide the best opportunities for comparing the inputs and outputs of customers (unpaid) and workers (paid).

SIC-type data on schools include teachers and administrators but not students; therefore, detailed data on enrollments and curricula would also be needed to reconstruct classroom behavior settings and incorporate the

occupancy times, contributions and rewards of students.
Churches and voluntary associations have few employees and
many members;   volunteers often occupy the central zones
(4, 5, and 6) of settings in these authority systems.   With
economic motives so attenuated, can interactions between
economic and eco-behavioral variables still be detected?
Perhaps so, if members' money payments (dues, tithes, dona-
tions) to support the paid officials, buildings, and other
expenses of their organizations are prorated down to the
levels of the individual settings. Finally, households are
an SIC industry only to the extent that they employ domestic workers.

We believe that all SIC industries which contain two
or more genotypes could be translated (partitioned for
accounting purposes) into their constituent genotypes. As
an example, we have cited the small manufacturing establishment in Midwest which consisted of settings from two
genotypes--Commercial Company Offices and Factory Assembly
Shops.   Settings of the first type may be found in small
enterprises in many sectors of the economy; settings of the
second type may be limited to a few durable goods manufacturing industries.

Barker identified 198 genotypes in Midwest in 1963-64.
Another 200 genotypes might be required to cover kinds of
settings in the rest of the United States not represented
in Midwest because of its small population and its geo-
graphic location. The complete set of (say) 400 genotypes,
including household genotypes, would encompass the living-
time of the U.S. population in a given year.   Two major
U.S. data systems based on the SIC, namely the 1972 BEA
input-output matrix and the 1970 and 1978 BLS industry-
occupation employment matrices, contain 496 and 260 industries respectively; each of these data sets accounts exhaustively for the gross national product and for all gainful employment.   Since the BLS matrix cross-classifies 425
Census occupations with its 260 industries (see Chapter 5)
it might be most useful to start from it.

We suggest the construction of a time-allocation
matrix, with a column for each of the 260 industries and a
row for each of the 400 genotypes. The time of gainfully
employed persons in each industry would be allocated to the
one or more appropriate genotypes in which they worked; if
other persons (customers, clients, students, patients,
spectators, onlookers) were also involved in the programs
of any genotypes in that industry, their estimated

occupancy times would also be recorded in the appropriate genotypes. Proceeding in this fashion, estimates of the living-time of all persons, gainfully employed and other, would be exhaustively allocated among the 260 industries, which include schools, hospitals, religious organizations, nonprofit organizations, government agencies, and private households along with many other nonmarket categories.

Such a matrix would provide a starting point for further conceptual and empirical research. Within a fixed population and total living-time, increases in occupancy time in some industries would have to be offset by decreases in other industries; these shifts in occupancy times among industry columns would also involve shifts in occupancy times among genotype rows.

The statisticians responsible for periodic revisions of the SIC must make decisions to include new industries and to delete old ones that have disappeared or dwindled to insignificance. Thus, changes in the SIC list of industries from (quinquennial) census to census reflect technological and economic change. Barker and Schoggen (1973) measured social change in Midwest from 1954-55 to 1963-64 partly in terms of the 'accretion and erosion of genotypes'--i.e., the introduction of new genotypes and the disappearance of old ones. The proposed genotype-by-industry matrix would provide a framework for the periodic joint updating of lists of industries and lists of genotypes within the framework of a comprehensive (and changing) allocation of time among industries and among genotypes.

NOTE

1. As in any exhaustive classification, one or more residual categories of 'behavior settings' may have to be created by definition to cover all situations in which any person may be living (and therefore behaving) at any moment--for example, walking alone on a prairie or repairing an underground telephone cable.

CHAPTER 5

THE CLASSIFICATION OF ROLES IN SOCIAL SYSTEM ACCOUNTS

In Chapter 4 we described how eco-behavioral data for behavior setting genotypes could be merged with economic data
for SIC industries. We suggested construction of a genotype-by-industry matrix of perhaps 400 genotype rows and
260 industry columns, the elements of which would contain
estimates of the time spent in each genotype within each
industry by (a) gainfully employed persons and (b) others.
The living-time of the U.S. population in a given year
would be allocated exhaustively among the genotype rows and
also among the industry columns (as augmented to include
the occupancy times of their customers, students, spectators, and--in the private household 'industry'--household
members). Over the years, technological, economic, and
social change would be reflected in the periodic joint
updating of industry and genotype classifications and the
jointly-shifting allocations of time among industries and
genotypes.
    In the present chapter we suggest that data on roles
and behavior mechanisms in genotypes can be merged with
data on occupations and the attributes of jobs and workers.
The occupational structure is central to the allocation of
life styles and the distribution of incomes in modern societies. It changes in response to technological and economic pressures and a great deal of education at and above
the high school level aims at preparing young people for
occupations in which employment is expected to grow. The
identification of roles in genotype programs with occupations can be made independently of the cross-classification
of genotypes by industries.
    In 1981 the U.S. Bureau of Labor Statistics published
updated versions of its National Industry-Occupation Employment Matrix for 1970, 1978, and projected 1990 at the
level of 425 occupations and 260 industries. The industries are, or can be translated into, the SIC categories.
The BLS matrix provides a basis for further development of

employment data cross-classified by occupation and industry.

Paid roles in the programs of Barker's genotypes can
be identified with specific occupations in the Census Bureau and BLS classifications, in the Standard Occupational
Classification (SOC) which has been increasingly emphasized
since 1977, and in the Fourth Edition of the Dictionary of
Occupational Titles (DOT). Three digits of the SOC and DOT
codes are identical, and these are the most important ones
for our purposes. We will refer most frequently to DOT
occupations, as we did a great deal of exploratory work
with them.

These three digits characterize each kind of job in
terms of the complexity of the worker's function in relation to data, people, and things. Each job is also characterized by the level of physical strength required. We
selected individual DOT ratings and groups of ratings corresponding approximately to the 441 occupations recognized
in the 1970 Census of Population and found that 68 percent
of the variance in mean earnings of male workers across
Census occupations was associated with the DOT ratings on
complexity of worker functions and heaviness of work.

Barker rated each behavior setting in Midwest on five
behavior mechanisms: thinking; talking; affective behavior; manipulation (use of the hands); and gross motor activity. It is tempting to equate thinking with complexity
of relations to data; affective behavior and talking with
complexity of relations to people; manipulation with complexity of relations to things; and gross motor activity
with strength required. Barker's rating for each mechanism
was the sum of subscale ratings on participation (the percent of total occupancy time during which the mechanism was
in evidence), tempo, and intensity. These ratings are too
coarse to measure the inputs workers are paid for in
specific occupations. A good deal of developmental
research would be justified to extend the DOT system to all
paid roles in behavior setting genotypes. As in Chapter 3,
the problem would be to identify and measure the contributions (and attributes) of workers which are rewarded in the
various genotypes.

Many people perform as amateurs in roles (athletes,
musicians, actors) that others fill as professionals. It
is by now clear that housework is work and equivalent monetary values can be imputed to its outputs; DOT ratings can
be applied to the various specialized tasks separately or

to a cluster of tasks for which a housekeeper might be
hired. It should be possible to develop complexity ratings
and strength required or 'heaviness of work' measures for
all roles in genotype programs, paid or unpaid, market or
nonmarket, even including those of customers and audience
members. It is also recognized that student roles at high
school and postsecondary levels involve hard work and the
foregoing of current income for the prospect of higher
earnings, more interesting jobs, and/or preferred life
styles at a later date.

The DOT and its supplements also characterize occupations by the levels of certain 'worker traits' required for
average performance in them. Among these are general educational development, specific vocational preparation, and
general, verbal, and numerical aptitude. Across occupations, the DOT ratings on worker traits are highly correlated with the DOT ratings on complexity of worker functions and with Census estimates of mean earnings. The
worker traits are human capital embodied in a person; the
complexity ratings refer to habitat-claims or jobs: the
demands imposed by behavior settings on anyone who tries to
fill a specified role.

If the demand for paid workers is really a demand for
worker functions and the supply of paid workers is really a
supply of worker traits, it should be possible to estimate
the implicit market values of worker traits. Extension of
complexity ratings to all roles in all genotypes and of
trait ratings to members of all relevant population subgroups would generalize these labor market concepts to
cover the demand for participant functions and the supply
of participant traits in all nonmarket activities. A good
deal of exploratory research would be justified to determine whether the trait-and-function approach can provide a
reasonable basis for imputing equivalent monetary values to
the contributions of unpaid participants in behavior settings.

5.1.   ROLES IN BEHAVIOR SETTINGS AND JOBS IN THE
       DICTIONARY OF OCCUPATIONAL TITLES: RELATIONSHIPS
       CITED BY BARKER AND HIS ASSOCIATES

Barker and Wright (1955, p. 39) made a passing reference to
the Dictionary of Occupational Titles (Second Edition,
1949), which we shall call DOT 2. They noted that a self-

employed plumbing and electrical contractor in Midwest performed tasks characteristic of at least a dozen of the DOT occupations and concluded that the DOT was not relevant to their immediate needs. They may have chosen an unfortunate test case, as many other members of Midwest's labor force (teachers, attorneys, barbers, and so on) might have fit very nicely into single DOT occupations.

In Barker's system, all gainful employment is conducted in the central zones of behavior settings: zones 6 (sole leader), 5 (joint leaders), and 4 (active functionaries). Workers are paid to implement the programs of work settings. Proprietors, managers, and self-employed professionals occupy zones 6 and 5; employees who work under direct supervision in a plant, store, or office but do not supervise others usually occupy zone 4.

Barker uses the same set of zones for behavior settings which are operated mainly or wholly by amateurs. For example, Barker and Gump (1964, p. 187) found that 86 percent of all the 'performance positions' (i.e., zone 4, 5, and 6 roles) occupied by high school students in Midwest town during 1959-60 could be identified in DOT 2 as "standard occupations in American culture." There were 77 such occupations listed; some performances were paid (service station attendant, waitress, sales clerk, and others) but most were not (actor and actress, athlete, musician, usher, and others in settings sponsored by the high school or by churches and voluntary associations). If the performance positions were weighted by the amounts of time devoted to each, the 86 percent cited by Barker and Gump would rise to 99 percent plus, as their complete list of performances not defined as occupations in the DOT is as follows: attendant, Methodist wedding; award recipients, high school awards assembly; bride, Methodist wedding; bride, charivari; club or school officer, high school student council meeting; initiation directors and planners, high school freshman initiation; king, queen, and attendants, Valentine formal (dance); offenders, city court; and witness, district court session.

It would seem from the above that nearly all of the time-consuming, recurrent unpaid roles in zones 4, 5, and 6 of behavior settings could be given names and code numbers corresponding to jobs listed in the Dictionary of Occupational Titles (DOT). If the unpaid performers were adults, it should be enough to add a digit to the job number indicating that they were unpaid. If the unpaid performers

were children, a second digit should be added to indicate
their age-range; most settings in which children have leadership and performing roles are age-graded.

5.2. CLASSIFYING OCCUPATIONS

The U.S. Manpower Administration's Handbook for Analyzing
Jobs (1972, pp. 4-5) states that "all job-worker situations
involve to some degree a relationship on the part of the
worker to data, people, and things.... These relationships
are expressed by 24 worker functions arranged in hierarchies according to level: the lower the identifying number, the higher the level....
     A combination of the highest functions which a worker
performs in relation to data, people, and things expresses
the total level of complexity of the job-worker situation."
(p. 4)
     The 24 worker functions are listed as follows on p. 5:

	DATA		PEOPLE		THINGS
0	Synthesizing	0	Mentoring	0	Setting up
1	Coordinating	1	Negotiating	1	Precision Working
2	Analyzing	2	Instructing	2	Operating-
3	Compiling	3	Supervising		Controlling
4	Computing	4	Diverting	3	Driving-Operating
5	Copying	5	Persuading	4	Manipulating
6	Comparing	6	Speaking-	5	Tending
			Signaling	6	Feeding-Offbearing
		7	Serving	7	Handling
		8	Taking		
			Instructions-		
			Helping		

The hyphenated terms (e.g. Taking instructions-Helping) are
regarded as single functions.
     The relations to data form a strict hierarchy. For
example, a worker capable of compiling is assumed to be
capable of computing, copying, and comparing; a worker
capable of synthesizing is presumed able to handle any or
all of the other six functions. 'Data' is construed broadly to include all kinds of information. The relations to

things also form a strict hierarchy. The data hierarchy is one of cognitive complexity; the things hierarchy, of psychomotor complexity.

The relations to people comprise a hierarchy only in a general sense. Berwitz (1975, p. 47) states that "Mentoring (advising, counseling) is a higher function than Persuading or Negotiating and may or may not involve the other two. Instructing is not necessarily higher than Supervising and therefore does not have a hierarchical relationship to it. Serving, however, is a lower level of complexity."

Relations to people involve affective as well as cognitive aspects, personality as well as intelligence. At any level from persuading to mentoring, a comparative advantage in intelligence for worker A may offset a comparative advantage in personality (affect) for worker B. It may or may not be possible to rate levels of 'personality' in a strict hierarchy, but in any event it seems unlikely that many promotion ladders could be based on personality alone.

Each job in the Dictionary of Occupational Titles (Fourth edition, 1977) is classified according to its levels of complexity in relation to data, people, and things. Thus, dentists are coded as 101: coordinating, mentoring, and precision working. Pharmacists are coded 161: coordinating, speaking-signaling, and precision working. Teachers in elementary and secondary schools are coded 227: analyzing, instructing, and handling. Scientists in experimental fields are usually coded 061 (synthesizing, speaking-signaling, precision working), while those in theoretical fields are usually coded 067 (synthesizing, speaking-signaling, handling); the 'handling' presumably consists of using pencils and paper and carrying books and briefcases.

We can easily translate Barker's programs for private enterprise genotypes into the occupations and DOT codes of their zone 4, 5, and 6 workers. The three grocery stores in Midwest town might have different numbers of employees but they would have the same set of DOT occupations (manager, cashier, butcher, stock clerk); hence, the labor force of each store would include at least one person in each of four occupations:

Occupation	Zone	DOT Code
Manager	6	167
Cashier	4	362
Butcher	4	681
Stock clerk	4	387

Each store has the program of Barker's Genotype 83 (grocery stores) built into its staffing pattern and job descriptions.

Similarly, Barker's program for Genotype 15 (banks) requires the following set of occupations:

Occupation	Zone	DOT Code
President	6	117
Vice-President	4	117
Cashier	4	362
Clerks	4	382

There was only one bank in Midwest town, but the banks in other towns no doubt required the same set of occupations.

It is quite possible to make a similar list for each setting in Midwest that contained one or more gainful workers. We might then visualize a matrix with a column for each genotype that contained at least one gainful worker and a row for each distinct occupation.

If the rows were arranged from top to bottom according to a pattern used in the 1970 U.S. Census of Population, 13 major occupational categories would appear in the following sequence: (1) teachers, elementary and secondary; (2) professional, technical, and kindred workers; (3) managers and administrators; (4) sales workers; (5) clerical and kindred workers; (6) craftsmen, construction; (7) mechanics and repairmen; (8) other craftsmen; (9) operatives, including transportation equipment; (10) laborers (excluding farm); (11) farmers and farm workers; (12) service workers; and (13) private household workers.

Within these categories, the 1970 census listed a total of 441 detailed occupations; the jobs in Midwest could be listed in the same order. In general, jobs requiring higher levels of education and cognitive skills would appear in the upper portion of the list; unskilled and semi-skilled jobs would appear in the lower portion.

The Dictionary of Occupational Titles (Fourth edition, 1977), which we will call DOT 4, lists approximately 20,000 occupations. The Third edition, DOT 3, listed nearly as many. Berwitz (1975) implies that some of the DOT listings are alternate names for the same occupations, for he describes DOT 3 as containing "the 14,000 basic jobs" in the U.S. economy as of the mid-1960s.

If the same amount of duplication exists in DOT 4, it includes three-digit complexity codes for about 14,000 distinct occupations. These same three digits are included in the Standard Occupational Classification (1977), which was developed in the United States to provide a common system for its various statistical agencies. We assume similar complexity ratings are included in the International Standard Classification of Occupations (ISCO), referred to in The OECD List of Social Indicators (1982, p. 20), or could be supplied by inference from DOT 4 or the SOC used in the U.S.

Supplements to DOT 3, published in 1966, listed several other attributes of jobs, one of which is 'heaviness of work' or the level of physical strength required. The levels recognized were sedentary, light, medium, heavy, and very heavy, which could be coded as 0, 1, 2, 3, and 4. Thus, in Midwest's grocery stores, the jobs of manager and cashier would be coded 0 (sedentary) and those of the butcher and stock clerk as 3 (heavy). All four of the occupations in Midwest's bank would be coded 0 (sedentary).

5.3.   CLASSIFYING UNPAID ROLES

We have already suggested in section 5.1 that nearly all unpaid roles in zones 4, 5 and 6 of behavior settings have paid counterparts somewhere in the society. If so, an unpaid role in those zones can be given the name of the corresponding paid occupation and also its SOC-DOT ratings on complexity and strength required. The coding system for unpaid roles performed by adults should indicate that they are unpaid; if the roles are performed by children, the coding system should indicate both the age-range of the children and the fact that they are unpaid.

People who accept unpaid leadership or performing
roles usually try to do them well according to the traditions of the community or organization sponsoring the relevant settings. Persons who are incapable of doing them are
usually not asked--at least they are not asked twice!
People who are ill-disposed toward the activity or genuine-
ly overcommitted will usually refuse to serve. A Sunday
School teacher seriously tries to teach; an amateur athlete, actor, or musician seriously tries to perform.

Children are encouraged, explicitly and implicitly, to
learn skills that are valued by their older siblings, parents, teachers, and other role models. The ultimate standards are set by professionals, even though the aspiration
levels of local children may be set by local high school
athletes and other talented amateurs in various fields.

DOT 4 (p. 88) and the SOC (p. 94) code professional
athletes as 341: compiling, diverting, and precision working. The heaviness of work is not coded in these publications, but in basketball, football, track, swimming, and a
number of other sports it must be rated 4 (very heavy).
'Compiling' evidently means that the athlete is continually
collating visual and other information about the state of
the game; 'diverting' or entertaining means that the game
is being played in front of spectators; and 'precision
working' means skillful handling of any behavior objects
that may be involved (for example, a basketball).

Hence, we see no incongruity in coding the roles of
Midwest's (or any other) amateur athletes as 341, along
with their age-range in each specific setting and the fact
that they were or are unpaid. Amateur actors, like professionals, would be coded 047: synthesizing, diverting, and
handling; amateur singers 047 (synthesizing, diverting,
handling); and amateur instrumental musicians 041 (synthesizing, diverting, precision working).

Roles in zones 3, 2, and 1 are always unpaid; at least
they are not paid by the leaders of the setting at hand.[1]
We believe that the DOT complexity codes can be adapted to
the description and classification of these roles also.

Table 5.1 is adapted from Table 2.4 in Barker and
Schoggen (1973, p. 37). It expresses their conception of
the functions and power associated with roles in each of
the six zones. It is clear that onlookers and loafers
(zone 1) have no function in the program of the setting and
almost no power in it. The least demanding paid jobs in
the data-people-things hierarchies of DOT 4 would be coded

Table 5.1. Penetration Zones of Behavior Settings: Their Functions, Power, Human Components and Examples

Penetration zone	Functions	Power	Human components	Examples
6	Control and implementation of program	Direct control of entire setting	Single leaders	Club president presiding at meeting
5	Control and implementation of program	Direct, but shared, control of entire setting	Multiple leaders	Team captain conferring with coach
4	Joint control (with zone 5 or 6) and implementation of subsystems of program	Direct, shared control of part of setting	Factors (functionaries, assistants, etc.)	Church organist playing for worship service
6-4	Control and operation of program	Direct control of entire setting	Operatives	Lawyer or his secretary answering query of clients
3	Implementation of major goal	Indirect control of most of setting	Members (customers, clients, etc.)	Store customer making purchase
2	Implementation of minor goal	Some influence on part of setting	Spectators (audience, invited guests, etc.)	Parade viewer watching parade
1	No functions	Almost no power	Onlookers (loafers, etc.)	Infant accompanying mother in grocery store
0	Recruiting and dissuading potential inhabitants	Region of influence external to setting	Potential inhabitants	Potential guest reading invitation

Source: Adapted from Table 2.4, p. 37, in Roger G. Barker and Phil Schoggen, Qualities of Community Life, San Francisco, Jossey-Bass, 1973.

687 (comparing, taking instructions-helping, and handling).
Such jobs often involve very heavy work and unpleasant
working conditions, always under close supervision.

Possibly onlookers could be given a provisional rating
of 798, implying simply that their relations to data, to
people, and to things (separately and collectively) fell
below the minimum levels of complexity which are compens-
able in the labor market.

Some zone 3 roles, particularly those of students,
may bear the same relationship to gainful occupations that
high school athletic roles bear to those of professional
athletes. Students (zone 3) in vocational classes are
practicing at the same data-people-things levels (computing, persuading, precision-working, or whatever) as are
required by the corresponding occupations. Students (zone
3) in academic courses at various levels are analyzing,
coordinating, and/or synthesizing data. Shoppers (zone 3)
in a supermarket are comparing, speaking-signaling, and
handling; their 'job' in the store should evidently be
coded 667.[2] If shoppers were not pemitted to handle the
merchandise, supermarket managers would have to hire additional workers to fetch and carry--in effect, to do the
shopper's 'job' in the store. In large lecture courses,
students occupy zone 2 (audience, spectators) but are still
'working' on data at various levels of the complexity
scale.

These examples should suffice to illustrate how roles
in zones 3 and 2 might be classified.

5.4.   BEHAVIOR MECHANISMS IN RELATION TO ROLE COMPLEXITY
       AND HEAVINESS OF WORK

Barker and Wright (1955, pp. 156-176) listed the prominent
behavior mechanisms (those rated 6 or higher) in each of
the 585 nonhousehold behavior settings that occurred in
Midwest during 1951-52. Some settings mainly involved a
single person: thus the prominent ratings for gross motor
activity and manipulation in setting 334 (Milk Company
Route) would apply to an individual milk deliveryman.
This was true also of Corliss Blacksmith Shop (prominent
ratings on gross motor activity and manipulation) and various other settings.

A setting like the Arkwright Garage may have involved
two or three auto mechanics all doing the same kind of

work: hence, its prominent ratings on gross motor activity, manipulation, and thinking may have applied equally to
each individual and in fact to the occupation 'Auto Mechan-
ic' as a whole. It is worth noting that the DOT 4 code for
automobile mechanics is 261 (analyzing, speaking-signaling,
precision working), implying a high level of cognitive
complexity and a very high level of psychomotor complexity.
As of 1951-52, at least, the work would have been rated as
heavy, coded 3 (next to the highest rating on a 0 to 4
scale).

In brief, when Barker and the compilers of DOT 3 and
DOT 4 looked closely at members of the same occupation,
they came to similar conclusions as to which behavior mechanisms were salient. Barker's behavior mechanism 'thinking' is associated with cognitive complexity—complexity of
relations to data. His mechanism 'manipulation' is associated with psychomotor complexity—complexity of relations
to things. 'Gross motor activity' is associated with heaviness of work or level of physical strength required.

Two of Barker's behavior mechanisms—'affective behavior' and 'talking'—involve relations to people; there is
no point in talking or displaying affect to data and
things. Midwest's largest behavior settings, in terms of
numbers of people present in the same enclosed space at the
same time, were devoted to recreation and social contact;
in such settings (for example, basketball games), moods may
change from dejection to elation in a matter of seconds and
loud, fast talking (shouting, cheering) means that the settings are going well.

It is not clear whether Barker's ratings on talking
and affective behavior are sensitive enough to measure
phenomena corresponding to DOT 4's complexity of relations
to people. In the 1951-52 survey of Midwest, affective
behavior and talking were prominent in Sunday worship services, in school lunch rooms, and in some church and school
music practices, but they were not prominent in stores,
offices, and other settings operated on a day-in, day-out
basis by gainfully employed adults.

It seems clear that DOT-SOC (or similar) ratings
should be adapted as widely as possible to the classification of roles in social system accounts. The occupancy
times of different individuals performing the same occupational role should be capable of simple 'adding up' in
social accounts for a nation or a community.

However, there are aspects of group behavior in settings that are designed for excitement, recreation, and
emotional expression that may be best approached by Barker's methods of rating behavior mechanisms for the setting
as a whole. Barker's present rating scales might need to
be modified for the purposes of a social accounting system
in which most elements, if not all, would be subject to the
normal rules of addition and subtraction.

5.5. RELATIONS BETWEEN DOT RATINGS OF WORKER FUNCTIONS,
      DOT RATINGS OF WORKER TRAITS, AND CENSUS DATA ON
      OCCUPATIONS AND EARNINGS

Table 5.2 shows some empirical associations between DOT 4
ratings on complexity of workers' relations to data,
people, and things (here labeled Y13, Y14, and Y15); ratings derived from DOT 3 (1965) and its Supplement (1966) on
heaviness of work (Y1), general educational development
(Y4), specific vocational preparation (Y5), training time
(Y50), cognitive aptitude (Y9), proportion of outdoor
rather than indoor work (Y2), and proportion of work environments which were hazardous and unpleasant (Y3); and estimates of the characteristics of male workers employed
during 1969 based on the special volume on occupations and
earnings in the 1970 U.S. Census of Population: median
years of schooling (X5), median age (X7), average hours
worked per year assuming 50 weeks of   employment (X15),
mean hourly earnings (X17), percent with 4 years college or
more (X23), and percent with less than 4 years high school
(X25).
      We spent a great deal of time during 1977–80 matching
occupations in DOT 3 with 460 occupations in the 1970 U.S.
Census of Population which accounted for total civilian
employment.[3] In some cases, we averaged the DOT ratings
from two or more detailed occupations to match a Census
occupation, since the Census classification is coarser than
the DOT. We made extensive use of data in the Supplement
(1966) to DOT 3; with the exception of Y13, Y14, and Y15
(data-people-things, based on DOT 4), all the Y-variables
are derived from the Supplement. As our work was exploratory, we made a number of ad hoc decisions as to how
certain DOT variables should be linearized, extrapolated or
combined.   However, the X-variables are almost exactly

Table 5.2. Weighted Averages of DOT and Census Variables for 13 Occupational Categories and Four Larger Aggregates: Males in the Experienced Civilian Labor Force, United States, 1970

Occupational category	N1 Number of male workers (1,000)	X1 Mean yearly earnings 1969 (dollars)	Y13 Data	Y14 People	Y15 Things	Y1 Heaviness of work (level)	Y4 General educational development (years)	Y5 Specific vocational preparation (years)	Y50 Training time (Y4+Y5) (years)	Y9 Cognitive aptitude (level)
			Worker functions relating to: (hierarchical level)							
1. Teachers, elem. & sec.	744	9,577	2.00	2.00	7.00	1.00	16.0	2.5	18.5	1.73
2. Professional, technical	6,249	13,481	0.89	4.50	4.30	0.66	16.6	5.2	21.8	1.75
3. Managers, administrators	5,395	13,689	1.08	4.17	6.96	0.45	15.1	4.9	20.1	2.01
4. Sales workers	3,364	10,735	3.14	5.60	7.00	0.96	13.5	1.0	14.5	2.89
5. Clerical	3,737	8,070	3.22	6.96	5.48	1.15	12.9	0.8	13.7	2.85
6. Craftsmen, construction	2,989	8,547	3.28	7.55	1.33	2.08	13.2	4.9	18.1	3.28
7. Mechanics, repairmen	2,466	8,073	2.04	7.12	1.03	2.40	13.8	3.9	17.7	3.11
8. Other craftsmen	5,104	9,134	2.79	7.65	1.12	1.95	13.3	3.5	16.8	3.17
9. Operatives (incl. transp. equip.)	9,776	7,416	5.15	7.02	3.65	1.99	11.3	0.7	12.0	3.72
10. Laborers (excl. farm)	3,433	6,074	6.00	7.75	6.18	3.06	10.0	0.2	10.2	4.06
11. Farmers and farm workers	2,213	5,586	2.85	6.70	1.74	2.92	12.9	1.5	14.4	3.45
12. Service workers	4,013	6,267	4.92	6.50	4.56	2.18	11.4	0.5	11.9	3.62
13. Private household workers	38	3,312	3.91	6.70	4.55	1.13	12.1	0.3	12.3	3.68
TOTAL, all occupations	49,518	9,179	3.27	6.31	4.14	1.66	13.2	2.5	15.6	3.02
Larger aggregates:										
Upper white collar (2,3)	11,643	13,577	0.98	4.34	5.53	0.57	15.9	5.1	21.0	1.87
Lower white collar (1,4,5)	7,844	9,356	3.09	5.90	6.28	1.06	13.5	1.0	14.5	2.76
Upper blue collar (6,7,8)	10,558	8,720	2.75	7.50	1.16	2.09	13.4	4.0	17.4	3.19
Lower blue collar and farm (9 through 13)	19,473	6,727	4.99	7.00	4.07	2.32	11.3	0.6	11.9	3.73
TOTAL, all occupations	49,518	9,179	3.27	6.31	4.14	1.66	13.2	2.5	15.6	3.02

Table 5.2. (Continued)

Occupational category	X5 Median years of schooling	X7 Median age (years)	X15 Hours worked per year (50 weeks)	X17 Mean hourly earnings (dollars)	Y2 Proportion of time spent in: Outdoor work	Y3 Proportion of time spent in: Hazardous or unpleasant work environment	X23 Percent with 4 years college or more	X25 Percent with less than 4 years high school
1. Teachers, elem. & sec.	17.7	33.2	2040	4.69	0.00	0.00	92.6	1.0
2. Professional, technical	15.8	38.3	2128	6.30	0.11	0.09	53.8	6.7
3. Managers, administrators	13.4	44.5	2374	5.84	0.07	0.02	25.0	22.2
4. Sales workers	12.9	39.8	2152	4.96	0.08	0.02	17.2	25.8
5. Clerical	12.6	37.0	1977	4.08	0.13	0.00	9.1	28.1
6. Craftsmen, construction	11.0	42.2	1979	4.32	0.62	0.98	1.0	57.3
7. Mechanics, repairmen	11.7	39.4	2184	3.71	0.12	0.63	1.1	50.1
8. Other craftsmen	11.8	41.9	2127	4.29	0.34	0.72	3.2	45.1
9. Operatives (incl. transp. equip.)	11.0	37.5	2083	3.56	0.20	0.70	1.0	59.3
10. Laborers (excl. farm)	10.3	33.8	1828	3.33	0.66	0.55	1.1	66.6
11. Farmers and farm workers	10.0	45.0	2423	2.27	0.99	0.96	3.0	64.3
12. Service workers	10.9	39.9	1937	3.21	0.29	0.40	2.4	57.2
13. Private household workers	9.2	45.0	1601	2.04	0.01	0.13	1.7	76.7
TOTAL, all occupations	12.2	39.5	2105	4.33	0.27	0.43	13.8	41.7
Larger aggregates:								
Upper white collar (2,3)	14.7	41.2	2242	6.09	0.09	0.06	40.4	13.9
Lower white collar (1,4,5)	13.2	37.8	2058	4.51	0.10	0.01	20.5	24.5
Upper blue collar (6,7,8)	11.6	41.4	2098	4.16	0.37	0.77	2.1	49.7
Lower blue collar and farm (9 through 13)	10.8	38.2	2046	3.30	0.39	0.64	1.5	60.8
TOTAL, all occupations	12.2	39.5	2105	4.33	0.27	0.43	13.8	41.7

Source: The Y variables were compiled from the Dictionary of Occupational Titles (1965) and its Supplement (1966). The X variables were compiled from the U.S. Census of Population, 1970.

derived from Census figures and the Y-variables were developed with very considerable care.

Only a few points in Table 5.2 need be noted; they may be observed most clearly in the four larger aggregates of occupations in the lower part of the table. The figures shown for the larger aggregates are weighted means of the relevant members of the set of 13 occupational categories, the weights being the numbers of male workers (N_1) employed in each category.

Cognitive complexity (complexity of relations to data) is greatest for the upper white collar group, at 0.98, and least for the lower blue collar, at 4.99. (Recall that the highest level of data complexity for a specific occupation is 0 and the lowest 6). Psychomotor complexity (complexity of relations to things) is highest for the upper blue collar group, at 1.16,; next highest for the lower blue collar, at 4.07; and very low, on the average, for both of the white collar aggregates. Complexity of relations to people shows a rather restricted range, as many upper white collar occupations with ratings of 0 or 1 on relations to data are rated only 6 (speaking-signaling) on relations to people; however, the upper white collar group averages 4.34 on relations to people, implying much greater complexity than is faced by the other groups: lower white collar 5.90, upper blue collar 7.50, and lower blue collar 7.00.

On heaviness of work, the upper white collar group averages 0.57 (midway between sedentary and light), the lower white collar 1.06 (light), the upper blue collar 2.09 (medium), and the lower blue collar 2.32 (a third of the way from medium toward heavy).

As noted in earlier sections, these four DOT variables are closely associated with Barker's five behavior mechanisms.

We have translated DOT's scales for general educational development and specific vocational preparation into approximate numbers of years. For the larger aggregates, estimated years of general educational development move similarly to the Census data on median years of schooling. Our estimates of specific vocational preparation average 5.1 years for the upper white collar group and 4.0 for the upper blue collar, but only 1.0 and 0.6 years respectively for the lower white collar and lower blue collar.

These two variables should be strategic in Barker's method of deciding that settings A and B belong to the same genotype if the zone 6 leader of B could learn to run

setting A in less than one-fourth of the time actually
taken by the leader of A to learn it starting from scratch,
<u>and</u> if the leader of A could take over setting B in less
than one-fourth of the training time originally needed by
its present leader.

Analogous calculations must be made by high school and
university advisers whenever a student considers changing
his major subject, and by adult workers when they contem-
plate retraining for another field. What is the 'curric-
ulum distance' in full-time student years from an M.S.
degree in physics to an M.S. degree in mathematics? Is the
'distance' the same in the reverse direction? How far is
it between two adjoining genotypes, High School Physics
Classes and High School Mathematics Classes?

In Table 5.2, mean yearly earnings show a strong positive association with cognitive complexity and with complexity of relations to people. Earnings also show a high
positive correlation with general educational development
and with cognitive aptitude (note that the highest level of
aptitude on this scale is 1.00 and the lowest is 5.00, so
the upper white collar is high at 1.87 and the lower blue
collar low at 3.73).

5.6. ROLES AND WORKER FUNCTIONS AS ATTRIBUTES OF THE
      ENVIRONMENT: WORKER TRAITS AS ATTRIBUTES OF INDIVID-
      UALS

In Barker's framework, a zone 4, 5 or 6 role in a behavior
setting is a <u>habitat-claim for an operative</u>; the habitat in
question is the behavior setting. The role is related to
other roles in the setting; the complexity of the demands
imposed on this particular role by the whole network of
relations involved in the setting's program is measured by
this role's DOT ratings in the data-people-things hierarchies.

Suppose now that an individual presents himself as
someone who can meet the demands of a particular role and
successfully operate the claim. To do so, he must have
certain attributes in appropriate degrees: general educational development, specific vocational preparation, cognitive aptitude, and perhaps others. In other words, he must
have the cognitive, psychomotor, and interpersonal skills
required for the role and the necessary level of physical
strength.

It is important to note that roles and worker functions are attributes of the environment of human behavior;
worker traits are attributes of individuals.

NOTES

1.   The farmer-customers of Midwest's animal feed mill
(Genotype 5) occupy zone 3 of that setting.   They are
gainfully employed in behavior settings of such genotypes
as 'Dairy Farms' and their work includes, on occasion,
driving to the mill to buy a truckload of feed.   The
possibility of double-counting their time at the mill must
be eliminated when a time-allocation matrix is constructed
which includes exactly 8760 -hours per year for each town-
and-trade area resident.   But from the standpoint of the
mill setting as such there is no problem: they are
customers (zone 3).

2.   Before coming to the store, the shopper probably did
some 'compiling' at home (data complexity level 3) and
perhaps some 'analyzing' (data complexity level 2).

3.   The Census Bureau spoke of 441 occupations, so some of
our 460 must be subdivisions of members of the official set
of 441.

CHAPTER 6

THE CLASSIFICATION OF STOCKS
OF PHYSICAL CAPITAL AND CONSUMER
DURABLES IN SOCIAL SYSTEM ACCOUNTS

In section 3.3 we gave our rationale for including stocks of physical capital in social accounts based on behavior settings, and in section 3.4 we described the recently-published BEA (Bureau of Economic Analysis) estimates of stocks of physical capital and consumer durable goods in the United States. The reader may wish to refer to those two sections as an introduction to Chapter 6.

6.1. PHYSICAL CAPITAL AND OECD SOCIAL INDICATORS

For further motivation, we noted in section 3.5 that eight of the OECD (1982) social indicators involve aspects of the physical environment. Three relate to housing conditions: indoor dwelling space, basic amenities, and access to outdoor space (e.g. a garden or roof garden, a balcony or terrace large enough for a table and chairs, an area of open space suitable for walking or sitting and resting such as a courtyard or park). A fourth is based on the proximity of homes, in minutes, to shopping facilities, a pre-primary school, a primary school, a post office, a public transport stop, a sports center offering a range of popular activities where pupils can participate, and medical services capable of offering emergency treatment day and night.

6.2. THE THREE OECD INDICATORS OF HOUSING CONDITIONS: THEIR RELEVANCE TO THE HOMES OF MIDWEST

It may be helpful to visualize these indicators in terms of the behavior settings of Midwest town. The first three indicators would describe physical aspects of the houses and yards of Midwest residents. With rare exceptions, each house was occupied by a single family and stood on its own lot. The lots averaged about 0.25 acres; as of 1950, only

37 of the nearly 300 dwellings were on lots smaller than 75 by 150 feet (Barker and Wright, 1955, p. 38). This pattern continued through the 1960s (when Barker's last survey was made) and the 1970s (when we drove through the town our- selves). The front yards had lawns and shade trees; the back yards provided additional space for gardens, for children to play, and for outdoor fmaily activities.

Barker and Wright (1955, p. 84) described the "common varieties of family behavior settings" as home meals, home indoors, home outdoors (the yard surrounding the house), home bathroom, and home festive occasions. The OECD indi- cator access to outdoor space would relate specifically to the existence of, and kinds of family activities feasible in, the behavior setting 'home outdoors.'

The OECD indicator indoor dwelling space is the "per- centage of the population in dwellings occupied by n per- sons per room." (OECD 1982, p. 39). For any one family, the ratio of persons to rooms would impinge mainly on the settings 'home indoors' (possibilities for privacy) and 'home bathroom' (possibility of congestion).

The indicator basic amenities is the "percentage of the population living in households not having exclusive use of" such amenities as "flush toilet inside the dwell- ing, piped water inside the dwelling, fixed bath or shower within the dwelling, kitchen or kitchenette." (OECD 1982, p. 40). These amenities would directly affect the livabil- ity and efficiency of the behavior settings 'home indoors', 'home bathroom,' 'home meals', and 'home festive occa- sions.'

6.3. THE OECD INDICATOR OF ACCESS TO SELECTED SERVICES: ITS RELEVANCE TO THE STORES, SCHOOLS, AND SERVICE ESTABLISHMENTS OF MIDWEST

The fourth OECD indicator mentioned, proximity of selected services, is the "percentage of the population having access to selected services within a stated time." (OECD 1982, p. 41). The time intervals suggested in connection with survey questions on this topic are: less than 3 min- utes; 3 to less than 10 minutes; 10 to less than 20 min- utes; 20 to less than 30 minutes; 30 minutes or more. The selected services to be asked about include:.

Store or stores satisfying daily needs. In Midwest, these would at least include those types of stores (SIC establishments) necessary for a 'minimum convenience retail trade center', as listed in the upper portion of our Table 7.1: a gasoline service station, a grocery store, a drug store, a hardware store, a bank, an eating place, a garage, a variety store, and a store offering meat, fish, and fruit; on the margin between minimum convenience and 'full convenience' would be a laundry or laundromat and a dry cleaning establishment. Midwest had one or more establishments of each of these types, mostly on or near the courthouse square in the center of town. The town occupied about two-thirds of a square mile. Few homes were more than a half-mile from courthouse square, or 10 minutes walking-time. All but a few families had automobiles; with these, starting up the automobile, driving, parking, and entering the store of one's choice should have taken only 3 to 5 minutes.

A primary school and a pre-primary school. Within its town limits, Midwest had a primary (elementary) school for children aged 6 to 13; also a day care center for children of working mothers, and kindergarten classes for 5-year olds.

A post office. Midwest had a post office on courthouse square.

A sports center offering a range of popular activities where pupils can participate. There is some ambiguity here. Midwest's high school offered a truly remarkable array of extracurricular activities involving practice sessions after school and performances or games on a good many evenings. The elementary school had playgrounds and a considerable number of extracurricular activities for the older children (ages 11 to 13). There were several bowling leagues for children and adolescents which met weekly at the Garland Lanes in Midwest during most of the year. Voluntary associations sponsored several baseball leagues for children and adolescents during the summer months, when the schools were closed. Automobile traffic on the residential streets was very light, so various games could be played in them by small groups of neighborhood children within sight of their own homes.

Medical services capable of offering emergency treatment day and night. During portions of the 1950s and early 1960s, Midwest had a physician living within the town limits and able to respond to emergencies day or night. Midwest was marginal in population relative to the service capacity and earning power of ambitious young M.D.s or of

established physicians in mid-career. During 1963-64 Midwest had no physician, but Barker and Schoggen (1973, p.
75) noted that there was an active demand and a continuing
effort on the part of Midwest community leaders to attract
another.

There may have been physicians, and perhaps a small
hospital, within 10 miles of Midwest. Barker and Wright
(1955, p. 27) noted that there were five cities within 20
to 55 miles of Midwest, including Kansas City and Topeka;
the nearest city, Lawrence (site of the University of Kansas), could be reached in 40 minutes. Nowhere does Barker
imply that access to medical services was a major problem.

In relating these four OECD indicators to Midwest, we
have implied a great deal about stocks of physical capital.
First, there are the basic structures of the houses themselves, the garages and driveways, the flush toilets, the
piped water, the fixed bath or shower, the appliances used
in the kitchen or kitchenette. Second, there are the commercial buildings housing essential retail stores, service
stations, garages, the bank, the laundry, and the dry
cleaning establishment; each of these buildings contains
equipment without which the intended behavior setting cannot function. Third is the building that houses Midwest's
public elementary school, along with its equipment and
grounds; to it may be added the building and equipment of
the day care center, a private enterprise. Fourth is the
building and equipment of the U.S. post office, operated as
of 1963-64 by the federal government. Fifth, although the
buildings and equipment for physicians' and hospital services are located elsewhere, Midwest's residents constitute
a claim on those services and routinely use them.

6.4. THE FURTHER IMPLICATIONS OF 'ACCESS' AND OF BASIC
AMENITIES: STREETS, SIDEWALKS, WATER SUPPLY AND
SEWAGE DISPOSAL SYSTEMS, TELEPHONES AND ELECTRIC
POWER

The structures and equipment already cited imply the existence of still others. To provide access to selected services, streets and sidewalks were built and maintained by
the town government. To provide piped water, the town
government built a water supply plant and distribution
system. The flush toilets imply other structures, private
and/or public, for waste disposal. De facto, 'access to

selected services' came to imply automobiles (which affected the construction and maintenance costs of Midwest's
streets) and a telephone system (built and operated by a
private enterprise). The OECD indicators do not mention
electric lights and appliances, perhaps because it was
inconceivable that (in and after 1982) any home in an OECD
country might be without them. At any rate, few behavior
settings in the homes and 'selected service' buildings of
Midwest could have operated successfully without electric
lights and the associated system for distributing electric
power. Finally, it should be said that part of the state
and county road system that made it possible for Midwesterners to visit physicians and hospitals should be charged
to their 'access to selected services.'

6.5. THE OECD INDICATORS OF EXPOSURE TO OUTDOOR AIR
      POLLUTANTS AND NOISE: THEIR RELEVANCE TO BEHAVIOR
      SETTINGS AND TO DEFENSIVE INVESTMENTS FOR POLLUTION
      AND NOISE CONTROL

Two more OECD indicators, exposure to air pollutants and
exposure to noise, are based on outdoor concentrations of
sulphur dioxide and particulate matter and on outdoor noise
levels in front of the most exposed facades of the relevant
buildings (a) between 6 a.m. and 10 p.m. and (b) from 10
p.m. to 6 a.m. Air pollutants and noise impinge directly
on the pleasantness and healthfulness of the settings 'home
outdoors' and 'trafficways'--Midwest's streets and sidewalks. If windows are left open, the same air pollutants
permeate the indoor settings and the outdoor noise pene-
trates the more exposed rooms of the dwellings.
    Homeowners may take individual defensive measures such
as installing air conditioners and filters and keeping
their houses tightly closed. Those responsible for retail
stores, schools, and other 'selected services' may do the
same. The town government may pass ordinances against
noisy vehicles or vehicles emitting above-average amounts
of exhaust fumes; against burning leaves; and for requiring
the larger public and private users of fuels and chemical
processes to install 'air scrubbers' or similar devices.
All of these measures involve physical capital--structures
and equipment; those affecting vehicles owned by households
involve consumer durable goods, as vehicles used only for
household purposes are so classified.

6.6.   SIX OECD INDICATORS AND THE RESIDENTIARY ENVIRONMENT
       OF MIDWEST TOWN

The specific types of services mentioned in connection with
access were described in OECD (1982, p. 41) as 'illustrative examples'--though no doubt some of the most urgent
ones.   The examples could well be extended to include opportunities for religious worship, for recreation (movies,
bowling alleys, taverns, billiard parlors, watching high
school athletic events), for social contact, and for the
use of libraries.   A fire station was close at hand, and
also police protection (in Midwest's case, provided by the
county sheriff's office on courthouse square).
     With these extensions, the homes, buildings, streets,
and air spaces of Midwest so far described probably contained (in 1963-64) at least 95 percent of the living-times
of town infants and children under 14, retired persons over
65, and housewives not otherwise employed.[1]   The same was
probably true of many employed residents who both lived and
worked within the town's limits.   Whatever was good about
Midwest's environment, as measured by these six OECD indicators under the rubric of 'Physical Environment,' was
presumably good for them.
     We may speak of these parts of Midwest town and its
air space as the residentiary environment; it contained
almost everything needful for life except an adequate array
of workplaces and jobs.   In addition to the things
already mentioned, this environment contained all the consumer durable goods with which the town residents had sur-
rounded themselves.[2]

6.7.   THE OECD INDICATOR OF WORK ENVIRONMENT NUISANCES

The OECD indicator of access to services expresses the
needs of shoppers and customers; the OECD indicator of work
environment nuisances reflects the health hazards and hard-
ships of workers.   The list of nuisances includes regular
exposure at one's place of work to one or more of the following: draught; high temperature; low temperature; mois-
ture, water; dusts of different kinds; polluted air;
vibration, heavy shaking; noise;   uncomfortable working
position; and heavy lifting.   These nuisances exist in the
micro-environments of particular production processes involving particular structures and equipment; mitigating

the nuisances might require investments in new plant and
equipment. In Midwest there were very few establishments
that seemed likely to involve such nuisances: possibilities as of 1963-64 <u>might</u> have been the animal feed mill,
the factory assembly shop, the lumberyards, the laundry,
the dry cleaning establishment, the state and county garages and machine shops, and the excavation and construction firms.

6.8. THE OECD INDICATOR OF TRAVEL TIME TO WORK

The social indicator of travel time to work is the "percentage of persons in employment taking stated amount of
time for one trip to (or from) work." (OECD 1982, p. 30).
The travel-time class intervals suggested for this indicator are (in minutes):   0, 1-15, 16-30, 31-60, 61-120, and
121 or more.
    In Midwest, the travel times for all persons who both
lived and worked within the town limits would have been
less than 15 minutes. However, as of 1951-52 some 55 town
residents (of about 300 residents who were gainfully employed) worked wholly or partly outside of the town: 18
commuted regularly to other towns; 20 worked in the immediately surrounding rural region as farmers, road workers,
and rural teachers; and 17 worked in and out of Midwest as
truck drivers, salesmen, and government officials (Barker
and Wright 1955, p. 28). Barker does not give similar data
for 1963-64, but Census figures on intercounty commuting in
that part of Kansas in 1960 suggest that the percentage of
out-commuters was considerably higher in the later year.
    Midwest residents working outside of the town had a
stake in several additional types of physical capital: the
county and state roads on which they traveled; the machinery used by county and state agencies (and private contrac-
tors) to build and maintain these roads; the buildings and
machinery of the farms on which some worked as farmers or
employees; and the buildings and equipment of certain industrial establishments in cities 20 to 55 miles away.

6.9. THE LARGER COMMUNITY OF MIDWEST: COMBINED INDICATORS
      AND STOCKS OF PHYSICAL CAPITAL FOR TOWN AND TRADE
      AREA RESIDENTS

Barker and Schoggen (1973, p. 61) estimated that Midwest
and the rural district within a four-mile radius around it

contained (in 1963-64) 1680 inhabitants, 830 in the town and 850 in the open country. The 830 town residents was an exact count, the 850 country residents only a rough estimate--possibly a bit high but close enough for present purposes.

Table 2.1 shows that town residents accounted for only 48 percent of total occupancy time in the school and church authority systems and 53 percent of that in settings sponsored by voluntary associations. In Genotype 58, elementary school basic classes, town residents accounted for 98,251 person-hours and nonresidents for 123,868. In high school English classes, town residents contributed 9,019 hours and nonresidents 7,904. Town residents provided 12,648 hours and nonresidents 13,787 to Genotype 161, religious worship services. At the self-service (coin-operated) laundromat, town residents spent 10,920 hours and nonresidents 12,050. The town residents and the nearby country residents were equally, no more, no less, dependent on these selected services available only within the boundaries of Midwest town.

The OECD indicators are intended for application to all population subgroups. In the present case, it seems clear that the eight social indicators discussed for town residents should also be applied to those nonresidents who live within the school, church, and voluntary association attendance areas served by facilities in the town. Thus, the survey questions about indoor dwelling space, basic amenities, access to outdoor space, proximity (in minutes) of selected services, exposure to air pollutants and to noise, work environment nuisances, and travel time to work should all be answered for the residents of the service area as well as those of the town.

Within the service area boundary, farm buildings and machinery, tractors, and trucks would constitute a large proportion of the stock of physical capital used in conjunction with gainful employment. All roads within this area (approximately 50 square miles) would be equivalent to a street system for the larger community of Midwest and its 1680 inhabitants.

The residentiary environment of the larger community would now include the houses, yards, and consumer durables of the country dwellers as well as the homes, buildings, and air space of the town.

6.10. THE EXPORT BASE OF THE LARGER COMMUNITY OF MIDWEST

The larger community of Midwest exported agricultural prod-
ucts, which were sold in national and international markets.   It was a net exporter of labor in the form of out-
commuters. The county government offices in Midwest served
11,000 people, of whom fewer than one-sixth lived in the
greater Midwest community.   The county offices of certain
state and federal agencies also exported services to other
parts of Midwest County.
      With these export revenues, members of the greater
Midwest community imported groceries, clothing, consumer
durables, building materials, and the myriad items retailed
by the drug and variety stores.   They had a stake in the
national transportation system that made these exchanges
possible.
      At the same time, the flows of exports and imports
transmitted price and cost impacts into the local economy,
some of which led to changes in the rates of accumulation
of the various categories of physical capital and in spend-
ing for current consumption.

6.11. MICROCOSM, U.S.A.:   STOCKS OF PHYSICAL CAPITAL AND
      CONSUMER DURABLES, 1929, 1954, AND 1979

The BEA (Bureau of Economic Analysis) estimates of the
value of stocks of physical capital and consumer durable
goods in the United States, annually from 1925 through
1979, apply to the nation as a whole. Their development is
a major achievement, and their publication in a comprehensive form was accomplished only in 1981.
      It is not easy to visualize the implications of 5878.4
billion dollars' worth of structures, equipment, and consumer durables for the livability and efficiency of behavior settings and for measures of individual well-being.
Therefore, we will describe their relative levels and movements over time in terms of a hypothetical community which
we will call Microcosm, U.S.A.
      Microcosm had a population of 1000 in 1929. Growing
in direct proportion to that of the United States, its
population reached 1338 in 1954 and 1848 in 1979. At three
persons per household, the community had 333 dwelling units
in 1929, 446 in 1954, and 616 in 1979.

The dollar values in Table 6.1 can be interpreted as follows. First, they are stated in terms of 1972 prices: they are constant-dollar values and their changes over time are real in the sense that an increase from 1929 to 1954 implies that the structures involved have become more numerous, and/or larger, and/or better equipped, and/or of higher quality materials or workmanship. Second, they are gross values: a house built in (say) 1940 is carried in the 1979 stock estimate at the (1972) cost of building a new house just like it--not at its depreciated value--until the 1940 house is destroyed or discarded. The 1929 community of Microcosm could be replicated (everything built new) for $12,433,000 in 1972 dollars; the 1979 community of Microcosm could be replicated (everything built new) for $48,261,000 in 1972 dollars.[3]

We may visualize Microcosm as a town rather like Midwest in its residentiary environment but with an export base consisting of small factories (like, for example, Midwest's assembly shop for aluminum doors and windows) rather than farms. The factories, residences, retail businesses, and all other structures in which Microcosm's people live and work are on a single square mile of land.

The 1929 figures in Table 6.1 are per capita values for the United States in that year. Thus, the figure of $12,433 in the 1929 column, Row F, was obtained by dividing the U.S. population (121.8 million) into BEA's constant-dollar gross value estimate ($1514.3 billion). The 1954 figures in Table 6.1 were obtained by taking the U.S. per capita stock estimates for that year (shown in Table 6.2) and multiplying them by 1.338, the ratio of U.S. population in 1954 (163.0 million) to that in 1929. Similarly, the 1979 values in Table 6.1 were derived by taking the U.S. per capita stock estimates for 1979 (shown in Table 6.2) and multiplying them by 1.848, the ratio of the U.S. population in 1979 (225.1 million) to that in 1929.

The first thing to note in Table 6.1 is the sheer magnitude of the accumulations of physical capital relative to the annual gross national product (called GCP or gross community product in the Microcosm context). The ratio of 3.97 in 1979 was obtained by dividing the gross national product of the United States (in 1972 dollars), namely $1479.4 billion, into BEA's estimate of the gross value of physical capital, namely $5878.4 billion! In other words, if all structures, equipment, and consumer durables in the

Table 6.1. Microcosm, U.S.A.: Constant-Dollar Gross
Values of Stocks of Physical Capital and Consumer
Durable Goods, Total and by Five Major Categories, with
Community Population Growing at the U.S. Average Rate:
1929, 1954, and 1979

Category of structures and equipment (including consumer durable goods)	Gross values in 1972 dollars with community populations as indicated		
	1929 1000 persons ($1000)	1954 1338 persons ($1000)	1979 1848 persons ($1000)
A. Residential structures and consumer durables (except automobiles)	5384	8128	19689
B. Central place structures and equipment	1755	2986	9746
C. Export base structures and equipment	3409	4362	8240
D. Public utility structures and equipment	768	1330	3362
E. Highway transportation structures and equipment	1117	2503	7222
F. Total, civilian structures, equipment, and consumer durables	12433	19311	48261
Addendum:			
G. Gross community product (GCP)	2592	5058	12145
Ratio, total stocks to GCP	4.80	3.82	3.97

Source: Special aggregations and computations by Karl
A. Fox and Shu Y. Huang from detailed data published by the
U.S. Bureau of Economic Analysis (1981).

U.S. as of 1979 had had to be built or manufactured again
new, the task would have absorbed the entire output of the
economy for four years!
    To put the Microcosm example most tangibly, assume
that a foundation with great foresight and an interest in
social measurement had built an exact replica of the 1929
community, an exact replica of the 1954 community, and an
exact replica of the 1979 community on adjoining square

Table 6.2. Microcosm, U.S.A.: Constant-Dollar Gross
     Values of Stocks of Physical Capital and Consumer
     Durable Goods per 1000 Persons, Total and by Five Major
     Categories: 1929, 1954, and 1979

Category of structures and equipment (including consumer durable goods)	Gross values per 1000 persons (in 1972 dollars)		
	1929 ($1000)	1954 ($1000)	1979 ($1000)
A. Residential structures and consumer durables (except automobiles)	5384	6075	10654
B. Central place structures and equipment	1755	2232	5274
C. Export base structures and equipment	3409	3260	4459
D. Public utility structures and equipment	768	994	1819
E. Highway transportation structures and equipment	1117	2871	3908
F. Total, civilian structures, ˙ equipment, and consumer durables	12433	14433	26115
Addendum:			
G. Gross community product (GCP)	2592	3780	6572
Ratio, total stocks to GCP	4.80	3.82	3.97

Source: Special aggregations and computations by Karl
A. Fox and Shu Y. Huang from detailed data published by the
U.S. Bureau of Economic Analysis (1981).

miles of land. In each community, every automobile, every
kitchen, every store, every factory would be replicated
exactly as it was in the specified year. What sorts of
things might be learned?
     Consider first the five broad categories in Table 6.1.
Category A consists of the residences, with their indoor
dwelling spaces, their basic amenities, and their access to
outdoor space (also their home appliances and other durables except automobiles). Category B consists essentially
of the 'selected services' which are needed frequently by
most residents; they tend to be centrally located in towns
like Microcosm, which we assume to be several miles away
from the nearest other town of the same or larger size. In

Microcosm, Category C consists exclusively of the small factories. Category D contains all the public utilities: water supply, sewage disposal, electricity, telephone, and natural gas. Category E contains the streets, the automobiles owned by households, and the automobiles and trucks owned by businesses and other organizations.

Category A (residences and consumer durables) constitutes about two-fifths of the total value in both 1929 and 1979; the 1979 stock was 3.7 times as large as that existing in 1929. Category B was only one-third as large as the house-and-durables aggregate in 1929 but increased more rapidly and became half as large by 1979; its 1979 value was 5.6 times the 1929 amount. Category E (automobiles, trucks, streets, and highways) increased most rapidly of all, reaching 6.5 times the 1929 base as of 1979. The rate of increase of Category D (utilities) was intermediate between the house-and-durables and the central place groups; its value in 1979 was 4.4 times the 1929 level. Category C (in Microcosm, the factories) grew most slowly, attaining 2.4 times the 1929 level by 1979.

The change in the total value of all five categories may be dramatized by pointing out that the 1929 stock could have been replicated with one year's gross community product at the 1979 level, while the 1979 stock would have required four years' GCP! The total stock was 3.9 times as large in 1979 as in 1929.

Table 6.3 shows constant-dollar gross value estimates for five types of central place buildings, with Microcosm's population growing from 1000 in 1929 to 1338 in 1954 and 1848 in 1979. These types seem to correspond roughly to several of Barker's action patterns: business, education, physical health, government, and religion. At this level of aggregation, the identification of action patterns with buildings is rather simplistic. Given our scenario, with replicas of each piece of furniture and equipment in each room of each building in Microcosm in 1929, in 1954, and in 1979, the exact relation of buildings to behavior settings and to action patterns could be established.

The ratios of 1979 to 1929 stocks in Table 6.3 are 3.1 for commercial buildings, 4.7 for educational, 6.9 for hospital and institutional, 8.4 for state and local government excluding schools and hospitals, and 3.9 for religious buildings. The ratio for the aggregate of the five types is 4.2.

Table 6.3.   Microcosm, U.S.A.:   Constant-Dollar Gross
    Values of Selected Types of Central Place Buildings,
    with Community Population Growing at the U.S. Average
    Rate: 1929, 1954, and 1979

	Gross values in 1972 dollars with community populations as indicated		
	1929	1954	1979
	1000	1338	1848
Type of building	persons ($1000)	persons ($1000)	persons ($1000)
1. Commercial	690	689	2170
2. Educational	365	618	1698
3. Hospital and institutional	99	211	676
4. State and local government (except schools and hospitals)	68	171	569
5. Religious	85	140	334
6. Total, five types	1307	1829	5448

    Source: Special aggregations and computations by Karl
A. Fox and Shu Y. Huang from detailed data published by the
U.S. Bureau of Economic Analysis (1981).

        The estimates in Table 6.4 are per capita figures for
the United States as a whole.   When multiplied by 1000,
they correspond to the values of Microcosm's stocks of
these buildings per 1000 persons.   The 1979 stock (aggregate of the five types) per 1000 persons was 2.3 times as
large as that in 1929.
        Table 6.5 shows a breakdown of residential structures
and consumer durable goods into the structures themselves
and seven categories of durables, including automobiles
owned by consumers.   The sum of Item 1 (residential structures) and Item 8 (total consumer durables except automobiles) constitutes Category A of Table 6.1 (e.g. 5384 in
1929, 8128 in 1954, and 19689 in 1979, in thousands of
dollars).   Line 9, automobiles owned by consumers, was a
component of Category F, the highway transportation complex, in Table 6.1.
        The ratios of 1979 stocks to those of 1929 are 3.0 for
the structures themselves and 3.4 for furniture, other

Table 6.4. Microcosm, U.S.A.: Constant-Dollar Gross
Values of Selected Types of Central Place Buildings per
1000 Persons: 1929, 1954, and 1979

| Type of building | Gross values per 1000 persons (in 1972 dollars) | | |
	1929 ($1000)	1954 ($1000)	1979 ($1000)
1. Commercial	690	515	1174
2. Educational	365	462	919
3. Hospital and institutional	99	158	366
4. State and local government (except schools and hospitals)	68	128	308
5. Religious	85	105	181
6. Total, five types	1307	1367	2948

Source: Special aggregations and computations by Karl
A. Fox and Shu Y. Huang from detailed data published by the
U.S. Bureau of Economic Analysis (1981).

durable house furnishings, and tableware.[4] These durables
are inert items which do a great deal to make a home com-
fortable and attractive but they don't 'do' anything;   for
the most part they have no motors or moving parts.   The
1979 to 1929 ratio for another relatively inert (and very
heterogeneous) category, jewelry, watches, and so on, is
6.4.

The 1979 to 1929 ratios for categories 3, 5, 6 and 7
range from 14 to 95!   Of course, their 1929 bases were
small.   However, by 1979 the absolute value of kitchen and
other household appliances exceeded the 1929 value of the
most traditional category—furniture, other durable house
furnishings, and tableware—by a substantial margin.   The
same was true of the radio and television group; the wheel
goods and sports equipment group was valued at $652,000 in
1979 and the 'other motor vehicles' group at $547,000,
compared with $678,000 for the furniture group in 1929.
For consumer-owned automobiles, the 1979 to 1929 ratio was
7.5.   For the entire residence-and-consumer durables complex, the 1979 to 1929 ratio was 3.9.

Table 6.6 shows the same categories on a per capita
basis (for the U.S.) and per 1000 persons for Microcosm.

Table 6.5. Microcosm, U.S.A.: Constant-Dollar Gross
    Values of Residential Structures and Consumer Durable
    Goods with Community Population Growing at the U.S.
    Average Rate: 1929, 1954, and 1979

Category	Gross values in 1972 dollars with community populations as indicated		
	1929 1000 persons ($1000)	1954 1338 persons ($1000)	1979 1848 persons ($1000)
1. Residential structures	4448	6409	13492
2. Furniture, tableware, and other durable house furnishings	678	981	2286
3. Kitchen and other household appliances	57	207	832
4. Jewelry, watches, opthalmic products, books, maps	140	286	885
5. Radio, TV, records, musical instruments	27	111	994
6. Wheel goods, durable toys, sports equipment, boats and pleasure aircraft	27	94	652
7. Other motor vehicles (excludes automobiles)	6	41	547
8. Total consumer durables, except automobiles (Items 2 through 7)	935	1721	6196
9. Automobiles owned by consumers	424	892	3201
10. Total, residential structures and consumer durables including automobiles owned by consumers	5807	9021	22889

    Source: Special aggregations and computations by Karl
A. Fox and Shu Y. Huang from detailed data published by the
U.S. Bureau of Economic Analysis (1981).

Table 6.6. Microcosm, U.S.A.: Constant-Dollar Gross
    Values of Residential Structures and Consumer Durable
    Goods Per 1000 Persons: 1929, 1954, and 1979

| Category | Gross values per 1000 persons (in 1972 dollars) | | |
	1929 ($1000)	1954 ($1000)	1979 ($1000)
1. Residential structures	4448	4790	7301
2. Furniture, tableware, and other durable house furnishings	678	733	1237
3. Kitchen and other household appliances	57	155	450
4. Jewelry, watches, opthalmic products, books, maps	140	214	479
5. Radio, TV, records, musical instruments	27	83	538
6. Wheel goods, durable toys, sports equipment, boats and pleasure aircraft	27	70	353
7. Other motor vehicles (excludes automobiles)	6	31	296
8. Total consumer durables, except automobiles (Items 2 through 7)	935	1286	3353
9. Automobiles owned by consumers	424	667	1732
10. Total, residential structures and consumer durables including automobiles owned by consumers	5807	6742	12386

Source: Special aggregations and computations by Karl
A. Fox and Shu Y. Huang from detailed data published by the
U.S. Bureau of Economic Analysis (1981).

The 1979 to 1929 ratios were 1.6 for the residential structures themselves, 1.8 for the furniture group, 8.2 for all
other consumer durables except automobiles, 4.1 for consumer-owned automobiles, and 2.1 for the residence-and-
durables complex as a whole.

In our scenario, it would be easily possible to visit
the three replicas of Microcosm--1929, 1954, and 1979--in
rotation.   Special studies could be made of kitchens, of
bathrooms, of bedrooms, of living rooms, of garages, driveways, and yards, of automobiles, boats, and recreational
vehicles. What activities feasible in 1979 were not feasible in 1954? In 1929?

Even without documentation, the three replicas of the
'hardware' of Microcosm should realize an archeologist's
dream--or an architect's, or a social and economic histo-
rian's. But what if our foundation had had the foresight--
and foreknowledge--to conduct a complete Barker-type survey
of Microcosm's behavior settings in each of the three
years? What might we learn about the interactions between
changes in the behavior objects and circumjacent milieus of
the settings, the attributes of the participating individuals, and the concomitant changes in their allocations of
time between settings and between types of roles within
settings?

A foundation with such foresight and objectivity would
certainly have obtained permission from zone 5 and 6 leaders in Microcosm's nonhousehold, mostly open-to-the-public
settings, to make documentary films and sound recordings of
sample occurrences of settings in each genotype--which
could be re-run in replicas of the rooms or other spaces in
which the activities occurred.   What was a grocery store
like in 1929? In 1954? In 1979? A house-building, or
street construction, or sewer line excavation site? And so
on.

We should note in passing that people not only behave
in behavior settings--they learn to behave in behavior
settings. The equivalent of four years of the community's
gross economic product is embedded in the buildings and
equipment in which and with which they live and work. The
houses last an average of perhaps 70 years, various other
structures 30 to 50, and various types of equipment and
consumer durables perhaps 8 to 15. Their persistence imposes a gyroscopic stability and continuity upon most of
the activities of daily life over periods of one or a few
years.

Nevertheless, human life expectancy is such that the
entire stock of factory and office equipment and consumer
durables is replaced several times during a typical person's life span, the stock of commercial and industrial
buildings twice, and the stock of residential structures

once. In the short run, physical capital enforces stability; in the long run it enforces change. The immediate
physical environment of our behavior changes in size,
shape, and technology and in its distribution over space.
We do not know where our environment is going but we must
go with it, for it contains us.

NOTES

1. In 1951-52, Barker and Wright (1955, p. 31) estimated
these percentages of total living-time as 97.5 and 98.5.

2. Estimates of the percentage of living-time spent in
Midwest during a survey year apply strictly to those
persons (about six-sevenths of the total) who do not change
their residences to or away from the town during the year.
Barker and Wright (1955, pp. 28-29) noted that 14 percent
of the persons living in Midwest on November 1, 1949 had
moved away by October 31, 1950; also, that 14 percent of
the persons living in Midwest on October 31, 1950 had moved
there in the preceding 12 months. But the 95 to 98 percent
estimates would apply even to their living-times during the
months when they were officially Midwest residents.

3. The BEA (1981) has also published estimates of net
values. Their relative movements over time are quite
similar to those of the gross values, and we prefer the
gross values for our present purpose.

4. The category titles in Tables 6.5 and 6.6 do not constitute an exhaustive list of the items included in them,
but are suggestive of the major types.

CHAPTER 7

THE CLASSIFICATION AND DELINEATION OF
COMMUNITIES AND REGIONS IN SOCIAL SYSTEM ACCOUNTS

We noted in Chapter 1 that social system accounting faces two major problems: how to measure and account for nonmarket activities and how to combine social and economic indicators. In Chapter 2 we used the concept of a 'closed' community to suggest that a system of social accounts based on behavior settings could accomplish both of these objectives at the level of a town and its trade area. In Chapter 3 we asserted that all of the objective indicators in the OECD List of Social Indicators (1982) could be picked up and/or incorporated in such an accounting system. In Chapters 4 and 5, we proposed methods for merging eco-behavioral data on genotypes and roles with economic data on industries and occupations at the national level.

In the present chapter we use central place concepts to show how the data systems and accounts described for a small community and for the nation as a whole could be applied to counties (under favorable circumstances), home-to-work commuting fields (functional economic areas or FEAs), and BEA Economic Areas. BEA Economic Areas constitute an exhaustive partitioning of the United States.

During the past decade, the U.S. Bureau of Economic Analysis (BEA) has succeeded in developing estimates of employment and earnings, by eleven economic sectors, for each of the 3000 or more counties in the United States. These county estimates add up to the corresponding official national totals, and could be added up for any cluster or category of two or more counties. Apart from the county estimates as such, the BEA has emphasized publication of estimates in greater industry detail for Standard Metropolitan Statistical Areas and BEA Economic Areas. Both types of areas consist of clusters of whole counties, and most of the BEA Areas are centered on SMSAs or clusters of contiguous SMSAs.

Each BEA Area consists of one or more home-to-work commuting fields. Few residents of a given BEA Area work in any other. Hence, the incomes of residents, with few

exceptions, are earned and spent in the same BEA Area; an
even larger percent of their time is spent in it, and nearly all of their participation in nonmarket activities occurs within its boundaries. Thus, a BEA Area approximates
a 'closed' community for social accounting purposes; if it
consists of two or more distinct home-to-work commuting
fields, the same is true of each field separately. The 173
BEA Economic Areas delineated as of 1969 constituted an
exhaustive partitioning of the United States into these
urban-centered, relatively self-contained regions.

The behavior setting approach to social accounts is
definitely an ecological one. At the community level it
has affinities with the work of rural sociologists such as
Galpin (1915), Kolb (1933), and Brunner (1933). If extended to BEA Areas, it has affinities with the work of human
ecologists such as McKenzie, Park, and Hawley, and particularly with McKenzie's (1933a, 1933b) studies of metropolitan regions. A series of steps from Barker's town and
trade area to metropolitan regions is provided by central
place theory, which has been developed mainly by geograph-
ers and economists.

Berry and Harris (1968) listed the successive steps in
the central-place or urban hierarchy as hamlet, village,
town, small city (often a county seat), regional capital,
regional metropolis, national metropolis, national capital,
and world city. BEA Economic Areas are centered on cities
ranging from the regional capital to the world city class
(e.g. New York). Borchert and Adams (1963) used a different terminology in classifying trade centers in a large
region surrounding Minneapolis: minimum convenience, full
convenience, partial shopping, complete shopping, secondary
wholesale-retail, and primary wholesale-retail. The first
four categories required successively wider arrays of types
of retail stores and service establishments; the last two
required successively wider arrays of wholesalers. We show
that most of the private enterprise genotypes in Midwest as
of 1963-64 corresponded exactly to the types of retail
stores listed by Borchert and Adams, and that Midwest qualified as a full convenience center in their classification
scheme.

We also consider the problem of defining a community's
'completeness' in terms of the arrays of nonmarket as well
as market genotypes it contains and the proportion of time
the residents of its town and trade area spend within its
boundaries. After studying retail trade data for all

communities in the Des Moines BEA Economic Area, we con-
clude that a full convenience center and its trade area
(which we assume to correspond with its school and church
attendance areas) constitutes the smallest community for
which a set of social accounts might reasonably be maintained.   Such centers usually include both an elementary
school and a high school as well as two or more churches
and the stipulated array of retail and service establishments.

Most county seat towns in the area can be classified
as either partial or complete shopping centers. The county
courthouse,   attorneys'   offices,   and   local   offices   of
certain state and federal agencies in such a town substantially increase the variety of its environment. If it is
(as usual) the largest town in the county and is located
near its center, the county as a whole forms a logical (and
ecological) accounting unit.   The next human-ecological
unit above such counties is a home-to-work commuting field
or FEA.

Midwest in 1963-64 had a town and trade area population of about 1680. Barker's measures of inhabitant-setting intersections (ISI) were particularly intriguing as
descriptions of the network of face-to-face associations
linking members of the community with one another. With
only one bank, one elementary school, and one high school
and with most of the retail stores clustered around courthouse square, there could be little doubt that a considerable portion of Midwest's environment was familiar to, and
shared by, most of these 1680 people. Barker developed an
index of the size or extent of the town's environment
(other than households) based on a weighted average of the
total number of its behavior settings, the total number of
their occurrences during the year, and the total number of
hours during which they were active. He used this index to
compare the sizes of the ecological environments of Midwest
in two different years and of the environments of Midwest
and an English town in each of those years.

It would be useful to know how the patterns of inhabitant-setting intersections change as between towns, small
cities, and regional capitals and whether appropriate measures of the sizes of their environments could be developed. In a regional capital of (say) 60,000 population, the
ISI networks might identify elementary school attendance
areas and neighborhood shopping centers as well as the high
school, the community college, and the central business

district. It would be much too expensive to determine
ISI's in such a city by census methods; it would be necessary to develop short cut methods based on maps of school
attendance areas, interviews with merchants, and perhaps
interviews with a sample of households.

Measures of the sizes of the environments actually
occupied (used) by poor, aged, or disabled persons could be
computed by Barker's methods and compared with those of
adults with good health and adequate incomes. ISI patterns
and measures of extent of the de facto environments in
distinctive urban neighborhoods should also be useful.

By using insights and data systems based on central
place theory, it should be possible to develop compatible
sets of social accounts and indicators at all levels in the
urban hierarchy from towns (in favorable locations) and
small cities to the largest metropolises and, of course,
for the nation as a whole.

7.1. THE CLASSIFICATION OF RETAIL AND WHOLESALE TRADE CENTERS

Borchert and Adams (1963) classified all of the towns and
cities in a multi-state region around Minneapolis according
to the arrays of retail and wholesale establishments they
contained. They arrived at the six-level hierarchy depict-
ed in Figure 7.1. The first four levels, in ascending
order, are based on retail trade: minimum convenience,
full convenience, partial shopping, and complete shopping
retail trade centers. The fifth and sixth levels are based
on wholesale criteria: secondary wholesale-retail and
primary wholesale-retail trade centers. The type or level
of center is indicated at the base of each bar. Types of
business are listed in the right-hand column. Businesses
that were required and optional in defining each type of
trade center are indicated by markings on each bar.

Table 7.1 applies the Borchert-Adams framework to
Midwest town as of 1963-64. To begin with, Midwest easily
satisfies the requirements for a minimum convenience trade
center on the basis of nine private enterprise genotypes:
gasoline service stations, grocery stores, a drug store,
hardware stores, a bank, eating places, garages, farm implement agencies, and a variety store. Each genotype is
also a Standard Industrial Classification (SIC) industry.

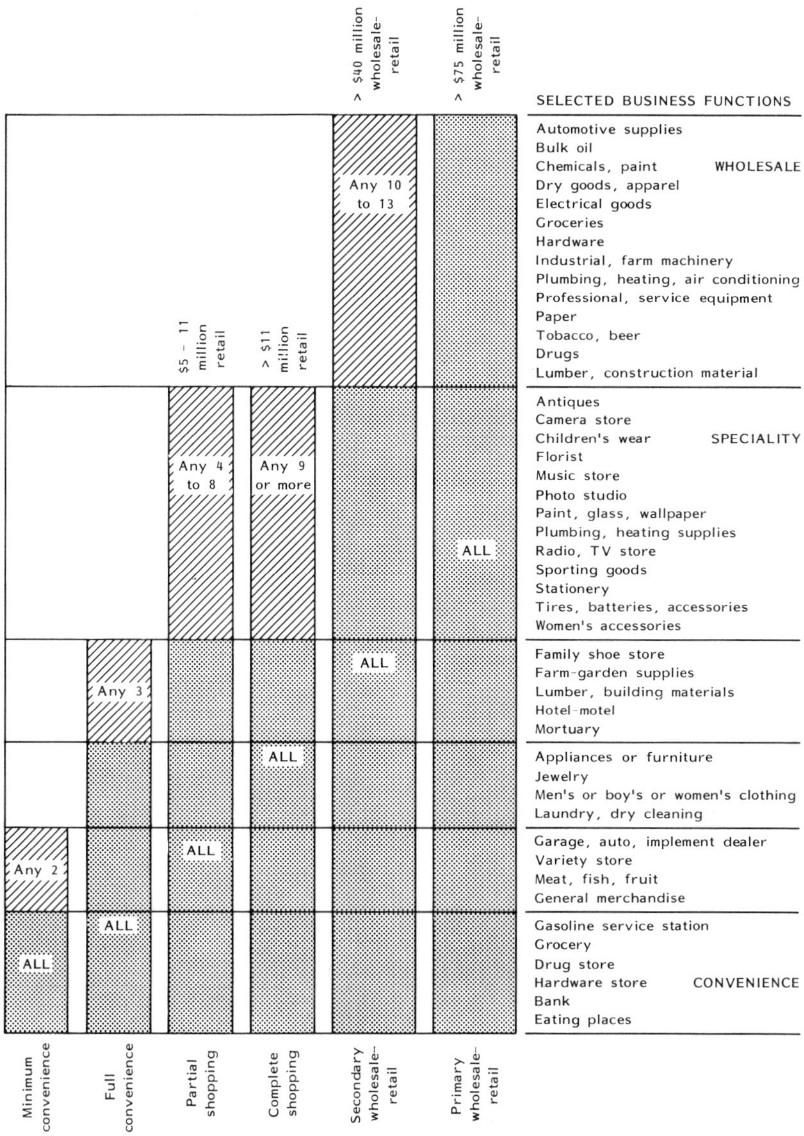

> $40 million wholesale-retail   > $75 million wholesale-retail

SELECTED BUSINESS FUNCTIONS

$5 – 11 million retail   > $11 million retail

Any 10 to 13

Automotive supplies
Bulk oil
Chemicals, paint   WHOLESALE
Dry goods, apparel
Electrical goods
Groceries
Hardware
Industrial, farm machinery
Plumbing, heating, air conditioning
Professional, service equipment
Paper
Tobacco, beer
Drugs
Lumber, construction material

Any 4 to 8   Any 9 or more

ALL

Antiques
Camera store
Children's wear   SPECIALITY
Florist
Music store
Photo studio
Paint, glass, wallpaper
Plumbing, heating supplies
Radio, TV store
Sporting goods
Stationery
Tires, batteries, accessories
Women's accessories

Any 3   ALL

Family shoe store
Farm-garden supplies
Lumber, building materials
Hotel-motel
Mortuary

ALL

Appliances or furniture
Jewelry
Men's or boy's or women's clothing
Laundry, dry cleaning

Any 2   ALL

Garage, auto, implement dealer
Variety store
Meat, fish, fruit
General merchandise

ALL   ALL

Gasoline service station
Grocery
Drug store
Hardware store   CONVENIENCE
Bank
Eating places

Minimum convenience | Full convenience | Partial shopping | Complete shopping | Secondary wholesale-retail | Primary wholesale-retail

Figure 7.1. Trade center types defined by business functions. (Source: John R. Borchert and Russell B. Adams, Trade Centers and Trade Areas of the Upper Midwest. Upper Midwest Economic Study, Urban Report No. 3, Minneapolis: University of Minnesota, September 1963, p. 4).

Table 7.1. Correspondences Between Barker's Retail Trade Genotypes
   (Midwest, 1963-64) and the Selected Business Functions Prescribed by
   Borchert and Adams (1963) for (a) Minimum Convenience and (b) Full
   Convenience Trade Centers

Type of retail trade center and business function (Borchert-Adams)	Genotype No.	N (number of settings)	Total	Average per setting	E (centiurbs of habitat*
Minimum convenience:					
Gasoline service station	177	4	39281	9820	2.80
Grocery	83	3	83187	27729	1.33
Drug store	54	1	39212	39212	0.61
Hardware store	85	2	12181	6090	1.03
Bank	15	1	36860	36860	0.43
Eating places (commercial)	162	5	[100000?]	[20000?]	2.18?
Plus any two of the following:					
Garage, auto, implement dealer:					
Garages	78	2	28578	14289	1.21
Farm implement agencies	65	2	13051	6526	0.86
Variety store	208	1	21330	21330	0.57
Meat, fish, fruit (included in Genotype 83, Grocery)					
General merchandise	---	-	-----	-----	----
Subtotal, Minimum convenience	9	21	373680	17794	11.02
Full convenience:					
Appliances or furniture	77	1	11976	11976	0.54
Jewelry	100	1	4606	4606	0.47
Men or boys or women's clothing	35	1	21330	21330	0.57
Laundry, dry cleaning:					
Laundry services	109	1	5467	5467	0.50
Laundry (self-service)	108	1	22970	22970	1.25
Dry cleaning	34	1	6770	6770	0.51
Plus any three of the following:					
Family shoe store	---	-	-----	-----	----
Farm-garden supplies	---	-	-----	-----	----
Lumber, building materials	114	2	10412	5706	0.98
Hotel-motel (Midwest Hotel)	92	1	[3000?]	[3000?]	0.57?
Mortuary	75	1	731	731	0.16
Increment for full convenience:	9	10	87262	8726	5.55
Total for Full convenience	18	31	460942	14869	16.57

*Computed from the formula implicit in Barker and Schoggen's
definition of a centiurb (i.e., one percent of the environment of a
"standard town" or urb): E = 0.049N + 0.0006030 + 0.0001113D, where N is
the number of settings, O (occurrences) the number of setting-days, and D
(duration) the number of setting-hours; the explicit formula was derived by
Fox as a computational shortcut. See Barker and Schoggen (1973, pp. 22-30)
for the definition of a centiurb and their rationale for using it
as a measure of habitat extent.
   Source: Compiled or reconstructed from Table 5.3, pp. 110-116, in
Roger G. Barker, Ecological Psychology, Stanford: Stanford University
Press, 1968 and Appendix A, pp. 448-494, in Roger G. Barker and Phil
Schoggen, Qualities of Community Life, San Francisco: Jossey-Bass, 1973.

The lower portion of Table 7.1 shows that Midwest also qualifies as a full convenience trade center on the basis of nine additional genotypes: a furniture store, a jewelry store, a clothing store, a laundry, a self-service laundromat, a dry cleaning establishment, lumberyards, a small hotel, and a funeral home. It is significant that, in eight of these nine genotypes, Midwest had only one establishment, indicating that Midwest and its trade area exceeded the threshhold population size and buying power for a full convenience trade center by a rather small margin. In contrast, Midwest had two or more establishments in six of the minimum convenience genotypes, and Barker notes somewhere that Midwest had also had two drug stores for many years until just before the 1963-64 survey.

It is worth noting that total occupancy time in the minimum convenience group averaged nearly 42,000 person-hours per genotype, compared with only 9,700 per genotype in the full convenience set. If the ratio of customer-hours to employee-and-proprietor hours is about the same in both groups, it appears that the locational 'pull' of a given number of consumers on a minimum convenience genotype is about four times as great as that on a full convenience genotype. If a full convenience genotype were displaced to another location ten miles away, it should displace only a fourth as much occupancy time from its orginal site as if a minimum convenience genotype were removed to the same distance.

Figure 7.2 shows the distribution of town population sizes in a 5,000 square mile area around Fort Dodge, Iowa, a city with 30,000 residents. Generally similar distributions exist in many agricultural regions of the United States.

According to the Borchert-Adams criteria, Fort Dodge as of 1963-64 was a secondary wholesale-retail trade center. It had all 13 types of retail specialty stores shown in Figure 7.1, all but one or two of the 14 wholesale categories, and annual retail sales of $66 million.

It seems intuitively clear that no other town or city in the area shown can rival Fort Dodge in the extent and variety of its central place functions. Of the 15 places shown other than Fort Dodge, 4 would be classified as complete shopping, 3 as partial shopping, and 8 as full convenience centers. Several other towns not shown would be

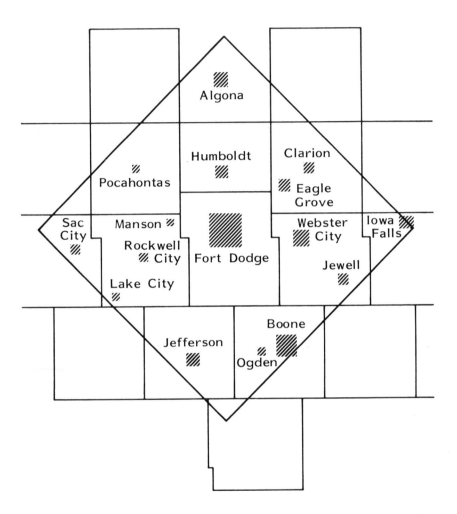

Figure 7.2. Distribution of town population sizes in the Fort Dodge area. Areas of squares are proportional to 1960 town populations. Only towns with retail sales of $2.5 million or more for year ending June 30, 1964, are shown.

marginal members of the full convenience class, and there were also several minimum convenience centers.

7.2. CLASSIFICATION OF TRADE CENTERS IN THE DES MOINES BEA ECONOMIC AREA

As of 1970, the Des Moines (Iowa) BEA Economic Area consisted of 26 whole counties extending over 14,000 square miles and containing nearly 800,000 people. Only 45 of the nation's 173 BEA Economic Areas had 1970 populations of 1,000,000 or more; methods of description and analysis that proved successful or helpful in the Des Moines area should be applicable to at least 120 other BEA areas and probably more.

     Figure 7.3 shows a classification, according to the Borchert-Adams criteria, of the 91 trade centers in the Des Moines BEA Economic Area which met the standards for minimum convenience or higher levels in 1969-70. Des Moines was the only primary wholesale-retail center, with taxable retail sales 9.6 times as large as the minimum for this category: $903 million as against $93.75 million.[1] Three other cities qualified as secondary wholesale-retail centers; 13 as complete shopping centers; another 13 as partial shopping centers; 25 as full convenience centers; and 36 as minimum convenience centers.

     Where numbers are shown on the map, they are sales taxes due (3 percent) in thousands of dollars; taxable sales equal 33.33 times taxes due. The symbols identify trade center levels as follows: Double rectangle, primary wholesale-retail; single rectangle, secondary wholesale-retail; oval, complete shopping; number underlined, partial shopping; C, full convenience; and dot, minimum convenience.

     By counties, the number of retail businesses reporting taxable sales in 1969-70 ranged from fewer than 300 in Ringgold, Clarke, and Davis counties to more than 6,000 in Polk. Taxable sales per business ranged from $28,200 in Van Buren County to $148,800 in Polk. Many individual stores in small towns are just above the threshhold sizes for their genotypes; while some units of threshhold size will also be found in larger towns and cities, the maximum and modal sizes will increase with city and trade areas populations until they strike an approximate balance

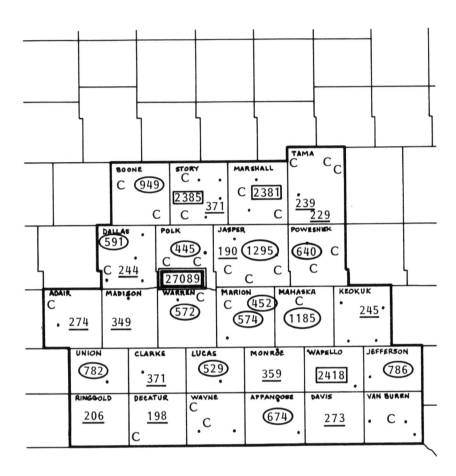

Figure 7.3. Trade centers in the Des Moines BEA Area
classified by Borchert–Adams types based on taxable retail
sales, 1969–70. Where numbers are shown, they are sales
taxes due (3 percent) in thousands of dollars; taxable sales
equal 33.33 times taxes. Symbols: Double rectangle,
primary wholesale–retail; single rectangle, secondary wholesale–retail; oval, complete shopping; number underlined,
partial shopping; C, full convenience; dot, minimum
convenience.

between internal economies of scale and external
limitations such as traffic congestion and population
density.

The Iowa sales tax data available were published in
such a form that we could not check each center's precise
array of 'selected business functions', so we used total
retail sales as the classifying variable. Total sales may
appear to be a crude criterion, but there is good logical
support for it in our study area. Consumers throughout the
area have had rather similar needs; they have all wanted
service stations, grocery stores, drug stores, banks, and
eating places near at hand, and open-country residents have
been willing, for convenience, to patronize small establishments in small towns. As town populations increase,
garages, variety stores, general merchandise stores, and
more specialized establishments have tended to enter at
their threshhold sizes, with the result that two towns
having the same total sales in 1969-70 tended to have the
same array of genotypes, about the same number and sizes of
establishments, and about the same proportional allocations
of total sales among product lines. Uniformity in consumer
purchases implies uniformity in retail sales.

In Figure 7.3, it will be noted that two counties,
Wayne and Van Buren, have no centers above the full convenience category. Nine other counties (Tama, Adair, Madison, Keokuk, Clarke, Monroe, Ringgold, Decatur, and Davis)
have at most partial shopping centers. Eleven counties
(Boone, Dallas, Jasper, Poweshiek, Warren, Marion, Mahaska,
Union, Lucas, Jefferson, and Appanoose) have complete shopping centers but no larger cities. Three more (Wapello,
Marshall, and Story) have secondary wholesale-retail centers, and Polk a primary wholesale-retail center.

Table 7.2 shows the (unweighted) means of certain
variables for each of these five groups of counties. Each
variable decreases monotonically from the primary wholesale-retail class to the full convenience category. Total
employment in retail trade is, of course, closely related
to the number of retail businesses. More significant are
the decline in number of workers per retail business from
3.47 in the primary wholesale-retail county to 1.27 in the
full convenience group and the corresponding decline in
taxable sales per retail business from $148,900 to $31,400.
Taxable retail sales per capita decline from $3327 in the
primary wholesale-retail county to $1312 in the full conve-
nience group; personal income per capita (1971) also

Table 7.2. Unweighted Means of Selected Variables for Counties Grouped According to the Borchert-Adams Types of Their Largest Trade Centers, Des Moines BEA Economic Area, 1969-70

Category of largest trade center	Number of counties	Retail sales tax due per capita, 1969-70	Taxable retail sales per capita, 1969-70	Personal income per capita, 1971	Number of retail businesses, 1969-70	Employment in retail trade, 1970	Number employed per retail business, 1970	Taxable retail sales per business, 1969-70
A. Original values of variables									
Primary wholesale-retail	1	$ 99.82	$3327	$4501	6399	22219	3.47	$148800
Secondary wholesale-retail	2[a]	65.54	2185	4126	1088	2648	2.44	83600
Complete shopping	10[b]	55.64	1855	3555	661	1506	2.25	57300
Partial shopping	9	44.29	1476	3325	380	702	1.83	41900
Full convenience	2	39.37	1312	3137	359	446	1.27	31400
B. Index numbers, primary wholesale-retail = 100									
Primary wholesale-retail	1	100.0	100.0	100.0	100.0	100.0	100.0	100.0
Secondary wholesale retail	2[a]	65.7	65.7	91.7	17.0	11.9	70.3	56.2
Complete shopping	10[b]	55.7	55.8	79.0	10.3	6.8	64.8	38.5
Partial shopping	9	44.4	44.4	73.9	5.9	3.2	52.7	28.2
Full convenience	2	39.4	39.4	69.7	5.6	2.0	36.6	21.1

a. Excluding Story because of large number (about 20,000) of university students in its population of 62,783.

b. Excluding Warren because more than half of its labor force works in Polk County and also does much shopping there.

Source: Compiled and computed by Karl A. Fox from Iowa Sales Tax Reports for 1969-70 and the 1970 U.S. Census of Population.

declines, but much less steeply, from $4501 to $3137, and sales as a percent of income decline from 73.9 to 41.8.

All these gradients imply that residents of counties having only full convenience or partial shopping centers made some of their purchases in counties having complete shopping centers and/or larger cities. In a regression analysis covering all 99 counties of Iowa for the year ending June 30, 1964, we found the following implicit gradients for Iowa towns and cities of successively larger populations:

Regression Estimates of Annual
Retail Sales per Capita
Based on Tax Collections

Town Population Size	Not Adjusted for Effects of per Capita Income	Per Capita Income Held Constant	Usual Type of Trade Center
1,000- 2,499	$ 854	$ 981	Full Convenience
2,500- 4,999	1,024	1,097	Partial Shopping
5,000-24,999	1,312	1,246	Complete Shopping
25,000 and over	1,640	1,405	Secondary Wh.-Retail
R^2	.57	.74	

Percentage Increase in
Estimated Retail Sales per Capita
from one Population Size
to the Next Attributable to

Town Population Size	Total	Higher per Capita Incomes	Wider Product Lines	Usual Type of Trade Center
1,000- 2,499				Full Convenience
2,500- 4,999	20	7	12	Partial Shopping
5,000-24,999	28	13	14	Complete Shopping
25,000 and over	25	11	13	Secondary Wh.-Retail

Estimated retail sales per capita increased an average of
24 percent from each population class to the next; an average of 11 percent was attributed to higher per capita
incomes in the next class and an average of 13 percent
(slightly more than half of the increase in per capita
sales) was attributed to wider product lines--or, in
Barker's terminology, additional behavior setting genotypes.[2]

It is perfectly obvious that open-country residents
must make their purchases, or most of them, in towns and
cities. In Table 7.3, we have listed 25 towns and cities
with particularly high retail sales per capita of their own
residents. Eighteen of them are county seats, and 16 of
these have the largest values of taxable retail sales in
their respective counties and presumably the widest product
lines. Nine of the 16 just mentioned are so dominant as to
account for 79.8 to 89.8 percent of all retail sales in
their counties!

If a town accounted for 100 percent of a county's
retail sales and only 50 percent of its population, the
town's sales per capita of its own residents would be
exactly 2.00 times the county's sales per capita of all the
county's residents. Chariton in Lucas County approaches
this situation; with (5009/10163)100 = 49.3 percent of the
county's population and 86.3 percent of its sales, Chariton's sales per capita of its own residents are 86.3/49.3
= 1.75 times those of Lucas County per capita of its residents. The respective per capita tax figures are $105.66
for Chariton and $60.52 for Lucas County.

Another way of viewing the matter is as follows: If
Chariton's own residents buy exactly as much per capita as
the county average, then Chariton must be serving the
equivalent of 1.75(5009) = 8,766 average consumers; 5009 of
these are residents of Chariton and 3,757 must be residents
of the open-country and the smaller towns.

On these assumptions, 16 of the trade centers served
at least as many nonresidents as residents; their sales per
capita of their own residents ranged from 2.00 to 2.91
times their counties' averages. Ratios for the other nine
centers ranged from 1.47 to 1.99.

If we classify the 25 centers into Borchert-Adams
categories, we find five complete shopping centers, ten
partial shopping centers, nine full convenience centers,
and one minimum convenience center (near the upper sales

Table 7.3. Sales Taxes Per Capita, County Average Sales Taxes,
     and Equivalent Average Consumers Served, 25 Trade Centers with
     High Sales Tax Collections Per Capita of Their Own Residents,
     Des Moines BEA Economic Area, 1969-70

County and trade center	Sales tax due per capita of trade center population (dollars)	Population of trade center (number)	Sales tax due per capita of county population (dollars)	Ratio, trade center to county tax per capita	Equivalent average consumers served by trade center (number)
Adair					
Greenfield*	$123.70	2212	$53.36	2.32	5132
Adair	134.20	750	53.36	2.51	1882
Clarke					
Osceola*	118.92	3124	54.64	2.18	6810
Ringgold					
Mount Ayr*	116.87	1762	40.32	2.90	5110
Mahaska					
Oskaloosa*	105.59	11224	62.87	1.68	18856
Lucas					
Chariton*	105.66	5009	60.52	1.75	8766
Appanoose					
Centerville*	103.14	6531	52.25	1.97	12866
Davis					
Bloomfield*	100.31	2718	41.56	2.41	6550
Keokuk					
Sigourney*	105.75	2319	41.11	2.57	5960
Wayne					
Corydon*	98.64	1745	41.33	2.39	4171
Humeston	94.86	673	41.33	2.30	1548
Van Buren					
Keosauqua*	89.74	1018	37.41	2.40	2443
Bonaparte	108.69	517	37.41	2.91	1504

limit for its class); these centers are grouped by types in
Table 7.4.
     The five complete shopping centers have an average
population of 7,943 and an average sales ratio (city per
capita to county per capita) of 1.69. They account for 43
to 61 percent of their counties' populations and 85 to 89
percent of their counties' retail sales. All five centers
are county seats. Three of the five counties are of the

124   Chapter 7

Table 7.3. (Continued)

County and trade center	Sales tax due per capita of trade center population (dollars)	Population of trade center (number)	Sales tax due per capita of county population (dollars)	Ratio, trade center to county tax per capita	Equivalent average consumers served by trade center (number)
Union					
Creston*	95.03	8234	64.85	1.47	12104
Decatur					
Leon*	92.38	2142	36.92	2.50	5355
Jasper					
Prairie City	90.59	1141	54.88	1.65	1883
Sully	105.03	685	54.88	1.91	1308
Dallas					
Adel*	100.00	2419	50.58	1.99	4814
Madison					
Winterset*	95.49	3654	42.34	2.26	8258
Monroe					
Albia*	86.42	4151	43.11	2.00	8302
Jefferson					
Fairfield*	90.23	8715	56.68	1.59	13857
Tama					
Toledo*	97.64	2361	45.24	2.16	5100
Traer	98.74	1682	45.24	2.18	3667
Poweshiek					
Montezuma*	96.11	1353	54.47	1.76	2381
Marshall					
Gilman	170.51	513	67.46	2.53	1298

*County seat.
Source: Compiled and computed by Karl A. Fox from Iowa Sales Tax Reports for 1969-70 and the 1970 U.S. Census of Population.

12-township type with land surfaces of 425 to 436 square miles.

The ten partial shopping centers have an average population of 2,686 and an average per capita sales ratio of 2.33. Four of them (Osceola, Mount Ayr, Bloomfield, and Albia) are strongly dominant in their counties, with 28 to 44 percent of their populations and 80 to 90 percent of their sales; in these respects they are much like the five complete shopping centers. The other six partial shopping

Table 7.4. Selected Data for 25 Trade Centers with High Retáil
Sales Per Capita of Their Own Residents, Classified by Trade
Center Types, Des Moines BEA Economic Area, 1969-70

Type of trade center	Ratio, trade center to county sales per capita	Popu- lation of trade center (number)	Popu- lation of county (number)	Trade center sales as percent of county total	Land area of county (square miles)
Complete shopping					
Oskaloosa*	1.68	11224	22177	85.0	572
Chariton*	1.75	5009	10163	86.3	434
Centerville*	1.97	6531	15007	85.7	523
Creston*	1.47	8234	13557	89.3	425
Fairfield*	1.59	8715	15774	87.8	436
Partial shopping					
Greenfield*	2.32	2212	9487	54.1	569
Osceola*	2.18	3124	7581	89.8	429
Mount Ayr*	2.90	1762	6373	80.2	538
Bloomfield*	2.41	2718	8207	79.8	509
Sigourney*	2.57	2319	13949	42.7	579
Leon*	2.50	2142	9737	33.0	530
Adel*	1.99	2419	26085	18.5	597
Winterset*	2.26	3654	11558	71.4	564
Albia*	2.00	4151	9357	88.7	435
Toledo*	2.16	2361	20147	25.3	720
Full convenience					
Adair	2.51	750	9487	19.8	569
Corydon*	2.39	1745	8405	49.6	532
Humeston	2.30	673	8405	18.4	532
Keosauqua*	2.40	1018	8643	28.3	487
Prairie City	1.65	1141	35425	5.3	731
Sully	1.91	685	35425	3.7	731
Montezuma*	1.76	1353	18803	12.7	589
Gilman	2.53	513	41076	3.2	574
Traer	2.18	1682	20147	18.2	720
Minimum convenience					
Bonaparte	2.91	517	8643	17.4	487

*County seat.
Source: Compiled and computed by Karl A. Fox from Iowa
Sales Tax Reports for 1969-70 and the 1970 U.S. Census of
Population.

centers account for 9 to 32 percent of their counties'
populations and 18 to 71 percent of their sales, and have
sales ratios of 1.99 to 2.57. All ten of the partial shopping centers are county seats.

The nine full convenience centers include only three
county seats. The average population of the nine centers
is 1,062 and the average per capita sales ratio is 2.18.
(Midwest town's population was 830, and the ratio of its
town-and-trade-area population to its town population,
1680/830 = 2.02, is conceptually equivalent to the ratio of
2.18 just cited for the Iowa full convenience centers).
Two of the county seats, Corydon and Keosauqua, account for
49.6 and 28.3 percent respectively of their counties'
sales; the third, Montezuma, accounts for only 12.7 percent
of its county's sales and is overshadowed within the county
by Grinnell. The other six centers account for 3 to 20
percent of their counties' sales and 1.2 to 8.3 percent of
their counties' populations; in all cases their sales are
surpassed by other centers within their counties.

Finally, the one center in the list which we have
classified as minimum convenience, Bonaparte in Van Buren
County, is just below our cutoff point for the full convenience centers. With 6.0 percent of its county's population and 17.4 percent of its sales, Bonaparte has a sales
ratio of 2.91, rivaled only by Mount Ayr's ratio of 2.90.

We do not propose to implement a complete set of trade
area delineations. However, a number of comments are in
order.

(1) In nine counties (Mahaska, Lucas, Appanoose,
Union, Jefferson, Clarke, Ringgold, Davis, and Monroe) as
of 1970, it appears that the trade area of the county seat
was approximately coextensive with the county itself. Only
10 to 20 percent of the taxable retail sales in those counties remained for smaller incorporated places, unincorpor-
ated hamlets, and open-country locations. Apparently, no
area smaller than the county itself would enclose the
retail businesses of the county seat and all or nearly all
of their regular customers.

Five of these nine counties are of the 12-township
type, with land surfaces of 425 to 436 square miles; the
other four have areas of 509; 523; 538, and 572 square
miles, to be compared with the Des Moines BEA Area average
of 13,985/26 = 538.

(2) In Madison County, with the county seat making
71.4 percent of the county's taxable sales, it would seem

appropriate to include about five-sixths of the county's townships in the trade area of the county seat and assign the remainder to another area or areas. In several other counties (Adair, Keokuk, Decatur, Wayne, and Van Buren) where county seats make 28.3 to 54.1 percent of the taxable sales, perhaps one-third to two-thirds of the counties' areas would constitute the trade areas of the county seats, leaving room for additional trade areas of the full convenience and/or minimum convenience types wholly or partly within the same county.

(3) The other three county seats (Adel, Montezuma, and Toledo) make only 12.7 to 25.3 percent of their counties' taxable sales. Adel and Montezuma are surpassed in their counties by Perry and Grinnell, and Toledo has a near rival in Tama; it appears that the trade areas of these three county seats would comprise from one-sixth to one-third of their counties' land surfaces.

(4) The remaining seven towns in Tables 7.3 and 7.4 are not county seats; six are full convenience centers and the seventh is just below our cutoff point for that class. They account for 3.2 to 19.8 percent of their counties' sales and appear to serve from 623 to 1985 average consumers in addition to their own residents; figures on open-country population densities and populations of the smaller incorporated places in their vicinities should permit reasonable approximations to their trade areas.

7.3. TRADE CENTER CATEGORIES AND THE OECD SOCIAL INDICATOR OF PROXIMITY TO SELECTED SERVICES

Sections 7.1 and 7.2 used only retail and wholesale trade criteria to classify and delineate communities. By definition, consumers have little contact with wholesalers; individual well-being is directly affected by the proximity of retailers.

The OECD indicator of proximity to selected services stresses, by implication, retail stores of the minimum convenience type, 'satisfying daily needs'. It also stresses proximity to a post office, a primary school, a pre-primary school, a sports center, a public transport stop, and medical services capable of offering emergency treatment day and night. In Barker's terms and under U.S. conditions, 'proximity' involves units of the school and government, as well as of the private enterprise, authority

systems.   Not mentioned by the OECD report, but certainly
implied, is proximity to a fire station and police protection.   Fire stations should be as close as possible to
potential fires and police stations to preventable crimes.

If we move up the scale from 'daily needs' to (approximately) 'weekly needs', we bring in full convenience
retail and service establishments, more sophisticated medical services, weekly worship services, some voluntary associations, and additional government services.   'Weekly
needs' is only a metaphor, as this level includes high
schools (secondary schools) which are used daily but by
well under 10 percent of the population;   many other organizations at this level are open daily but are visited
('needed') by a minuscule percentage of the total population on any one day.

Borchert and Adams (Figure 7.1) seem to imply that few
additional retail trade genotypes are introduced above the
complete shopping center level.   The numbers of establishments per genotype continue to increase and perhaps the
sizes of the largest units.   Cities which satisfy secondary
wholesale-retail criteria usually have community colleges
(postsecondary schools) and substantial concentrations of
medical specialists in addition to general practitioners.
Residents of such cities should find in them behavior settings of nearly all genotypes that are regularly visited by
members of the public as distinct from paid employees of
the setting leaders.

The great metropolises have some additional cultural
treasures that are valued highly by many but are visited by
few more frequently than once or twice a year.   Apart from
these treasures, there is a certain redundancy in having
18,000 restaurants or 6,000 bars!   Many behavior settings
in the spectacular skyscrapers are involved, directly and
indirectly, in large-region, national, and multinational
coordination, negotiation, finance, and control; we cannot
extend this book in this direction.

7.4.   SOCIAL ACCOUNTING MATRICES FOR SUCCESSIVELY LARGER
COMMUNITIES AND URBAN-CENTERED REGIONS

In Chapter 2 we described a conceptual model of a small
community in which the second-by-second activities of each
resident could be represented (1) by his locational coordinates in three-dimensional space, (2) by his location in

some well-defined architectural entity (e.g. Room 15 of the high school), (3) by his presence in a specific behavior setting (the 9:00 A.M. algebra class is in session in Room 15), and (4) by his behavior within that setting (his behavior indicates that he is the teacher). His life-path during the year would literally intersect a series of behavior settings, each in a particular role; the number of different nonhousehold settings intersected would be his ISI and the number of hours he spent in each setting would be his contribution to its occupancy time (OT).

Fox and van Moeseke (1973) represented a rational individual as trying to choose an optimal life style (the time-allocation vector $\underline{x}^*$) during the coming year subject to the limitations of his endowment (the vector $\underline{b}$) and his environment (the matrix $\underline{A}$). Each column of $\underline{A}$ represents a specified role in a specified behavior setting. The elements $\underline{a}_{ij}$ of column $\underline{j}$ ($\underline{j}$ = 1, 2, ..., n) are input coefficients; a unit of time spent in the $\underline{j}$th role-and-setting absorbs $\underline{a}_{ij}$ units of $\underline{b}_i$, the $\underline{i}$th element of the endowment vector ($\underline{i}$ = 1, 2, ..., m). Thus, the individual seeks to maximize his utility function $\underline{u}(\underline{x})$ subject to $\underline{Ax} \leq \underline{b}$, $\underline{x} \geq 0$. If $\underline{x}$ is measured in hours, the elements of the optimal life style vector $\underline{x}^*$ will sum to 8760 hours in a 365-day year. The elements of $\underline{b}$ would include time (8760 hours), income from property and transfer payments, occupational skills, health status, and some others.

The actual allocation of an individual's time among behavior settings, as observed in a Barker-type survey, should reveal his preference structure for behavior settings just as his actual purchases of consumer goods should reveal his preference structure for them. Thus, observed changes in the occupancy times of behavior settings by well-defined population aggregates should be subject to study by the methods of statistical demand analysis, as presented in Fox (1958), but with appropriate adjustments in the price and income concepts as described in Fox and van Moeseke (1973) and Fox (1974a).

Within a given community, residents having a number of attributes (age, sex, years of schooling completed) and statuses (in school or not; employed or not; living in private homes rather than nursing homes) in common could be grouped for purposes of accounting and modeling. We believe the 830 residents of Midwest could be classified into about 150 attribute-and-status groups which would also be applicable to other U.S. communities. Barker's 884

behavior settings could be grouped into authority systems;
within each authority system multiple settings in any genotype could be aggregated to the genotype total and in some
cases two or more genotypes could be combined; genotypes
accounting for very small amounts of occupancy time could
be consolidated into 'miscellaneous' categories. The
resulting time-allocation matrix (TAM) for the community
might have about 150 columns (groups of behavior settings)
and a similar number of attribute-and-status rows.

As many genotypes are designed specifically for children or adolescents and many workplaces are entered only by
adults, the TAM would contain many zero elements; each row
would represent the time-allocation vector (TAV) of a particular attribute-and-status group in Midwest in 1963-64.
Given the distribution of persons among attribute-and-
status groups in another community in the same region, we
could compute an expected TAM for it on the explicit assumption that its TAVs per person were the same as those of
Midwest for each group (row) i, i = 1, 2, ..., 150. Communities at successively higher levels in the central place
hierarchy of the region would have successively wider
arrays of genotypes; this has been amply documented for
retail trade and consumer-oriented services--see, for
example, Fox and Kumar (1965) and Fox (1974a)--and is probably true for the nonmarket authority systems as well.
The 'expected TAM' for a previously unsurveyed community
could then be modified and interpreted on the basis of a
limited amount of information specific to that community.

The 'expected TAM' approach could probably be extended
upward successfully from small towns like Midwest, through
small cities (often county seats of 5,000 to 25,000 population) with trade areas approximating counties, to FEA central cities (usually with 30,000 to 300,000 people) and
complete FEAs (typically with 150,000 to 500,000 residents). BEA Economic Areas of up to 2,000,000 people could
be accounted for as clusters of FEAs plus some additional
industries and genotypes in the largest city if its population exceeded 300,000. Fullerton and Prescott (1975) developed a simulation model for Iowa with 120 geographical
units (counties or parts of counties) which could be clustered to form FEAs, BEA Economic Areas, or other types of
regions. 'Expected TAMs' for Iowa counties and FEAs could
be compared, and possibly linked with, components of the
Fullerton-Prescott model for the same areas.

Alternatively, published data from the U.S. censuses of population and housing could be used to extend some elements of a social accounting system from the national level through BEA Economic Areas, FEAs, and counties down to townships, villages, and towns in rural areas and to census tracts and enumeration districts within SMSAs and urbanized areas. These same data are used by local governments currently, in conjunction with primary data needed for their various functions (street, water, and sewer system maintenance; planning and zoning; traffic control; public health; police and fire protection; public school administration; parks and playgrounds; abatement of excessive noise levels and air pollution; and perhaps others). Local governments could, if they choose, adapt behavior setting accounts to the analysis of alternative policies in their own departments. Within a comprehensive behavior setting and time-allocation framework, they should be better able to distinguish between policies which merely shift a problem between neighborhoods or departmental jurisdictions and policies which are likely to solve a problem in situ and/or with minimal adverse effects on other neighborhoods and programs.

NOTES

1. Borchert and Adams set this minimum at $75 million as of 1962, but consumer prices were 25 percent higher in 1969-70; hence we raised the threshhold to $93.75 million (equals 1.25 times 75).

2. This analysis was based on a rather sophisticated interpretation of data for counties rather than for individual towns and cities, and does not conflict with our following paragraphs about specific central places.

CHAPTER 8

A BEHAVIOR SETTING APPROACH TO MICROANALYTICAL
SIMULATION MODELS AT THE COMMUNITY LEVEL

James R. Prescott

Barker's social accounting system for the town of Midwest is unique in both coverage and conception. Though official data systems exist for private enterprises and government, his includes churches, voluntary associations and a good deal more on schools than is found in the U.S. Census of Governments. The individual reporting unit distinguished in most official systems (manufacturing establishments, stores, etc.) may also contain many behavior settings. Similarly, the variables collected and structural detail on the internal characteristics of behavior settings extend well beyond traditional financial accounting variables that are given most emphasis in government data systems.

Though comprehensive, structural comparisons seem to be the strength of Barker's system; less power is found in specifying causal interrelations among behavior settings and norms for assessing both individual setting and system performance. Thus, Barker and Schoggen (1973) are able to provide penetrating contrasts of Midwest and Yoredale (a small English town), and similarly well-documented structural comparisons of small and large schools are found in Barker and Gump (1964). It is, however, less easy to analyze the degree of success in individual setting operation and the major variables influencing performance. [The theory of manning is an exception here so will be reviewed briefly below; see, Wicker (1979).] Also, there are dimensions of intersetting structure and intersetting relationships which could usefully be added to Barker's system. The ultimate objective would be causally specified hypotheses which could be empirically modeled.

In this chapter we propose an empirically-based dynamic simulation model at the community level. We begin with a general discussion of modeling strategies and some comments on the unique nature and promise of Barker's data for modeling the community of Midwest. Successive sections deal with the theory of manning, behavior setting operation, prototype settings and causal relationships. The

132

final section discusses some anticipated problems and provides concluding remarks.

8.1. MODELING THE BARKER COMMUNITY OF MIDWEST

With the National Science Foundation's support during 1974-
80, Fox and his associates have made extensive uses of data
systems at the community, regional, national and world
levels. At the community level Fox (1980) has synthesized
a data set from secondary data sources published by Barker
[termed the Fox-Barker (FB) data set] to illuminate the
socioeconomic structure of this community. Despite these
extensive empirical applications, the primary data from the
1963-64 survey of Barker's community have not yet been used
to comprehensively model the town of Midwest. Indeed, we
know of no comprehensive sociometric model of a community
of any size.
    In our view such a model should (1) specify causal
relationships within Barker's behavior setting structure
and (2) provide a comprehensive set of social accounting
tables for a small community. The value of a social accounting system is substantially enhanced if such causal
hypotheses are testable; if they are not, we shall never
know if or why attendance at the Boy Scout meeting is ab-
normally low or high, why a community has an unusually high
drop-out rate in the school authority system, or the relative importance of parental attitudes and the quality of
teaching in determining high school grade distributions.
The power of a data system depends (at least in part) on
showing how specific variables in specified tables can be
used to test accepted theories; this is often lacking even
in well-established government data systems.

8.1.1. Modeling Strategies

The alternative types of model structures depend on research objectives. Land use-transportation models of the
type discussed by Brown et al. (1972) have been applied to
larger urban regions with very specialized land uses and
transit networks. Regional simulations that combine input-
output and demographic cohort-survival techniques also have
been applied to labor markets, states and larger regions
(see, for example, Fullerton and Prescott, 1975). Though

time use accounts incorporated into these types of models
would render them capable of testing numerous hypotheses of
interest, they are very economics-oriented and designed for
larger regions than the small town studied by Barker. For
the town of Midwest our objectives would be the following:
     (1) Expand the FB data set to include assignments of
time to all of Barker's behavior settings and allow for re-
aggregation of these activities into approximations of the
87 time use categories employed by the SRC (Survey Research
Center) in its study of Americans' use of time in 1975-76
(see SRC, 1977, 1978). Utilize the Barker data set in
conjunction with the FB data.
     (2) Provide a typology for the operation of behavior
settings along with measurable performance norms. This
would include both the internal and external influences on
a given setting in achieving specified objectives.
     (3) Provide a modeling typology and flowcharts for
sets of behavior settings within each of Barker's five
authority systems (church, school, private enterprise,
government and voluntary associations). The typology might
include ten to twelve major types of settings within each
authority system. The flowcharts would specify the predetermined and/or exogenous variables that causally influence the dependent variables (social indicators or performance norms) which, in turn, become predetermined variables
in future simulated periods.
     (4) Combine the modeling elements in (3) above with
the assignments in the FB data set to simulate behavior
settings and the resulting use of time by individuals in
Barker's community.
     These objectives suggest the use of two computer-
modeling packages. (1) MICROSIM provides a capability for
using all individuals in the FB data set and simulating
life histories of members of the community; this is a
modern version of the original work initiated by Guy Orcutt
(1961) at Harvard University. (2) The Forrester-type of
model structure provides for dynamic simulation by specifying tabled functions between causally related variables.
It is quite flexible, allowing the models to set constraints (variable limits) and identify poorly specified
equations which might be causing counterintuitive results.
 This type of model would be more applicable to objectives
(2) and (3).
     Caldwell (1980) provides a case for the use of micro-
analytical simulation as an appropriate methodology for

modeling social accounts. First, it allows for direct
representation of individuals and families. Thus, stock
attributes can be accumulated over time (e.g., experience
in leadership roles, skills, experiences, educational at-
tainment, etc.); these cannot be carried in currently implemented regional and land use-transportation models.
Second, life histories can be represented so individual
comparisons can be made over time. We might want to know
how behavioral capacities change (and how diffuse they are
throughout the community) when certain behavior settings
are added, deleted or replaced by other settings. Third,
the complexity of society should be representable so that
assumptions as to behavior setting causal relationships can
be varied. As indicated below, the modeling would have to
include new behavioral hypotheses with varied impacts on
the individuals in Barker's community as represented in his
1963-64 data.

The Forrester-type model seems appropriate for modeling the operation of behavior settings. In Urban Dynamics,
Forrester (1969) was able to attain a believable representation of a very complex social organism; as in his effort,
various data gaps might be present in specifying causal
hypotheses. Analogous to his major systems for population,
housing and enterprises, we could envisage the five Barker
authority systems plus a household sector with prototypes
(as discussed below) within each of these systems. The FB
and Barker data sets are extremely rich and disaggregated,
but many of the causal relationships might have to be
judgmentally specified as was the case in Forrester's work.
The Forrester framework allows for such specifications as
well as the individual testing of smaller model components.

Alternative spatial and temporal bases might be considered for the community simulation. Fox has chosen to
close the FB data set by bringing certain out-commuting
activities within the region's boundaries, but it would
seem desirable to preserve some spatially competitive jobs
and residential locations; these adjustments should not be
difficult to make. A daily simulation could be considered
with highly disaggregated locations for households and
behavior settings; this would allow one to analyze individual person-and-setting intersections as well as placing
individuals in specific settings at particular times.
Several seasonal and within-week prototype simulations
could be developed. However, it seems that the most needed

work is on the determinants of behavior setting attendance
(and related performance measures), and this suggests a
longer time unit without the locational detail.

8.1.2. Data Sources

Barker and his associates have produced a community data
set which is unparalleled in detail (see, e.g., Barker and
Schoggen, 1973). By implication from published sources
this data set includes detailed ratings on action patterns
and behavior mechanisms for all behavior settings, the
number of participants by zone in these settings and the
distribution of time spent in the settings for each individual. Any model which utilized either individuals or
behavior setting data would substantially benefit from his
unpublished information.
     Even if some data for individual time use were not
available, a complete time use file could be generated from
the FB data set. Fox (1980) describes his synthesis as
follows in an unpublished manuscript (see Appendix 2, Reference Notes, Volume I, Chapter 9):
     "In Table 9.1, while observing these distributional
     constraints, I have allocated the 830 town residents
     among 285 households and a nursing home. The entries
     in the table indicate the age, sex, marital status
     and relationship (to the household's head) of each
     member of the household. The entries 1, 2 and 3
     above the household indentification numbers represent
     Barker's Socioeconomic Classes 1, 2 and 3, with the
     number of persons in Class 3 increased by 26 to in-
     clude the black residents. The entries below each
     household column indicate years of education com-
     pleted by each household member (head, wife, parent
     or other relative) aged 20 years or over."
     In this reference, Fox goes on to describe similar
assignments to the rural farm sector and the specific allocation of jobs to households. He conjectures that there
might be something like 2,000 constraints in Barker's published data for 1963-64 alone. These would be more than
sufficient to replicate a complete time use distribution
for each of the 1,500 individuals in town and trade area.
The data set need not exactly replicate the time use distributions of Midwest's residents in a given year but only
be believable; 2,000 constraints in the form of time use

control totals for 884 behavior settings in 198 genotypes
should suffice. Data gaps in the Barker set should be
estimable in a consistent framework.

8.2. STRUCTURAL AND CAUSAL HYPOTHESES

Prior to specifying causal relationships, it is useful to
review some normative concepts due to Barker and analyze
several ways by which behavior settings could be classified. The 'theory of manning' does examine some of the
consequences of under- and overmanned behavior settings as
they relate primarily to the participants within the setting itself. Also, there are structural characteristics
used primarily in economics and regional geography which
offer a way to categorize settings (and genotypes) for
modeling purposes; another possibility is to use Barker's
authority systems and group distinctive clusters of genotypes. In a final section, we illustrate possible causal
structures for several prototypes of settings.

8.2.1. Theory of Manning

Wicker (1979) provides a discussion of manning theory with
the effects of under-, optimally and overmanned behavior
settings. When a setting is undermanned, people take various actions to protect the setting program from disruption.
There are also secondary impacts which are a consequence of
the primary actions designed to preserve the adequate com-
pletion of the setting's program; additional psychological
impacts may occur because of interpretations given to the
primary and secondary reactions to undermanning. Wicker
suggests that small schools tend to have undermanned behavior settings with the result that students feel more chal-
lenged, experienced and valued in these activities.
    Manning theory distinguishes between the 'maintenance
minimum' (the smallest number of people needed to carry out
the program) and 'capacity' (the largest number of persons
that can be included and still sustain the program). (This
is somewhat analogous to the minimum and maximum range of a
good in central place theory.) When the number of participants is less than the maintenance minimum, presumably the
setting's program must be modified, and this would also be
true for overmanned settings where participant numbers

exceed capacity. Between these limits are adequately manned settings. [See Wicker (1979, p. 140) for a more detailed discussion of the theory.] Empirical measures include, for example, students per behavior setting and responsible roles per student; the applied research discussed in this reference primarily relates to schools and churches.

Several comments are pertinent here. (1) Attendance is a performance norm consistent with the manning studies cited in Wicker (1979) and is used (with others) in the flowcharts discussed below. (2) The consequences of under- and overmanned settings relate primarily to the individual setting's operation and interrelationships among partici- pants. Thus, individuals in undermanned settings perform more diversified tasks, feel more significant, apparently have little time to be concerned over differences among other participants and tend to think of themselves in terms of their jobs. While this emphasis may be appropriate to the psychologist, there are many intersetting relationships which will also influence setting attendance. For example, setting complementarities may exist where an overmanned school play try-out is due in part to the private drama lessons given by a highly-regarded teacher. Additional characteristics are suggested in the next section.

8.2.2. Behavior Setting Operation

Barker provides static measures of action pattern and be- havior mechanism ratings in each behavior setting; less attention is paid to structural characteristics within and among settings which might be useful in distinguishing prototypes for modeling purposes. Fourteen setting charac- teristics are distinguished below and are split into (1) individual setting attributes, (2) determinants of the number and sizes of settings and (3) among-setting rela- tionships. Rating scales could be developed for these characteristics with cluster analyses grouping behavior settings into prototypes for modeling.

Individual setting attributes. These include (1) task organization (horizontal and vertical), (2) task special- ization (common or committee activities), (3) sequential dependence, (4) input complexity, (5) output complexity, and (6) zonal satisfaction.

The first three attributes relate to internal organization and the interdependence of successive occurrences
for given settings. The den meetings during the Cub Scout
pack meeting are horizontally integrated; if subcommittee
chairpersons are on the executive committee, then we have a
vertically integrated setting. Some settings may combine
both organizational attributes, increasing the setting's
complexity and the preparation times of leaders. The pro-
liferation of subcommittees may be efficient if both the
specialized tasks and skills of members exist; a common
meeting will usually suffice for simpler setting objectives. Sequential dependence may also influence setting
attendance. Missing a single class period may be much more
crucial to good student performance in a mathematics course
than in one on art history. The ability of setting leaders
to find appropriate organizational structures may have a
substantial influence on the participation by all zonal
members in the setting's occurrences.

The last three characteristics include the production
technology of the setting and various measures of zonal
satisfaction. For input complexity, we distinguish fixed
and variable inputs in addition to inputs required outside
the formal occurrence and hence unmeasured by Barker's
methods. The church bake sale and playing tag in the
vacant lot provide sharp contrasts in input complexity,
with the former requiring substantive efforts before and
outside of the setting itself. Fixed inputs are essential
to the production of setting outputs, whereas variable
inputs may be adjusted to relative scarcities. Carnivals
are multiproduct settings with a wide array of outputs,
whereas the ice cream stand in the park has a more limited
product line. Also, note that outputs of some settings
will be inputs to future occurrences in the same (or
another) setting. Finally, zonal satisfaction will influence setting attendance but should be related to numerous
facets of the setting's operation; this may include the
leader's enthusiasm, organizing ability, attention to
members' complaints, and the like.

Number and sizes of settings. The determinants of
these include (7) scale economies, (8) setting divisibility, (9) market thresholds, and (10) setting competition.

The first two attributes relate to technological constraints on the size of individual settings. Scale economies may be exhausted when Wicker's 'capacity' is reached,

so added competitive settings are likely to develop when
settings are overmanned. At scales where adequate manning
occurs, there is a lower probability that new competitive
settings will be successful. Membership divisibility may
also set limits on the size (or growth) of individual settings. The bridge club should ideally be divisible by four
and the chess club by two, with similar constraints placed
on the various athletic settings distinguished by Barker.
Eleven players are required to have the A football team,
but an additional eleven must be found for the B team. The
required inputs for these activities may show similar dis-
continuities. If the bridge club grows by four members, an
additional four chairs and a card table are needed.

The last two characteristics influence the existence
and number of settings that will be found in communities of
alternative sizes. The market threshold is analogous to
the 'maintenance minimum' number of participants in manning
theory; there must be some minimum community size which
will produce enough participants to enact the setting's
program. This concept suggests that there are probably
hierarchies of settings among communities of different
sizes in the four authority systems excluding private enterprises; hierarchies in the latter are well documented in
central place studies. Setting competition will also influence attendance. There appears to be only one option
for young boys in Cub Scouts, whereas girls may be Blue-
birds or Brownies. Competition may stimulate leaders in
organizing setting activities, or it may produce too many
poorly manned settings in which programs are inadequately
executed.

Among-setting relationships. These include (11) substitutes and complements, (12) linkages (forward and backward), (13) benefit incidence, and (14) policy channels.

Relationships among settings appear to be the least
well studied by the ecological psychologists thus far.
School dances are complementary with the private teacher
giving dance lessons; the quality and quantity of both
mutually reinforce the attendance at both settings. Settings within genotypes, alternatively, may be highly competitive so are close substitutes. The barbershop, beauty
salon and grocery store employees of a community probably
would place themselves in this category. High tavern attendance may reduce movie house ticket sales and could even
decrease the production of outputs in work-related

settings.   Settings may also have significant forward
(demand) and backward (supply) linkages.   The talented
ninth-grade pianist is a product of the combined efforts of
pupil and teacher and supplies a valuable input to the
school operetta.   The quality of the latter is dependent on
numerous linkages in the community such as dance lessons,
drama coaching and music lessons on numerous instruments.
The quality of the inputs to the operetta depends on the
variety of settings and the abilities of their teachers
over a number of years prior to the production.
     The last two characteristics are concerned with pol-
icy.   Some settings produce outputs that are more generally
linked to other settings or individuals in the community.
In 1950-51 the town of Midwest had a chest X-ray unit and
cancer control clinic providing free examinations to citizens.   These settings are usually publicly-supported, and
their number and output levels are a partial measure of the
community's interest in redistributing behavioral income
(in this case the enjoyment of good health) among residents.   We also may want to distinguish key settings (or
individuals active in these settings) through which important policy actions are implemented.   These may be settings
with key community leaders, citizens' committees, elected
bodies such as the municipal council, and the executive
committees of public-spirited organizations.

8.2.3.   Prototype Settings

The fourteen characteristics discussed above are only one
way to group behavior settings for modeling purposes.   A
priori, we should be able to reduce the number of setting
prototypes far below the 884 settings in 198 genotypes that
Barker distinguished in his 1963-64 survey.   The ninth
and tenth grade English classes will probably not differ
substantially in the educational processes internal to
these settings; other settings differing only by age group
include athletic contests, school classes, Cubs through Boy
Scouts, and so on.   It might be possible to group different
athletic contests (e.g., football and basketball) together
for modeling purposes.   The following suggests major prototypes within each of the five authority systems.
     Schools.   School classes are the major educational
settings, and it may be necessary to distinguish classes on
the basis of input complexity (e.g., science and shop

classes versus lecture sections). Athletic practices and
performances and club meetings will be important extracurricular activities in the school system. Special events
(class plays, band concerts, assemblies, dances, etc.) will
comprise several prototypes with perhaps two others for
educational and noneducational excursions. The occupancy
time in a rather broad class of settings may be primarily
determined by the activity groups discussed above; this
would include the various administrative offices distinguished by Barker, time in hallways, etc.

Churches. Worship services and Sunday School classes
are the two most important prototypes. Special events will
include weddings, funerals, social events and fund raisers
(e.g., the church bake sale). Additional settings include
study groups, fellowship meetings and prayer and meditation
services; it seems likely that these can be modeled in a
common 'meetings' format.

Private enterprises. As discussed below, separate
models could be specified for the demographic and economic
systems, the latter to include profits, sales, costs and
the equilibrium number of enterprises in each genotype.
Many of Midwest's enterprises are residentiary with sales
levels influenced by export income in farming and, to a
much lesser extent, manufacturing; business implement and
services sales are probably even more closely related to
export earnings. Since the latter is exogenous, it might
be simpler to handle the economic characteristics in a
single prototype model. Some enterprises may have significant social influences. Cafes and restaurants provide
social gathering places for the town's inhabitants; a
drugstore near the high school provides a similar function
for students after school is over. Bars, pool halls and
movie theaters are often settings where interpersonal con-
flicts are resolved. Perhaps three or four prototypes
would be developed in addition to the economic model.

Government. Several groups of activities can be distinguished here. Some offices provide regular services to
virtually every household. Auto license bureaus and tax
assessment offices are examples, and visitations will be
primarily determined by economic and demographic variables.
Police, fire prevention and the courts are 'social control'
activities. The age-quality of the housing stock, school
drop-out rates, unemployment rates and income are some
variables that we expect to influence police and fire-pre-
vention activity levels. Other governmental activities

will influence other settings and draw on the community for
leadership. The agricultural extension agent will give
presentations at various agricultural clubs and business
meetings, and the mayor (and the other elected officials)
will be expected to appear at numerous community functions.
Modeling the election process is suggestive here; polling
places are a separate genotype in the 1963-64 survey.

Voluntary associations. A wide variety of motivations
probably typifies this system. Sewing clubs and bridge
parties accommodate the social and specialized interests of
members. Voluntary work in charitable organizations probably provides some prestige in leadership roles and
'public-spirited' rewards to lower-zone participants in
collecting door to door, etc. Professional and business-
related interests probably typify participants in the
Junior Chamber of Commerce, Rotary Club, Lion's Club and
others. Thus, attendance (or membership) may depend on
annual dues, the level of budgetary allocations to
publicly-oriented projects and the extrinsic premium in the
private sector to membership (or leadership) in such organizations.

This discussion suggests the presence of about 30
basic prototypes; perhaps double this number would emerge
ultimately. Cluster analysis applied to Barker's ratings
on action patterns and the fourteen rating categories discussed above would be another method in identifying prototypes. Though some prototypes may include common variables, the modeler would want to specify plausible differences in parameter values that might occur among settings;
a given percentage decline in farm income may have a larger
impact on twelfth grade compared to ninth grade drop-out
rates, for example.

8.2.4. Causal Relationships.

After specifying model prototypes, the next task would be
to compile flowcharts which specify causal relationships.
Figure 8.1 provides an example of how one prototype (basketball game at the high school) might be modeled. As
above, we assume the existence of separate economic and
demographic models to provide explanatory variables. Some
of these are listed as possible predetermined variables on
the left hand side of the flowchart with the dependent

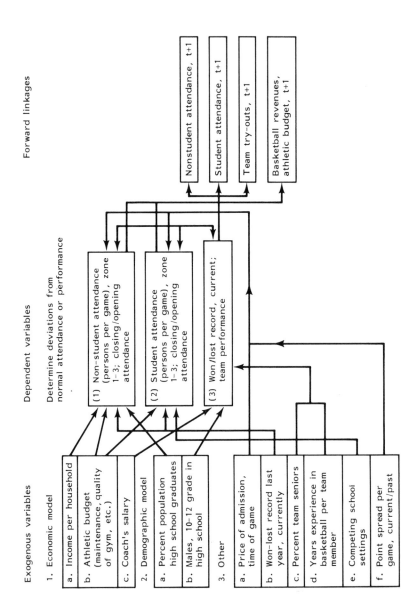

Figure 8.1. Athletic contests flowchart: basketball game at the high school.

variables including various performance measures; the latter include attendance, membership, won-lost record, and
others and can be modeled as deviations from 'normal' magnitudes.

Figure 8.1 is illustrative of possible variables that
might influence this setting's performance norms. In the
basketball game, we distinguish nonstudent attendance,
student attendance and the team won-lost record. Persons
per game is the attendance norm, though the ratio of
closing to opening attendance is another measure of
interest. Non-student attendance may be influenced by
income, price of admission and other variables measuring
'interest' (percent of town population who graduated from
the high school, last year's won-lost record and/or average
point spread per game). Student attendance may be influenced by these variables in addition to the scheduling of
competing extracurricular activities. Other attendance
determinants may include the quality of the gymnasium (age
and seating capacity) and coaching ability. The team's
won-lost record will be determined by coaching ability,
experience of the team (percent seniors and basketball
experience per team member) and perhaps by the size of the
potential player pool (males in grades 10-12). The three
dependent variable categories are simultaneously determined, with the current won-lost record influencing attendance and vice versa through the enthusiasm and size of
audience. The current dependent variables then influence
attendance, team try-outs and basketball revenues in future
time periods.

Figure 8.2 provides another example of possible variables that might influence the 'school classes' prototype.
Here we distinguish average daily attendance, the drop-out
rate and grade distributional measures (e.g., percent of
high grades) as performance norms. (Other measures are
possible; standard test scores and percent of seniors with
college scholarships are examples.) Educational attitudes
(occupational or socioeconomic distribution or percent of
population with twelve or more years of education) may
influence both average daily attendance and grade performance. Measures of how the local economy is performing
(farm income and/or unemployment) may at least partially
determine the drop-out rate. Illnesses or major flu epi-
demics will lower average daily attendance, with native
intelligence of the students a partial determinant of
grade performance. Births, deaths and net-migrants

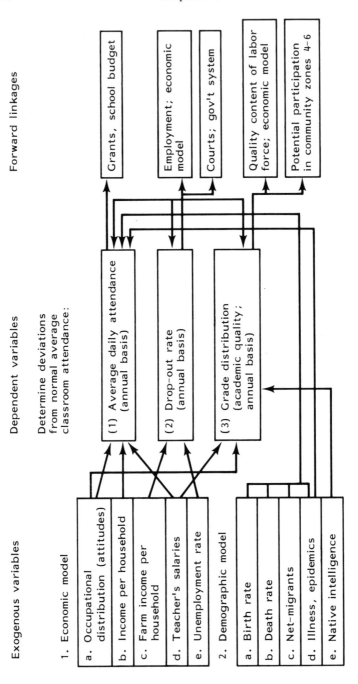

Figure 8.2. School classes flowchart.

determine the size of enrollments, and the three dependent variables have forward linkages to variables listed on the right hand side of Figure 8.2.

A final flowchart (Figure 8.3) suggests relationships which might be present in attendance at church worship services. Age groups are distinguished as well as revenues attained from collections at the service. Age distributions from the demographic model determine potential participants, while parental influence (percent with surviving parents in the community) and personal tragedies (percent widowed and/or percent with deaths in the immediate family) condition religious attitudes. The latter may also be influenced by both occupational hazards and the extent to which natural phenomena determine family income (percent in blue collar occupations and/or farming). Income per household and percent aged 65 and over have influences of opposite sign on worship service collections while zone 4, 5 and 6 preparation times influence attendance [pastor's variables (zone 6) and zone 4 and 5 performers' preparation times]. The dependent variables are again jointly determined, though church income may be less important in determining attendance than the opposite causal relation.

The above are initial examples of plausible causal linkages involved in behavior setting prototypes. If related to individuals' time use, such a system would include both individual household and behavior setting time uses as the basis for a community's social accounts. Consideration should also be given to administrative control prototypes which allocate resources among behavior settings; the elementary school's academic offerings and activities are something more than just the operation of its individual behavior settings. In addition, we note that by establishing causal linkages we have gone a long way towards specifying believable re-allocations of time use in the household data set. If a farm income decline of 20 percent increases drop-outs by a fixed number of males in the tenth through twelfth grades, then farm families with the qualifying progeny are debited time in school and credited with time in primary job; other effects are also possible, of course.

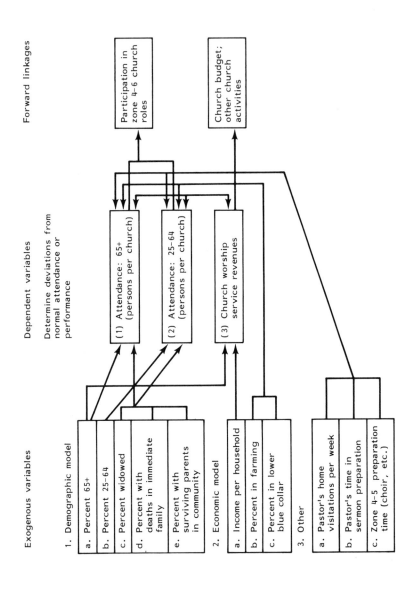

Figure 8.3. Church worship services flowchart.

8.3. CONCLUDING COMMENTS

In this chapter we have sketched a modeling strategy for empirically estimating a system of time-use social accounts for a community. Though Barker's system includes a substantial number of behavior settings, specifying prototypes would be one way to make the task more manageable. Several other problems might concern the modeler of such a system:

(1) Generality may be limited with the data based on the activities and social structure of a small midwestern town. A counter argument is that the meticulous distinction of 884 behavior settings most surely covers the overwhelming percentage of settings common to communities of a similar size across the United States. Also, if we believe in a hierarchical theory of central places as applied to noneconomic settings, then the Barker settings are found in nearly all U.S. urban communities of Midwest's population or larger. The modeler using Barker's data will miss the New England town meeting, but little more.

(2) Data availability could be a problem in specifying flowcharts similar to those discussed above. Detailed data were collected by Barker, but logical specifications of causal relationships may reveal new data needs. The pastor's sermon preparation time is clearly not available in Census publications and also may be excluded in Barker's data. However, even just the specification of these causal linkages would be of substantial value in future empirical work on community social accounts.

A final point should be noted. Had we a widely-accepted system of causal equations describing every important aspect of human behavior, we would be much closer to a consensus on what should constitute a system of social accounts. As all human behavior occurs in behavior settings, the latter must be a logical contender as the basic unit of such accounts. As yet, the causal linkages and their impact on setting performance in Barker's system must be specified.

CHAPTER 9

SOME BROADER IMPLICATIONS OF
BEHAVIOR SETTINGS FOR THE SOCIAL SCIENCES

Chapters 1 through 8 have been concerned with the two major
problems facing social system accounting: how to measure
and account for nonmarket activities and how to combine
social and economic indicators. These chapters developed
various aspects of our proposed solution--accounts based on
behavior settings--including the merging of eco-behavioral
data with data on industries and occupations in a comprehensive time-allocation framework. This framework could be
implemented consistently at the national level, at the
level of a town and its trade area (under favorable geographical conditions), and at the levels of successively
larger urban-centered regions including BEA Economic Areas
which constitute an exhaustive partitioning of the United
States.
    This chapter outlines some of the broader implications
of behavior setting concepts for the social sciences.
These implications are far-reaching.

9.1. DISTINCTIVE FEATURES OF THE BEHAVIOR SETTING CONCEPT

The behavior setting is not coextensive with any other unit
in the social and behavioral sciences. It is the basic
unit of the ecological environment of human behavior. As
Schoggen (1983) observes, the ecological environment is
more than the physical environment, it is more than the
social environment, it is not the psychological environment, it has structure and organization, and it is the
source (through behavior setting programs) of powerful
forces which determine much of the behavior of persons in
its constituent settings.
    The behavior of a particular person in a setting will
be influenced by its physical aspects (walls, furnishings,
counters, equipment, temperature, noise level), its social
aspects (the numbers and kinds of people in it, its program, the goals of its prominent action patterns), and the

demands it places on this person (the expectations govern-
ing his particular role). These various aspects of the
setting influence the person's behavior to the extent that
they are present in his life space (his awareness) at any
given moment, but this appears to be the case with most
people most of the time.

The other people in the setting are part of this
person's environment, as he is of theirs; if only for this
reason, the contents of the life spaces of different persons in the setting will be somewhat different. Each
person's outline is (for him) the environment's 'in-line';
the environment of each organism begins where that particular organism ends.

The dictionary definition of ecology is "the science
of the relationships between organisms and their environments". Psychology is "the science of mental processes and
behavior". When Barker and Wright (1955) made detailed
observations of the behavior of a particular child, they
were still within the domain of psychology; the fact that
they observed this behavior in the child's 'natural'
environment rather than in a laboratory or clinic led them
to describe this type of research on individual behavior as
ecological psychology, to distinguish it from experimental
and clinical psychology.

In experimental psychology, the 'environment' is
created by the research worker to study a particular type
of behavior under controlled conditions; if the experiment
is well done, its results can be reproduced by other scientists who replicate those conditions. Barker and Wright
had to accept the actual environment as something that must
be studied, described, and understood conjointly with the
behavior that occurs in it. Their professional identification with psychology was so strong that Barker's 1968 book
on behavior settings and behavior setting surveys was
entitled Ecological Psychology; Barker (1978, p. 2) would
now classify its subject matter as eco-behavioral science:
"We were slow to discover that psychology is not enough
when one seeks to explicate behavior that occurs in reading
classes, grocery stores, and worship services, that an
extraindividual behavior science is essential.... To fully
elucidate behavior and its environment both ecological
psychology and eco-behavioral science are required."

9.2. SOME RELATIONSHIPS OF BEHAVIOR SETTINGS AND ECO-
BEHAVIORAL SCIENCE TO ESTABLISHED DISCIPLINES

Table 9.1 is compiled and rearranged from a table in
Bechtel and Ledbetter (1976, p. 2) in which they compare
the units covered by a behavior setting survey with those
covered by other approaches and disciplines. They say that
the largest unit of study in gathering behavioral information is a culture; this unit is the traditional province of
anthropology. Their own table does not show behavior setting surveys as covering cultures, but they point out that
such surveys have been used for cross-cultural comparisons
by Barker and Barker (1961); cross-cultural comparisons are
also a major theme of Barker and Schoggen (1973).

     Next to cultures, Bechtel and Ledbetter list community
and above (presumably up to and including nations), neighborhoods, and organizations. They view sociology as covering all three of these units, anthropology and community
psychology as covering the first two, economics as covering
the first and third, and social psychology and management
sciences as covering the third (organizations). Behavior
setting surveys cover all three; therefore, they have
interfaces with anthropology, sociology, economics, community psychology, social psychology, and management
sciences.

     Next come three units which are exclusive to behavior
setting surveys: authority systems, genotypes, and behavior settings; these units are shown as having no interfaces
with established disciplines. A smaller unit, synomorphs,
is covered by behavior setting surveys and also by human
engineering and proxemics (see Hall, 1966).

     We have not used the terms 'synomorph' or 'syno-
morphic' explicitly in Chapters 1 through 8, but the associated concepts have permeated all of our expositions.
Barker and Wright (1955, p. 46) use 'synomorphic' as an
adjective meaning 'of similar structure (shape, form).' In
particular, "the structure of the behavior pattern and the
structure of the milieu of a behavior setting are seen to
be congruent, to fit, to be synomorphic. The criterion of
this synomorphism is perceptual; it is directly seen....
One frequent condition is congruence between the boundary
of the behavior and the boundary of the milieu."

     Barker (1968, p. 20) speaks of the parts of a behavior
setting as "behavior-milieu synomorphs, or, more briefly,
synomorphs. Structurally a behavior setting is a set of

Table 9.1. Behavioral Units Covered by a Behavior Setting Survey and by Other Approaches and Disciplines

Behavioral units	Behavior setting survey	Anthro-pology	Socio-logy	Econ-omics	Comm-munity psycho-logy	Social psycho-logy, manage-ment sciences	Human engin-eering, prox-emics	Person-ality, clinical psycho-logy
Cultures		X						
Community and above	X	X	X	X	X			
Neighborhoods	X	X	X		X			
Organizations	X	X	X	X		X		
Authority systems	X							
Genotypes	X							
Behavior settings	X						X	
Synomorphs	X							
Individuals								X

Source: Compiled and rearranged from Robert B. Bechtel and C. Burgess Ledbetter, The Temporary Environment: Cold Regions Habitability (U.S. Army Cold Regions Research and Engineering Laboratory, Hanover, New Hampshire, 1976, Special Report 76-10, October 1976, Table 1, p. 2.

such synomorphs." For example (p. 24, Fig. 3.2), Midwest's drugstore consists of three synomorphs: (1) the pharmacy, with its work area and counter and the associated behavior of the pharmacist and his customers; (2) the fountain, with its work area and counter and the associated behavior of food service workers and their customers; and (3) the variety department, with its merchandise-display tables and the associated behavior of the salespersons and their customers.

In its concern with the immediate physical environment of human activities, eco-behavioral science has affinities with architectural design. Robert Bechtel, in his book Enclosing Behavior (1977), reports substantial progress in collaboration with architects. His message is that "Behavior, not space, is enclosed by architecture.... In order for the planner or architect to know the purpose of his design, he must know thoroughly the behavior he will enclose.

Behavior for architectural programming is best studied by the techniques of ecological psychology [Barker would now say 'eco-behavioral science'. K.F.]. These techniques are the K-21 scale and the behavior setting survey ...." (p. vii)

The environment of human behavior includes hallways, sidewalks, streets, malls, and open spaces as well as the interiors of individual buildings. The proximity of residences to shops, schools and other services affects the overall efficiency of the environment, and levels of exposure to air pollutants and noise in residential areas are aspects of its quality. Thus, eco-behavioral science has affinities with urban planning.

Several disciplines deal partly with the location of human activities in space: location theory, central place theory, human geography, human ecology, and others. All of these have interfaces with eco-behavioral science; so do urban-regional economics, urban sociology, and regional science.

There are a good many interdisciplinary fields which can absorb and integrate ideas from different pure sciences. If we date ecological psychology from 1947, it is as old as all but one or two of these fields and older than most: small group theory, group dynamics, organization theory, administrative sciences, general systems theory, regional science, quantitative geography, environmental psychology, and others. People active in these

fields could absorb and disseminate very rapidly those
behavior setting concepts and applications which seemed
important to them. The planning fields, much older than
ecological psychology, could also readily absorb, disseminate, and develop applications of behavior setting concepts.

The work of Barker and his associates is quite widely
known and frequently cited--by architects, by child development specialists, by students of school size and organization, by community psychologists, by environmental psychologists, and others. However, few of the references
point toward a deep commitment to, and cumulative development of, behavior setting concepts. If such concepts were
now to receive greater emphasis in social system accounting
and in microanalytical simulation models of communities and
organizations, the latent awareness of the earlier work by
Barker, Wright, Gump, Schoggen, Willems, Wicker, Bechtel,
and others might quicken to enthusiasm.

9.3. BARKER ON THE NEED FOR AN ECO-BEHAVIORAL SCIENCE, 1969

In our view, the eco-behavioral science Barker proposes can
contain all economic behavior and its claims to comprehensiveness in describing human activities in social systems
are as legitimate as those of sociology and anthropology.

We will cite two chapters by Barker in Barker and
Associates (1978) as particularly important in this connec-
tion: Chapter 5, pp. 36-48, "Need for an Eco-Behavioral
Science" and Chapter 19, pp. 285-296, "Return Trip, 1977."

In Chapter 5, first published in 1969, Barker contrasts the concerns of scientific psychology with those of
the proposed new science as follows:

> "Questions about the effects of the environment
> on human behavior and development are being put with
> increasing frequency and urgency. What are the conse-
> quences for human behavior of poverty? of controlled
> climate in factories, offices, and homes? of con-
> gested cities? of transient populations? of high
> population density? of computer technology? of
> ghettos? of large schools? of 'bedroom' communities?
> Behavior scientists often respond hopefully to these
> questions with the promise that, given time and

resources, answers will be provided by the tried and
true methods, concepts and theories of the psychological sciences that have answered so many questions
about human behavior: about perception, about learning, about intellectual processes, and about motivation. The view presented here is, on the contrary,
that the methods, concepts, and theories of the psychological sciences cannot answer the new questions,
that a new science is required to deal with them." (p.
37)

The new eco-behavioral science Barker envisages "that
will answer the questions society faces today requires,
above all, concepts and theories appropriate to the phenomena involved" (p. 43); it will be "an eco-behavioral
science independent of psychology" (p. 43). It will require data archives--archives of "atheoretical, phenomena-
centered data" (p. 46). And, it will need "textbooks and
handbooks of data-reduction methods culled from quantitative botany, demography, geography, physiology, and economics" (p. 46).

9.4. BARKER'S MATURE VIEW OF AN ECO-BEHAVIORAL SCIENCE, 1977

In Chapter 19 (of Barker and Associates, 1978) Barker contrasts his initial (1940) view of what he hoped to learn by
studying people in towns with his mature view as of 1977:
"In 1940 I only asked, 'What do people do in these
towns?' In 1977 I ask in addition, 'What do these towns do
to people?' In 1940 I looked on the towns as a psychologist; in 1977 I also see them as an eco-behavioral
scientist." (p. 285). He elaborates this theme in a very
important passage which we shall quote in full:

"Nevertheless, in 1940 I saw the towns as collections of people, each person a dynamic entity freely
carrying out his plans within the environment the town
provided, an environment that was beneficient with
respect to some of his plans, deficient with respect
to others, and resistant to still others, but an environment that, although frustrating and constraining
to some extent, was a relatively stable, reliable
ground for action. In 1977, I see the towns as

assemblies of dynamic, homeostatic entities (drug-
stores, city council meetings, third-grade music
classes, and so forth) where people are essential
components (among other classes of components, such as
drugs, a gavel, and music books). These are behavior
settings, and within them people do not act in relation to a relatively fixed, dependable environment of
benefits, deficiencies, and constraints, because
stores, meetings, classes, and all other behavior
settings have plans for their human components and
armories of alternative ways of enforcing their plans.
Although according to this new understanding people
are less free in the immediate present than in the
older view, they are not diminished; quite the
contrary. When people understand behavior settings
and learn to create and operate them, they increase
their power by managing the environment that has so
coercive an influence over them. And in the new view
people are more important than in the earlier one:
As essential parts of ongoing behavior setting enterprises that are larger than their personal under-
takings, they have a hand in providing satisfactions
(and dissatisfactions), not only for themselves and
their immediate associates but for all others involved
in the setting. As essential components of behavior
settings, people have significance for more than those
with whom they have direct contact.
     The fundamental significance of behavior settings
for the behavior sciences comes from their position
within the topological hierarchy of entities ranging
from cell, to organ, to person, to behavior setting,
to institution (in some cases), and to community.
Within this included-inclusive series, behavior settings are proximal and circumjacent to people (people
are components of behavior settings), and behavior
settings are proximal and interjacent to institutions
and communities (they are components of institutions
and communities). Although we have only the beginning
of an understanding of behavior settings, we can see
that enlightenment must move in two directions:
inward to relationships between behavior settings and
their human components and outward to relationships
with institutions and communities. In both directions, there are important potential applications.
People control their lives to an important extent

(1) by creating and influencing the programs of the
behavior settings of their communities and (2) by
selecting, so far as possible, the settings into which
they allow themselves to be incorporated. A person's
greatest strength is at the boundary of a setting;
once he 'joins,' he has to cope with much greater
forces than those operating at the boundary. Knowledge of a community's behavior settings should be a
strong weapon in the armory of those professionals who
counsel individual persons." (pp. 286-287)

9.5. THE RELATION BETWEEN OBJECTIVE AND SUBJECTIVE SOCIAL INDICATORS: BARKER'S BEHAVIOR SETTINGS AND LEWIN'S LIFE SPACE?

The relation between objective and subjective social indicators is a topic of continuing concern. We suggest that
some new insights might be obtained from research combining
Barker's behavior settings with Kurt Lewin's concept of an
individual's life space. Lewin (1951) held that a person's
behavior at a given moment depends only on the content of
his life space at that moment. The life space includes
only the objects, people, and intentions of which the individual is aware at the moment--the things that are 'in his
mind.' He may be conscious of only a portion of a behavior
setting and he may experience even that portion somewhat
differently than do other people in the setting.
      In this view, a person's life experience is the his-
tory of his life space--the things he actually paid attention to. We might call this the person's subjective life.
His objective life would be the history of his activities
in behavior settings as recorded by neutral observers in
terms of eco-behavioral concepts. If his objective life is
completely enclosed in a series of behavior settings from
birth up to his present age, the repetitive patterns of
behavior setting occupancy which constitute his life style
should certainly be associated with repetitive patterns in
his subjective life.
      Research on these patterns should help answer some
important questions: How coercive are changes in the physical environment (for example, new office machines) upon
overt behavior? How coercive are they perceived to be by
the workers involved? We propose these questions in the

context described at the end of Chapter 6, namely, that the
complete stock of factory and office equipment and consumer
durables in the United States may be replaced four or five
times during an individual's working life and six or seven
times during his life span.   Ibn Khaldun noted 600 years
ago that it was exceedingly difficult to retrain a skilled
craftsman once--let alone three or four times.   Are we
expecting too much of today's workers? Or can we so manage
technological change that experienced workers may continue
to operate at their existing complexity levels in relation
to data, people, and things while the economy as a whole
turns out a rapidly changing product mix?

9.6. POTENTIAL USES OF BEHAVIOR SETTING CONCEPTS BY SOCIAL
      AND ECONOMIC HISTORIANS

The conceptual framework used by Barker in his behavior
setting surveys of existing communities could also be extended with profit to the study of social and economic
history.   Rostovtzeff (1926, 1941), in his magnificent
works on the social and economic histories of the Roman
empire and the Hellenistic world, juxtaposed pictures of
buildings and chambers, plans of cities, ancient paintings,
mosaics, bas-reliefs illustrating the activities of trades-
men and artisans, and evidence based on many kinds of docu-
ments and records.   So far as possible, he sought to reconstruct comprehensive pictures of life as it was lived in
successive generations in the various regions and prov-
inces.   Mumford (1961) made a similar attempt in The City
in History.   The comprehensiveness of behavior setting
surveys and their accounting (implicitly or explicitly) for
all of the living-time of all members of a community may
provide criteria of completeness and closure for historians
and archaeologists in identifying gaps in their information
and deciding when their work of description or reconstruction of a particular society is in some sense 'done'.
     As a further example, Vitruvius' The Ten Books on
Architecture, written nearly 2,000 years ago, is full of
prescriptions for building houses, temples, Greek theatres,
public baths, treasuries, prisons, and other structures,
and of explanations as to how they will expedite specific
kinds of behavior.   The ruins of Pompeii, buried by a vol-
canic eruption in 79 A.D., are essentially the shells of
behavior settings.   (It is true, of course, that some

structures were flexible enough to accommodate more than
one kind of behavior setting, so not every setting has left
a recognizable shell).

Braudel has entitled Volume I of his great work on
civilization and capitalism (1400 to 1800) The Structures
of Everyday Life (1981). He deals with the food and drink
of different social classes, their clothing, their furniture, their utensils and tableware, the interiors of their
dwellings, their technology, their agriculture, and their
towns and cities in different parts of the civilized world
and in different centuries within his chosen period; the
volume is profusely illustrated and achieves a remarkable
coherence. Braudel's objective in the three-volume work as
a whole is a 'total history' of material civilization, the
economy, and capitalism over the four centuries--'total' in
scope and in attention to the interrelations of technology,
economy, and society.

In a small book of 'afterthoughts' written while the
three-volume work was in press, Braudel (1977) urges young
historians concerned with that period to apply the modern
methods of national income accounting, and also to develop
estimates of national wealth, to make possible a total,
global economic history of that period. If data sufficient
for these purposes are developed, it may also be possible
to reconstruct social accounts based on behavior settings.

9.7. POTENTIAL USES OF BEHAVIOR SETTING CONCEPTS IN SOCIAL
      AND ECONOMIC DEVELOPMENT PLANNING

In Chapters 1 through 8 our concrete illustrations were
based on the U.S. data and social system with which we are
familiar; however, we made clear our judgment that behavior
setting concepts could be applied with the same ease or
difficulty in all member countries of the OECD. Some genotypes would be specific to one or a few countries, but they
should fit readily into larger categories or clusters of
genotypes.

We believe that behavior setting concepts are applicable to all existing societies that practice settled agriculture and have villages, towns, and cities. They should
be particularly useful in social and economic development
planning, where the aspirations of the people are for improved life styles and not simply for increased money
incomes.

9.8.   POTENTIAL USES OF BEHAVIOR SETTING CONCEPTS IN RECON-
STRUCTING   AND   REINTERPRETING   EARLIER   COMMUNITY
SURVEYS

Galpin (1915), Kolb (1933), Brunner (1933), and other U.S.
rural sociologists made surveys of many rural communities
from about 1912 into the 1930s and later.   It should be of
methodological as well as historical interest to find out
whether certain of these surveys could be reconstructed in
terms   of   genotypes   or   groups   of   genotypes   and   time-
allocation matrices.
    We know less about the various urban studies.   War-
ner's (1963) Yankee City studies <u>might</u> lend themselves to
such a reconstruction.   So <u>might</u> some of McKenzie's (1933a,
1933b) studies of metropolitan communities from the view-
point of human ecology.

9.9.   USES OF BEHAVIOR SETTING CONCEPTS IN VARIOUS FIELDS
OF MATHEMATICAL SOCIAL SCIENCE

Finally, we describe several recent papers, published and
unpublished, which relate behavior settings to various
fields of mathematical social science.   Fox (1969a, 1974a)
combined Barker's behavior settings with Parsons' concept
of generalized media of social interchange to derive a
measure of an individual's total income.   The individual
allocates his time among behavior setting-and-role combinations so as to maximize his expected utility.   His choice
ascribes shadow prices to the various media;   since one of
these is his money income, the imputed values of the other
(social) media can also be expressed in dollars and the sum
of these imputed values and his money income is defined as
his total income.   Fox also characterized the problems of
optimization within a behavior setting, optimization for
groups of interrelated settings, and optimization for a
small community.
    Fox and van Moeseke (1973, 1974a) reformulated the
above model in mathematical programming terms.   This model
theoretically allows the derivation of a scalar measure,
called social income (SI) and expressed in dollars, of the
individual's rewards in terms of all social media of exchange, and resulting from his activities in all relevant
behavior settings.   Summation over individuals would then
yield a figure, expressed in dollars, for the social income

of any specified population aggregate (nation, region, age, sex, occupation, or other grouping). <u>Total income</u> is the sum of social income and income from current personal services, i.e., gainful employment. Incomes from (a) gainful employment and (b) property and transfer payments are separately identified in the model; these are standard variables in the national income and product accounts, so the behavior settings and valuations of social media are firmly joined to those accounts.

In 1980, Jati K. Sengupta completed three papers, not yet published, on dynamic and theoretical social system models for a community. These papers are written at an advanced level. They forge links between Barker's concepts (as such and as extended by Fox) and those of advanced economic theory such as present-future jointness (Hicks), subjective expectations about future prices (Hicks, Tintner, Morishima), Slutsky effects, and many others. They also point out that a behavior setting may be viewed as a composite good with many attributes, as in Lancaster's new approach to demand theory.

The first paper examines the dynamic implications of three types of tests of the viability of clusters of behavior settings in a community: (a) the economic test through input cost and output value measures; (b) the ecological or structural test through linkage with other behavior settings; and (c) the demographic or stability test in terms of the transitions of individuals from one cluster of settings to another. The true state of the community is most likely to be a combination of all three aspects: the economic, the socio-ecological, and the demographic.

The second paper deals with the structure, stability, and efficiency of the distribution of behavior capacity in a community. It reviews a number of economic concepts (general equilibrium theory, disequilibrium systems, the formation of coalitions and hierarchies from a game-theoretic standpoint, distributions of preferences among consumers) and relates them to specific aspects of Barker's system and Fox's extensions of it. It then discusses the distribution of behavior capacities in a community in a production and transaction framework. A final section points out that six types of distributions, sometimes overlapping, require careful analysis in a community or <u>social ecosystem</u>: (1) the distribution of behavior capacity (inputs); (2) the distribution of behavior settings (activities); (3) the distribution of rewards from behavior settings (outputs); (4) the distribution of individuals according to age, sex, and other demographic characteristics; (5) the distribution of total income and expenditure; and (6) the distribution of individuals in terms of a composite socioeconomic score based on social status, income, power, and influence.

The third paper develops a theory of the allocation of behavior capacity in a community. It compares two models which seek to encompass all human activities, one by Becker (1965) and the other by Fox-van Moeseke (1973), suggesting some extensions of both, and presents a basic generalization of the Fox-van Moeseke model to accommodate the data network for behavior settings implied by the Fox-Barker (FB) data set mentioned in Chapter 8.

In 1977 Arnold M. Faden published his pathbreaking work, Economics of Space and Time: The Measure-Theoretic Foundations of Social Science. In it, he introduced a system of concepts involving measure theory which he claims to be a universal descriptive framework for social science. Fox has maintained that Barker's approach has, in principle, the capacity to classify, describe, and measure all of the usual, recurrent types of human behavior in existing and past societies. If both claims are valid, it should be possible to translate Barker's concepts into measure-theoretic form.

Faden addresses this task in a 1980 paper, as yet unpublished. He begins with a brief outline of the measure-theoretic approach in social science. He then develops the problem of description in terms of three underlying sets: physical space, S, the set of locations; time, T, the set of instants; and resource space, R, the set of possible quality types. (To this may be added the space of activities, O, which he says is less fundamental). A 'history' is a mapping from an interval of T to R X S, yielding a description of a specified entity over time. The actual world may be described as a measure μ over Ω, the set of all histories.

The final section applies these concepts to Barker's framework. Barker deals with certain distinguished subsets (regions) of S called behavior settings. These regions are identified by the kind of activity going on in them. These activities are space-time configurations of elementary acts, which may be identified with points of Q. Faden then considers the concrete measures, and units of measure, that should be appropriate to Barker's system.

James R. Prescott (1980) wrote a research proposal for developing a microanalytical simulation model of a small community based on Barker's 1963-64 data for Midwest. The basic units were to be 'prototype behavior settings' patterned after the more important settings in Midwest and capturing the essential features of the town's 884 settings in perhaps 60 representative submodels. Chapter 8 of this volume is a revised version of Prescott's 1980 proposal.

Paul van Moeseke (1981) has outlined, and obtained the basic results for, two papers on interfaces between economy and society which we shall characterize here simply as a social cost model and an objective consumption model.

In brief, behavior settings offer many challenges to mathematical social scientists. Barker's basic theory of behavior settings (pp. 136-185 in his Ecological Psychology, 1968) is intellectually profound but is developed in terms of diagrams and verbal statements. Barker's analysis of information flows in a behavior setting seems quite compatible with Marschak's (1971, 1974) economic theory of information. It appears also that Barker's theory of behavior settings could be reformulated in game-theoretic terms.

Fox (1984a,b) has addressed a two-part paper to mathematical social scientists in an effort to interest some of them in the development of mathematical-theoretical aspects of behavior settings and eco-behavioral science. Many linkages with established branches of mathematical social science should be feasible and fruitful.

CHAPTER 10

SOCIAL SYSTEM ACCOUNTS BASED ON
BEHAVIOR SETTINGS: SOME NEXT STEPS

According to Barker and Wright (1955, p. 9), "behavior
settings are prominent units of extra-individual behavior
identified with a high degree of agreement by independent
observers... They are features of the phenomenal worlds of
both laymen and scientists, and a description of the community in terms of behavior settings corresponds to common
experience."

Behavior settings are as visible and tangible as Census establishments. In fact, many behavior settings in the
private enterprise sector are Census establishments. The
identity is almost certain for establishments in which most
of the action occurs in a single room (a small store, a
repair shop, a small restaurant) and/or involves only a few
employees. In Midwest town, each of the grocery stores,
each of the service stations, and each of the attorneys'
offices consisted of a single behavior setting. The bank
was a single setting, but it contained an average of 21
people; the drug store, also a single setting, contained an
average of 12. In these last two cases, half of the people
(perhaps more) were customers.

Establishment data are the mainstay of economic censuses and also of many economic time series on employment,
retail sales, and the like. As every establishment consists of at least one behavior setting, every statistic
routinely collected about an establishment is also a statistic about a behavior setting or a (usually rather small)
cluster of behavior settings. Hence, if a pilot subsample
of establishments were selected for observation as behavior
settings using Barker's data sheets (see Figure 4.1), we
could learn a great deal about the potential usefulness of
such information at a very moderate cost.

Establishment reports contain information about those
components of behavior settings which belong to the economy. Customers as people are left out (their economic
footprints are recorded in the establishment's gross
sales); the action patterns and behavior mechanisms,

165

rewards and contributions, of workers and managers are reflected only in records of wages, salaries, and hours
worked. This is what economic data systems are and this is
perhaps all that economic data systems should be.

So, we ask economic questions and we get economic
answers. The danger is that we may come to believe that
there is nothing 'out there' except an economy. But: in
1976 the people of the United States worked (i.e. were
'gainfully employed') about 165 billion hours; they lived
about 1,910 billion! Our establishment data accounted for
less than 9 percent of our living-time. If we count waking
hours only, 'gainful employment' rises to 13 percent.
Should our data systems ignore the rest? Can we afford to
know so little about ourselves and our society?

True, there are quite a few data sets about particular
social concerns: crime, education, health, housing, energy, transportation, and others. We know from experience
that, in the United States as of 1980-81, it was impossible
for a single investigator, working without substantial help
from data experts in the various agencies and without substantial resources for special computations, to organize
these data sets into a coherent model of factors affecting
individual well-being. It is possible to show how existing
data sets might be organized into a preliminary version of
such a model. The United Nations (1975), in a report prepared by Richard Stone, demonstrates how much could be done
with existing social and demographic statistics to clarify
problems of social policy without going all the way to
formal models or comprehensive social accounting systems.

Publication of The OECD List of Social Indicators
(June 1982) should now provide the basis for cumulative
improvements in measures of individual well-being in many
countries. Our recommendations for social system accounts
based on behavior settings should complement the OECD
efforts.

10.1. WHAT WOULD A SYSTEM OF SOCIAL ACCOUNTS BASED ON
       BEHAVIOR SETTINGS INCLUDE?

Strictly speaking, an accounting system requires a unit of
account. In the national income and product accounts, the
unit (in the U.S.) is dollars. In demographic accounts,
the unit is persons. In time-use accounts, the unit is
person-hours.

A system of social accounts based on behavior settings would, in the first instance, include estimates of person-hours of occupancy time in each of an exhaustive array of genotypes and for all members of the population. The total person-hours spent in each genotype would be subdivided by demographic groups (age and sex); demographic accounts would supply estimates of the number of persons in each age-and-sex category whose living-time (in person-hours per year) must be allocated exhaustively among genotypes.

Genotypes would be cross-classified with industries, and in each genotype-by-industry 'cell' gainfully employed persons could be separated from unpaid ones; payrolls and property-type incomes which add up to the GNP across industries would also add up to the GNP across genotypes. Interindustry flows of goods and services could be translated into intergenotype flows. Stocks of physical capital on an industry basis could be allocated to genotype-by-industry 'cells' and thence aggregated to genotype totals. The unit of account for all these economic magnitudes would, of course, be dollars. But the economy would be embedded in an array of genotypes which included all living-time in a given year and hence all noneconomic activities as well as the economic ones.

Each specific behavior setting within a genotype is a complex entity existing in four dimensions--occupying, on each occurrence, a three-dimensional physical space and extending over a certain interval of time. All inputs to the social system are made in or to behavior settings and all outputs from the social system are produced in behavior settings. The inputs are contributions made by members of the society and the outputs are rewards received by them. The total value of the inputs _is_ the total value of the rewards; the gross social income _is_ the gross social product.

Up to this point, our proposed system of accounts is completely objective--an allocation of person-hours of occupancy time among age-and-sex categories, among occupations and quasi-occupations (unpaid roles), and among behavior setting genotypes cross-classified with SIC-type industries augmented to include the occupancy times of customers, students, household members, and other persons in unpaid roles. The problems of classification and measurement are inherently no more difficult than those dealt with in the economic censuses, the Census of Population and Housing, the Standard Industrial Classification, and the

Standard Occupational Classification. Monetary values are
referred to only (1) within those genotype-and-industry
'cells' which are included in the national income and product accounts and (2) in connection with estimates of the
values of physical capital (including consumer durable
goods) allocable to each cell and hence to each genotype.

10.2. LISTING AND CLASSIFYING THE OUTPUTS OF A SOCIAL SYSTEM

The next step is more difficult but still inherently objective: to list and classify the outputs of a social system
which constitute its gross social product and to define a
unit of measure for each output. The list would include
changes in the health, education and skills of individuals;
changes in stocks of physical capital, including consumer
durable goods; current consumption of purchased services
and nondurable goods; current consumption of services and
nondurable goods produced in households and nonmarket organizations for their own use; numbers of crimes and acci-
dents of various types; person-hours of exposure to specified levels of noise and air pollutants; and other outputs
initially more difficult to define.
    At this stage, the gross social product would be a
vector of outputs, each measured in its own natural or
customary unit. Most of the 33 OECD indicators could be
included in or derived from this output vector, interpreted
to include the distributions of the various outputs among
households. Each output could be disaggregated to the
level of genotype-and-industry cells. Within each cell, a
very basic problem could be studied: Can the vector of
outputs from each cell (and hence from a typical behavior
setting in the relevant genotype) be shown to result from
the vector of inputs in or to that cell? Are there structural relationships between inputs and outputs such that
changes in the amounts of specified inputs would lead to
predictable changes in the amounts of specified outputs?

10.3. INPUT-OUTPUT RELATIONSHIPS AND SOCIAL POLICIES

If such input-output relationships could be demonstrated,
and if proposed public policies could be interpreted as
increasing the amounts of inputs in some cells and reducing

them in others, then alternative policies could be compared
in terms of the changes in output vectors expected from
each contemplated set of changes in input vectors. As in
Jan Tinbergen's (1952) theory of economic policy, a policy-
maker could then apply his own relative weights (values or
pseudo-prices) per unit to each of the relevant inputs and
outputs and take the action that seemed most desirable in
those terms. If the choice among policies required prior
debate in a parliament or similar body, members with different value systems might arrive at different rankings of
the alternatives. However, the demonstration of stable
relationships between inputs and outputs would help to
separate questions of fact from questions of values.

10.4. PSEUDO-PRICES, EXCHANGE RATES, OR 'BARTER TERMS OF
TRADE' BETWEEN PAIRS OF SOCIAL SYSTEM OUTPUTS

A further step, and one which should not be taken lightly,
would be to specify a unique system of prices or pseudo-
prices for all social system inputs and outputs. A unique
price system would permit the computation of a single numerical value for the gross social product in a given year.
The unit of account need not be financial; it could, for
example, be years of life expectancy, or days per year free
from disease or disability, or the unit of measure of some
other social indicator. However, a unique price system
would imply that a unit of one output would be worth stated
numbers of units of all other outputs; the exchange rates
or 'barter terms of trade' between all possible pairs of
outputs would be fixed.

If the exchange rates were held constant over a ten-
year period, changes in the numerical value of the gross
social product would be due entirely to changes in the
quantities (numbers of natural or customary units) of
social system outputs. However, different sets of exchange
rates would lead to different time-paths of the numerical
values computed for the gross social product; extreme differences in exchange rate patterns could make the differ-
ence between upward and downward trends in the computed
product. If a certain set of exchange rates was appropriate in 1980, it would probably need revision in 1985 or
1990 as differential rates of improvement or deterioration
in various indicators over the intervening years might lead

to changes in the relative importance attached to further
improvements or retrogressions.

Another group of alternatives might be weights based
on the proportions of total occupancy time spent in each
genotype-and-industry cell.   One alternative would be to
assign equal weights per person-hour to all age-and-sex
categories in all activities.   Other alternatives would
include (a) assigning different weights to the person-hours
of various age groups, (b) assigning different weights to
person-hours spent in activities requiring different inten-
sities of effort, and (c) differentiating weights per
person-hour both among age groups and among types of activities.

Still another possibility is that different units of
account and different exchange rates would apply in different authority systems or clusters of genotypes.   If so,
outputs within each cluster might be weighted to yield a
numerical measure of the gross product of that cluster.
One cluster might include genotypes in which 'religion' is
the dominant pattern;   another might be dominated by 'education';   a third by 'physical health';   and so on.   If com-
mensurability were established beyond reasonable doubt
within each cluster, value judgments would be limited to
assigning relative importance weights to the units of account of the different clusters.   Consensus might be
reached that the gross social product is the vector of
outputs from the respective clusters;   beyond that point
differences in value judgments might preclude a unique
scalarization of the gross social product into a single
number.

10.5.   POSSIBILITIES FOR EXPERIMENTATION WITH SOCIAL SYSTEM
        ACCOUNTS AND MODELS BASED ON BEHAVIOR SETTINGS BY
        INTERNATIONAL AGENCIES, BY LOCAL GOVERNMENTS, AND BY
        MARKET AND NONMARKET ORGANIZATIONS

Experimentation with social accounts based on behavior
settings could proceed at several levels and on many independent initiatives.   We have emphasized the national
level, at which official data systems are most fully developed.   Comparability among the official data systems of
many countries has been promoted by international organizations (United Nations, OECD) since the late 1940s, so that
experimental accounts for one country would demonstrate

potentials and problems that would be relevant to many others. At some stage, international organizations might undertake the task of promoting a consensus as to those aspects of the accounts which were ready for widespread implementation at a given time.

One specific project should be pursued at the community level. This is the project described by James R. Prescott in Chapter 8. It would make use of the unique data sets for the community of Midwest which were developed by Roger Barker and his associates over a twenty-five year period. All persons and firms were given code names in these data sets and the most recent complete survey of the behavior settings of Midwest was made in 1963-64, so no issues of privacy are involved.

The present author also spent a great deal of time and effort during 1975-78 developing the partly-hypothetical Fox-Barker (FB) data set mentioned briefly in Chapter 8. Each paid role in each of Barker's 1963-64 settings was given the appropriate DOT-SOC occupational code number and the incumbent of that role was credited with a characteristic level of education and assigned to a household of the most probable socioeconomic status. Firms and other organizations were given the appropriate SIC industry codes. Rough, preliminary versions of a complete set of time-allocations of the various age-and-sex categories of the town and trade area population among an exhaustive set of 84 genotypes and clusters of genotypes were developed. However, the FB data set was left incomplete as deadlines for other research outputs loomed. This task also should be completed, to provide empirically-based prototypes of the various matrices and accounts described in this and previous chapters.

The FB data set would be completed in a social accounting mode. Prescott's proposed microsimulation model would make use of Barker's basic data plus whatever components of, or insights gained from, the FB data set proved useful. Prescott's work would shed a great deal of light on the inputs and outputs of behavior settings and the factors which lead to changes in levels of attendance and participation in nonmarket, as well as market, settings. Dynamic linkages among the various prototype settings would be explored and modeled. The constraints imposed on participation in individual settings by the total time available for allocation in each age-and-sex category of the community's population would be constantly in view. Firms and other organizations would be shown as competing, intentionally or not, for all inputs available in or to the community as a social system.

As the Midwest community was very nearly self-contained in terms of the time-allocations of its residents, many of the problems likely to be encountered in implementing conceptually-similar models at the national level could be anticipated and clarified in Prescott's community model.

Whether or not these particular projects go forward, local governments could experiment with similar accounts to see if they clarify some of their planning and administrative decision problems. Hopefully, unintended consequences of proposed changes in the physical, economic, or social environments of the community could be recognized and demonstrated within a behavior setting and time-allocation framework for the community as a whole or for any subdivision of it which was nearly self-contained with respect to a proposed change and its more obvious impacts.

An independent line of experimentation and research, which might be called <u>microsocial accounting</u>, could be carried on within organizations. It would involve attempts to identify and measure the inputs and outputs of each type of setting in an organization using Barker's rating scales, SOC-DOT measures of job complexity and worker traits, the lists of 'nonfinancial rewards' and 'work values' put forward by Belcher (1974) and Zytowski (1970), and the organization's financial and other accounts and output measures. The matrices and accounts we have suggested at national and community levels, if applicable there, should also be applicable to organizations.

Barker and his former students and colleagues have made extensive applications of behavior setting concepts to schools, hospitals, churches, and some other kinds of organizations. However, they have not yet tried to link these concepts with the economic accounts of organizations or with the organizational counterparts of comprehensive social accounts. Organizations would be justified in implementing and maintaining such accounts if they were sufficiently helpful in planning and decision-making and in explaining themselves to employees, members, and other constituencies. Progress in measuring trade-offs between economic and noneconomic rewards should be most rapid in private enterprises. However, the long-run contribution of

microsocial accounting to social productivity may be greatest in the nonmarket organizations.
    Finally, there is need for a major expansion in basic
research on the properties of behavior settings and the
prospects for an eco-behavioral science.

10.6. ROGER BARKER'S CONTRIBUTION TO SOCIAL SCIENCE: AN
      APPRAISAL AND A DEDICATION

Roger Barker made classic contributions to recognized
fields of psychology in early career but his later work led
him away from the mainstream of that discipline. His work
has become widely, but superficially, known in fields as
diverse as sociology, anthropology, child development,
education, and architecture, and in several subfields of
psychology; it has not yet been studied in depth by
scholars in most of these fields.
    Official data systems and social accounts are not
discipline-oriented. Barker's description of human activities and communities in terms of behavior settings is
singularly free of borrowings from sociology, anthropology,
economics or any traditional field of psychology. He
started from a base in experimental psychology under Calvin
Stone and Kurt Lewin and psychological measurement under
Lewis Terman, but he turned his skills in a direction entirely his own--to the systematic observation of naturally-
occurring human behavior in complete communities. He continued in this direction from 1947 to 1972 with substantial
research support and is still professionally active at age
81. Until 1968 he described his research as ecological
psychology--i.e. as a distinctive field within psychology.
Since 1969 he has recognized the need for "an eco-behavioral science independent of psychology" but certainly not
coextensive with any other established science.
    Barker's research program has been one of the most
original in the recent history of the social and behavioral
sciences. Its legacy is an eco-behavioral view of human
societies that is comprehensive in scope yet concrete and
operational in detail.
    We believe Barker's concept of behavior settings may
come to play as important a role in the social sciences as
the cell concept does in biology. In this belief we have
dedicated our book to him.

REFERENCES

Barker, R. G.: 1968, Ecological Psychology: Concepts and
 Methods for Studying the Environment of Human Behavior,
 Stanford University Press, Stanford, California.
Barker, R. G.: 1969, 'Wanted: an Eco-Behavioral Science',
 in E. P. Willems and H. L. Raush (eds.), Naturalistic
 Viewpoints in Psychological Research, Holt, Rinehart and
 Winston, New York. Reprinted with revisions in Barker
 and Associates (1978).
Barker, R. G. and Associates: 1978, Habitats,
 Environments, and Human Behavior, Jossey-Bass, San
 Francisco.
Barker, R. G. and L. S. Barker: 1961, 'Behavior Units for
 the Comparative Study of Culture', in B. Kaplan (ed.),
 Studying Personality Cross-Culturally, Harper and Row,
 New York.
Barker, R. G. and P. V. Gump (eds.): 1964, Big School,
 Small School: High School Size and Student Behavior,
 Stanford University Press, Stanford, California.
Barker, R. G. and P. Schoggen: 1973, Qualities of
 Community Life: Methods of Measuring Environment and
 Behavior Applied to an American and an English Town,
 Jossey-Bass, San Francisco.
Barker, R. G. and H. F. Wright: 1955, Midwest and its
 Children: The Psychological Ecology of an American Town,
 Harper and Row, New York. Reprinted in 1971 by Archon
 Books, Hamden, Connecticut.
Barker, R. G., L. S. Barker and D. D. M. Ragle: 1967, 'The
 Churches of Midwest, Kansas, and Yoredale, Yorkshire:
 Their Contributions to the Environments of the Towns', in
 W. J. Gore and L. C. Hodapp (eds.), Change in the Small
 Community: An Interdisciplinary Survey, Friendship
 Press, New York.
Bauer, R. A. (ed.): 1966, Social Indicators, M.I.T.
 Press, Cambridge, Massachusetts.
Bechtel, R. B.: 1977, Enclosing Behavior, Dowden,
 Hutchinson and Ross, Stroudsburg, Pennsylvania.

174

References 175

Bechtel, R. B. and C. B. Ledbetter: 1976, The Temporary Environment: Cold Regions Habitability, U.S. Army Cold Regions Research and Engineering Laboratory, Hanover, New Hampshire. Special Report 76-10.

Becker, G.: 1965, 'A Theory of the Allocation of Time', Economic Journal 75, 493-517.

Belcher, D. W.: 1974, Compensation Administration, Prentice-Hall, Englewood Cliffs, N.J.

Berry, B. J. L. and C. D. Harris: 1968, 'Central Place', in International Encyclopedia of the Social Sciences, Volume 2, Macmillan Company and the Free Press, New York.

Berwitz, C. J.: 1975, The Job Analysis Approach to Affirmative Action, John Wiley, New York.

Borchert, J. R. and R. B. Adams: 1963, Trade Centers and Trade Areas of the Upper Midwest. Urban Report No. 3, Upper Midwest Economic Study, University of Minnesota, Minneapolis, Minnesota.

Braudel, F.: 1977, Afterthoughts on Material Civilization and Capitalism, Johns Hopkins University Press, Baltimore, Maryland.

Braudel, F.: 1981, The Structures of Everyday Life: The Limits of the Possible. Translation from the French revised by Sian Reynolds. Collins, London. Volume 1 of Material Civilization and Capitalism, 15th-18th Century.

Brown, J. H., J. R. Ginn, F. J. James, J. F. Kain and M. R. Straszheim: 1972, Empirical Models of Urban Land Use: Suggestions on Research Objectives and Organization, National Bureau of Economic Research, New York.

Brunner, E. de S. and J. H. Kolb: 1933, Rural Social Trends, McGraw-Hill, New York.

Caldwell, S. B.: 1980, 'Choosing among Modeling Strategies for Social Accounts', paper presented at the Social Science Research Council Workshop on Social Accounting Systems, Washington, DC (March 24-26).

Duesenberry, J. S., G. Fromm, L. R. Klein and E. Kuh (eds.): 1965, The Brookings Ouarterly Econometric Model of the United States, North-Holland, Amsterdam.

Durnin, J. V. G. A. and R. Passmore: 1967, Energy, Work and Leisure, Heinemann Educational Books, London.

Faden, A. M.: 1977, Economics of Space and Time: The Measure-Theoretic Foundations of Social Science, Iowa State University Press, Ames, Iowa.

Faden, A. M.: 1980, 'Translating Behavior Setting Concepts into Measure-Theoretic Form: Measures over Space, Time,

Resources, and Activities', unpublished manuscript, Department of Economics, Iowa State University, Ames, Iowa.

Felson, M.: 1979, 'How Should Social Indicators be Collected, Organized, and Modeled?', Contemporary Sociology 8 (January), 40-41.

Forrester, J. W.: 1969, Urban Dynamics, M.I.T. Press, Cambridge, Massachusetts.

Fox, K. A.: 1956, 'Econometric Models of the United States', Journal of Political Economy 64, 128-142.

Fox, K. A.: 1958, Econometric Analysis for Public Policy, Iowa State University Press, Ames, Iowa. Reissued 1977.

Fox, K. A.: 1969a, 'Operations Research and Complex Social Systems', Chapter 9 in J. K. Sengupta and K. A. Fox, Optimization Techniques in Quantitative Economic Models, North-Holland, Amsterdam and American Elsevier, New York.

Fox, K. A.: 1969b, 'Toward a Policy Model of World Economic Development with Special Attention to the Agricultural Sector', in Erik Thorbecke (ed.), The Role of Agriculture in Economic Development, Columbia University Press, New York.

Fox, K. A.: 1974a, Social Indicators and Social Theory: Elements of an Operational System, John Wiley, New York.

Fox, K. A.: 1974b, 'Combining Economic and Noneconomic Objectives in Development Planning: Problems of Concept and Measurement', in Willy Sellekaerts (ed.), Economic Development and Planning: Essays in Honor of Jan Tinbergen, Macmillan Company Ltd., London.

Fox, K. A.: 1983, 'The Eco-Behavioural View of Human Societies and Its Implications for Systems Science', International Journal of Systems Science 14, 895-914.

Fox, K. A.: 1984a,b, 'Behavior Settings and Eco-Behavioral Science: A New Arena for Mathematical Social Science Permitting a Richer and More Coherent View of Human Activities in Social Systems:
    Part I, Concepts, Measurements, and Linkages to Economic Data Systems, Time-Allocation Matrices, and Social System Accounts', Mathematical Social Sciences 7 (2), 117-138.
    Part II, Relationships to Established Disciplines and Needs for Mathematical Development', Mathematical Social Sciences 7 (2), 139-165.

Fox, K. A. and S. K. Ghosh: 1980, 'Social Accounts for Urban-Centered Regions', International Regional Science Review 5, 33-50.

Fox, K. A. and S. K. Ghosh: 1981, 'A Behavior Setting
    Approach to Social Accounts Combining Concepts and Data
    from Ecological Psychology, Economics, and Studies of
    Time Use', in F. T. Juster and K. C. Land (eds), Social
    Accounting Systems: Essays on the State of the Art,
    Academic Press, New York, pp. 131-217.
Fox, K. A. and T. K. Kumar: 1965, 'The Functional Economic
    Area: Delineation and Implications for Economic Analysis
    and Policy', Regional Science Association Papers 15, 57-
    85.
Fox, K. A. and P. van Moeseke: 1973, 'Derivation and
    Implications of a Scalar Measure of Social Income', in H.
    C. Bos, H. Linnemann and P. de Wolff (eds.), Economic
    Structure and Development: Essays in Honor of Jan
    Tinbergen, North-Holland, Amsterdam and American
    Elsevier, New York.
Fullerton, H. H. and J. R. Prescott: 1975, An Economic
    Simulation Model for Regional Development Planning, Ann
    Arbor Science Publishers, Ann Arbor, Michigan.
Galpin, C. J.: 1915, The Social Anatomy of an Agricultural
    Community, Agricultural Experiment Station Research
    Bulletin No. 34, University of Wisconsin, Madison,
    Wisconsin.
Gross, B. M.: 1966, 'The State of the Nation: Social
    Systems Accounting', in Raymond A. Bauer (ed.), Social
    Indicators, M.I.T. Press, Cambridge, Massachusetts.
Gump, P. V.: 1971, 'The Behavior Setting: A Promising
    Unit for Environmental Designers', Landscape Architecture
    61(2),130-134.
Hall, E. T.: 1966, The Hidden Dimension, Doubleday, New
    York.
International Labor Office: 1969, International Standard
    Classification of Occupations: Revised Edition, 1968,
    ILO, Geneva.
Iowa Department of Revenue: 1970, Retail Sales Tax Data,
    July 1, 1969-June 30, 1970, Iowa Department of Revenue,
    Des Moines.
Keynes, J. M.: 1936, The General Theory of Employment,
    Interest and Money, Harcourt, Brace, Jovanovich, New
    York.
Kolb, J .H. and E. de S. Brunner: 1933, 'Rural Life', in
    President's Research Committee on Social Trends, Recent
    Social Trends, McGraw-Hill, New York, pp.497-552.

Kuznets, S.: 1937, National Income and Capital Formation, 1919-1935, National Bureau of Economic Research, New York.

Leontief, W. W.: 1936, 'Quantitative Input and Output Relations in the Economic System of the United States', Review of Economics and Statistics 18 (August), 105-125.

Lewin, K.: 1951, Field Theory in Social Science. Edited by D. Cartwright. Harper, New York. Reprinted 1975 by Greenwood Press, Westport, Connecticut.

Marschak, J.: 1971, 'Economics of Information Systems', Journal of the American Statistical Association 66 (March), 192-219.

Marschak, J.: 1974, Economic Information, Decision, and Prediction: Selected Essays, three volumes, D. Reidel, Dordrecht. See especially Volume II, Economics of Information and Organization.

McKenzie, R. D.: 1933a (1967), The Metropolitan Community, Russell and Russell, New York. First published in 1933; reissued by Russell and Russell, 1967.

McKenzie, R. D.: 1933b, 'The Rise of Metropolitan Communities', in President's Research Committee on Social Trends, Recent Social Trends, McGraw-Hill, New York, pp. 443-496.

Mumford, L.: 1961, The City in History: Its Origins, Its Transformations, and Its Prospects, Harcourt, Brace and World, New York.

Orcutt, G., M. Greenberger, J. Korbel and A. Rivlin: 1961, Microanalysis of Socioeconomic Systems: A Simulation Study, Harper, New York.

Organization for Economic Cooperation and Development: 1973, List of Social Concerns Common to Most OECD Countries, OECD, Paris.

Organization for Economic Cooperation and Development: 1982, The OECD List of Social Indicators, OECD, Paris.

Prescott, J. R.: 1980, 'A Behavior Setting Approach to Microanalytical Simulation Models at the Community Level', unpublished manuscript, Department of Economics, Iowa State University, Ames. A revised version is published as Chapter 8 of this volume.

Rostovtzeff, M.: 1926 (1957), The Social and Economic History of the Roman Empire, Oxford University Press, Oxford. Second edition, 1957.

Rostovtzeff, M.: 1941, The Social and Economic History of the Hellenistic World, Oxford University Press, Oxford.

Schoggen, P.: 1983, 'The Ecological Environment of Molar
    Human Behavior', paper presented at the 91st Annual
    Convention of the American Psychological Association,
    Anaheim, California (August 29).
Sengupta, J. K.: 1980a, 'A Dynamic Theory of Behavior
    Settings in a Small Community', unpublished manuscript,
    Department of Economics, University of California, Santa
    Barbara.
Sengupta, J. K.: 1980b, 'Structure, Stability, and
    Efficiency of the Distribution of Behavior Capacity in a
    Community', unpublished manuscript, Department of
    Economics, University of California, Santa Barbara.
Sengupta, J. K.: 1980c, 'A Theory of Allocation of
    Behavior Capacity in a Community', unpublished
    manuscript, Department of Economics, University of
    California, Santa Barbara.
Stone, R.: 1971, Demographic Accounting and Model-
    Building, Organization for Economic Cooperation and
    Development, Paris.
Stone, R.: 1981, 'The Relationship of Demographic
    Accounts to National Income and Product Accounts', in F.
    T. Juster and K. C. Land (eds.), Social Accounting
    Systems, Academic Press, New York.
Stone, R. and A. Brown: 1962, A Computable Model of
    Economic Growth, Chapman and Hall, London. Paper No. 1
    in Programme for Growth series, published for the
    Department of Applied Economics, Cambridge University.
Survey Research Center: 1977, 1978. Data Tapes from the
    Survey of Americans' Use of Time in 1975-76. Survey
    Research Center, University of Michigan, Ann Arbor,
    Michigan.
Terleckyj, N. E.: 1975, Improvements in the Quality of
    Life: Estimates of Possibilities in the United States,
    1974-1983, National Planning Association, Washington, DC.
Tinbergen, J.: 1939, Statistical Testing of Business
    Cycle Theories: Volume I, A Method and Its Application
    to Investment Activity; Volume II, Business Cycles in
    the United States of America, 1919-1932, League of
    Nations Intelligence Service, Geneva.
Tinbergen, J.: 1952, On the Theory of Economic Policy,
    North-Holland, Amsterdam.
United Nations: 1968, International Standard Industrial
    Classification of All Economic Activities (Third
    Edition), Statistical papers, Series M, No. 4, Rev. 2,
    United Nations, New York.

United Nations Department of Economic and Social Affairs:
1975, Towards a System of Social and Demographic
Statistics, United Nations, New York. Prepared by R.
Stone.

United Nations Economic, Social, and Cultural
Organization: 1976, International Standard
Classification of Education, UNESCO, Paris.

U.S. Department of Commerce, Bureau of the Census: Census
of Population and Housing, 1970:
   a. 1971. Occupations and Earnings, PC:2-7A, Government
      Printing Office, Washington, DC.
   b. 1972. Census Tracts: Final Report PHC(1)-57, Des
      Moines, Iowa SMSA, Government Printing Office,
      Washington, DC.

U.S. Department of Commerce, Bureau of the Census:
Censuses of Retail Trade, 1967 and 1972; Censuses of
Manufactures, 1967 and 1972; Census of Governments, 1972;
and others, Government Printing Office, Washington, DC.

U.S. Department of Commerce, Bureau of Economic Analysis:
1976, Local Area Personal Income, 1969-1974, Government
Printing Office, Washington, DC. See also issues for
subsequent years.

U.S. Department of Commerce, Bureau of Economic Analysis:
1977, BEA Economic Areas (Revised 1977): Component
SMSA's, Counties, and Independent Cities, Government
Printing Office, Washington, DC.

U.S. Department of Commerce, Bureau of Economic Analysis:
1979, The Detailed Input-Output Structure of the U.S.
Economy: 1972, two volumes, Government Printing Office,
Washington, DC.

U.S. Department of Commerce, Bureau of Economic Analysis:
1981, Revised Estimates of Capital Stocks and Related
Measures for Fixed Non-Residential Private and
Residential Capital, Government-Owned Fixed Capital, and
Durable Goods Owned by Consumers, 1925-79, National
Income and Wealth Division, Bureau of Economic Analysis,
Washington, DC.

U.S. Department of Commerce, Office of Federal Statistical
Policy and Standards: 1977, Standard Occupational
Classification Manual, Government Printing Office,
Washington, DC.

U.S. Department of Labor, Bureau of Labor Statistics:
1981, The National Industry-Occupation Employment Matrix,

1970, 1978, and Projected 1990, two volumes, Government
Printing Office, Washington, DC.

U.S. Department of Labor, Employment and Training
Administration: 1977, Dictionary of Occupational Titles:
Fourth Edition, Government Printing Office, Washington,
DC.

U.S. Department of Labor, Manpower Administration: 1965,
Dictionary of Occupational Titles, Volume I: Definitions
of Titles; Volume II: Occupational Classifications:
Third Edition, Government Printing Office, Washington,
DC.

U.S. Department of Labor, Manpower Administration: 1966,
Selected Characteristics of Occupations (Physical
Demands, Working Conditions, Training Time): Supplement
to the Dictionary of Occupational Titles, Third Edition,
Government Printing Office, Washington, DC.

U.S. Department of Labor, Manpower Administration: 1968,
Selected Characteristics of Occupations(Worker Traits and
Physical Strength): Supplement to the Dictionary of
Occupational Titles, Third Edition, Government Printing
Office, Washington, DC.

U.S. Department of Labor, Manpower Administration: 1972,
Handbook for Analyzing Jobs, Government Printing Office,
Washington, DC.

U.S. Executive Office of the President, Council of Economic
Advisers: 1983, President's Economic Report, Government
Printing Office, Washington, DC.

U.S. Executive Office of the President, Office of
Management and Budget: 1978, Standard Industrial
Classification Manual, 1972, Government Printing Office,
Washington, DC.

U.S. Senate, 90th Congress, 1st Session: 1967, Hearings
before the Subcommittee on Government Research of the
Committee on Government Operations on S.B.S. 843, The
Full Opportunity and Social Accounting Act. Part 1 (June
26, 1967), Part 2 (July 19, 20, and 26, 1967), and Part 3
(July 28, 1967).

Van Moeseke, P.: 1981a, 'A Social Cost Model', unpublished
manuscript, Department of Economics, Massey University,
Palmerston North, New Zealand.

Van Moeseke, P.: 1981b, 'An Objective Consumption Model',
unpublished manuscript, Department of Economics, Massey
University, Palmerston North, New Zealand.

Vitruvius, The Ten Books on Architecture (c. 14 B.C.).
   Translated by Morris Hicky Morgan. Dover edition, 1960,
   Dover Publications, New York.
Warner, W. L.: 1963, Yankee City, Yale University Press,
   New Haven, Connecticut. Abridged edition.
Warner, W. L., M. Meeker and K. Eells: 1949, Social Class
   in America, Science Research Associates, Chicago.
Wicker, A. W.: 1979, An Introduction to Ecological
   Psychology, Brooks/Cole, Monterey, California.
Zytowski, D. G.: 1970, 'The Concept of Work Values',
   Vocational Guidance Quarterly 18, 176-186.

BEHAVIOR SETTINGS, ECOLOGICAL
PSYCHOLOGY, AND ECO-BEHAVIORAL SCIENCE:
SOME ANNOTATED REFERENCES TO THE BASIC LITERATURE

In Chapters 1, 2 and 4 of the text, we introduced 70 or 80 terms that are unique to the literature on behavior settings or have special technical meanings in this literature. We illustrated and discussed these terms as we introduced them and trust that we made their relevance to social system accounts sufficiently clear.

The present author was the first person (beginning in 1966) to extend Barker's concepts systematically in the direction of comprehensive social accounts that could incorporate, or be linked with, existing economic, social, and demographic data systems; references to this work are cited in Appendix 2. Readers will find little or nothing published by Barker and his associates before 1982 that specifically mentions behavior settings as a basis for social accounts. However, there are many statements by Barker and his associates, beginning in the early 1950s, that imply a broader and more fundamental, if less structured, view of ecological psychology as the science concerned with the distribution of patterns of naturally-occurring behavior among human populations--in principle, anywhere and everywhere.

Readers of this book will presumably have had a variety of backgrounds in the social and behavioral sciences, statistics, environmental design, planning, administration, and other fields. Hopefully, they will want to know more about behavior settings and eco-behavioral science than has been conveyed in the text. The following references and annotations should help them to acquire this knowledge efficiently.

1. Wicker, Allan W., 1979, An Introduction to Ecological Psychology (Monterey, Cal.: Brooks/Cole).

This is the first (and as of 1984 still the only) textbook on ecological psychology. The style is personal, somewhat informal, and easily readable. The book is suitable for a

wide audience, including people with no formal coursework
in psychology. The presentation of the material is roughly
chronological, beginning with Roger Barker and Herbert
Wright's call in 1949 for an ecological orientation in
psychology and tracing the subsequent growth and refinement
of the field.

Wicker was associated with Barker during the mid-1960s
and has been an active and original contributor to ecological psychology since that time. Wicker's book draws extensively on Barker's work (there are 51 page-references to
Barker, more than twice as many as to any other scientist)
and has Barker's approval as indicated in his (Barker's)
foreword to the book.

2. Barker, Roger G. and Associates, 1978, <u>Habitats,</u>
    <u>Environments, and Human Behavior</u> (San Francisco:
    Jossey-Bass).

This book is a comprehensive survey of ecological psychology and eco-behavioral science—two fields directly concerned with the effects of the environment on human behavior. Information spanning twenty-five years is presented
by those who first worked in the field—staff members of
the Midwest Psychological Field Station of the University
of Kansas, who conducted research from 1947 to 1972 and who
obtained data from two towns, one in England and one in
Kansas. Roger Barker and his associates began their studies with a concern for how living conditions affect children's behavior and development. Ecological psychology was
devised to deal with these behavioral and psychological
conditions as they occur 'naturally', without the stimula-
tion and questioning of investigating psychologists. The
authors present procedures, conceptual problems, and
pertinent findings in this field.

As the work of the Field Station progressed, it became
apparent that children could not be effectively considered
apart from those around them and that psychology alone was
not adequate to explain behavior occurring in everyday
habitats. Eco-behavioral science evolved to explain the
behavior of people in terms of <u>behavior settings</u> in homes,
stores, churches, schools, hospitals, and towns. The authors describe the discoveries that led to the development
of this important new science, detail its unique methods
and concepts, and show how both ecological psychology and

eco-behavioral science are necessary to fully understand behavior and its environment.

The nineteen chapters consist mainly of abbreviated versions of journal articles and chapters in collective volumes, plus excerpts from two or three of the basic books by Barker, Wright, and Schoggen cited in our text. The editing has made all chapters relatively nontechnical and very readable;   details of procedures and statistical tests, necessary in the original versions, have been deleted from the revised ones.

Chapters 1, 2, 6, 7, 8, 9 and 10 deal with the naturally-occurring behavior of individuals (children) in terms of streams of behavior, behavior episodes, environmental force units, social actions, disturbances, and interactions with behavior objects.   These chapters are all within the domain of ecological psychology as distinct from eco-behavioral science.   Some readers will find these chapters interesting for their own sakes; they also demonstrate that a good deal of research has been done on the behavior of individuals reacting to micro-events occurring in behavior settings as well as to the settings' overall programs. This research can be linked with accumulated knowledge in many other fields of psychology.

The remaining chapters are studies in eco-behavioral science.

The preface and Chapter 19, 'Return Trip, 1977,' should be read together. They contrast the question Barker asked himself about towns in 1940 ("What do people do in these towns?") with the question he asks in 1977: "What do these towns do to people?"   In 1940 he looked on the towns as a psychologist; in 1977 he also sees them as an ecobehavioral scientist.   Chapter 19 is one of Barker's most explicit statements of the nature and potentials of ecobehavioral science.

Chapter 5 by Barker, 'Need for an eco-behavioral science,' a revision of a paper published in 1969, should be read carefully in conjunction with Chapter 19.   Barker states that eco-behavioral science will require several kinds of facilities that have not been developed by psychologists, and perhaps are not needed by them: (1) archives of primary data comparable to those accumulated by geologists, economists, and biologists over long periods of time and accessible to individual scientists who can study and analyze them in their own ways; (2) facilities for collecting, preserving, and retrieving ecological data

("atheoretical, phenomena-centered data") which "will continue to be of use in connection with problems not yet con-
ceived;" (3) data analysis methods appropriate to ecological data (methods adapted from "quantitative botany, demography, geography, physiology, and economics"); and (4)
field stations.

Chapter 11, 'An eco-behavioral approach to health
status and health care,' by Edwin P. Willems and Lauro S.
Halstead, reports convincing uses of behavior setting surveys in a hospital rehabilitation center for patients with
spinal cord injuries. They found that patients not only
performed differently in different settings (showed different degrees of initiative and independence); they also
changed in different ways and at different rates in different settings. The authors state (p. 186) that:

"When these central principles of behavioral ecology
really sink in, they will affect human behavioral
science in profound ways. One area that will be affected strongly is the area of human assessment. It
will no longer be so tenable or defensible to assess a
person's performance. Rather, we will have to assess
performance by settings, simply because variations in
settings produce variations in performance."

Chapter 13, 'Impact of the Agricultural Extension
Service on Midwest,' by Dan D. M. Ragle, Roger Barker, and
Arthur Johnson, analyzes the behavior settings sponsored by
this organization in Midwest during 1954-55 and 1963-64,
using the various measures we described in Chapters 1, 2
and 4 of our text. Similar analyses could be made of the
impact of almost any organization in Midwest or of particular genotypes of settings sponsored by one of its larger
organizations (e.g. the high school or the elementary
school).

Chapter 16, 'Big schools, small schools,' by Paul V.
Gump, demonstrates the usefulness of behavior-setting concepts in analyzing the consequences for students of differences in high school enrollments ranging from an average of
40 in the two smallest to an average of 2,105 in the two
largest of eleven Kansas high schools surveyed. The two
smallest had an average of 12.5 genotypes of academic and
commercial classes; the two largest had 28.5. Two high
schools with an average of 339 students offered an average
of 21.5 genotypes of instruction. Gump comments (p. 246)

that "it takes a lot of bigness to add a little variety. On the average, a 100 percent increase in size yielded only a 17 percent increase in variety." Students from small schools had over twice as many operating roles per student as those from large schools. Students from small schools reported more satisfactions from participation; students from large schools reported more vicarious satisfactions from being associated with an imposing institution.

Gump's chapter, and the book by Barker and Gump (1964) to be cited below, are relevant not only to high schools as such but to the study of organization size generally as a factor affecting the contributions made and rewards experienced by organization members.

Chapter 17, 'Importance of church size for new members,' by Allan W. Wicker, addresses the effects of organization size as evidenced by a small church and a large church of the same denomination in the same metropolitan area.

Chapter 14, 'Theory of behavior settings,' by Roger Barker, is a reprint of part of an article on 'Ecology and motivation,' first published in 1960. Barker notes (pp. 219-220) that:

"A behavior setting is a place where most of the inhabitants can satisfy a number of personal motives, where they can achieve multiple satisfactions. In other words, a behavior setting contains opportunities. Furthermore, different people achieve different clusters of satisfactions in the same setting. The unity of a behavior setting does not arise from similarity in the motives of the occupants. In the behavior setting 'football game', for example, the quarterback will experience a complex system of social-physical satisfactions, depending on what kind of a person he is; his mother in the bleachers will at the same time have quite a different set of satisfactions; and the coach will have still others. But unless these and other inhabitants of a football game are at least minimally satisfied, they will leave, or will not return on another occasion, and the setting will cease. In other words, a setting exists only when it provides its occupants with the particular psychological conditions their own unique natures require. Heterogeneity in the personal motives of the individ-

ual inhabitants of a setting contributes to the stability of the setting.

Behavior settings impose obligations on their
occupants, too. These obligations are consequences of
the intrinsic structure of behavior settings. If the
inhabitants of a setting are to continue to attain the
goals that bring them satisfactions, the setting must
continue to function at a level that each occupant
defines for himself in terms of his own satisfactions.
Every occupant of a setting is, therefore, faced with
three routes: One is the immediate, direct route to
his goals; the others are toward operating and toward
maintaining the setting so that his goals and the
routes to them will remain intact." (pp. 219-220)

Chapter 15, 'Measures of habitat and behavior output,'
by Roger Barker and Phil Schoggen, is adapted from Barker
and Schoggen (1973, pp. 22-48). The adaptation is clear
and relatively brief. Barker and Schoggen define many of
the terms described in Chapters 1, 2 and 4 of our text, and
they do it with a lighter and surer touch, as befits the
creators of these terms and measures.

3. Barker, Roger G., 1979, 'Settings of a Professionsl
   Lifetime,' Journal of Personality and Social Psychology, 37(12):2137-2157.

This article summarizes Roger Barker's career as a psychologist from 1928 (when he commenced graduate study in psychology at Stanford University) until 1978. It is organized (appropriately) around fifteen behavior settings or
clusters of settings which were crucial to his scientific
activity. In temporal order of their occurrence and with
their institutional connections, these were: Stanford
University, 1929-1935 (Lewis Terman's Seminar, Walter
Miles's Later Maturity Facility, Calvin Stone's Animal
Laboratory); University of Iowa, 1935-1937 (Kurt Lewin's
Offices, Nursery School Laboratory, Topology Meetings);
Harvard University, 1937-38 (Henry A. Murray's Clinic,
Child Psychology Class, Edwin Boring's Sack Lunch); Uni-
versity of Illinois, 1938-1942 (Study at Home, Extension
Classes); Stanford University, 1942-45 (Office of Disabil-
ity Survey); Clark University, 1946-47 (Office at the
University); University of Kansas, 1947-72 (Office of
Department Chairman, Field Station in Oskaloosa).

In early career, Barker did original research on child psychology, certain problems of aging, and psychological aspects of the rehabilitation of the physically disabled. His years at Stanford and Harvard gave him a broad acquaintance with psychology and psychologists. His two years (1935-1937) as a postdoctoral research associate with Kurt Lewin, one of the most brilliant and innovative psychologists of the century, were crucial to Barker's scientific development; he states (p. 2145) that Lewin's ideas "have remained at the center of all my subsequent work." Equally important was the new, higher level of intellectual effort to which he became adapted.

This article also gives Barker's reasons for leaving his endowed chair as G. Stanley Hall Professor of Child Psychology at Clark University in 1947 to establish the Midwest Psychological Field Station of the University of Kansas and to serve as Chairman of the Psychology Department there for a time. From 1950 on, he was able to devote all, or nearly all, of his efforts to the research program of the Field Station. The town of Oskaloosa proved ideal for the research program he had designed (though other midwestern towns twenty miles or so from a university might also have been suitable); the small settlements accessible to him from Clark University in Massachusetts were strung out along streams or across forested ridges, and the children in these straggling settlements did not have a common community environment—unlike the children of the towns in Illinois which had attracted his research interest in 1940.

4.   Barker, Roger G. and Herbert F. Wright, 1955, Midwest and Its Children: The Psychological Ecology of an American Town (New York: Harper and Row).   Reprinted 1971 by Archon Books, Hamden, Connecticut.

This is the first major book resulting from the research program of the Midwest Psychological Field Station;   it is dedicated "to Kurt Lewin and the People of Midwest."

Pages 1-176, 491-495, and 505-509 relate to behavior setting surveys.   Chapter I (pp. 1-19) describes the general problem and methods of 'psychological ecology.'   Chapter II (pp. 20-44) gives an informal, realistic description of the town of Midwest as of 1950 and reasons why Midwest was not isolated from, or atypical of, the mainstream of

American culture; the title of this chapter is 'Midwest and
the U.S.A.'

Chapter III (pp. 45-83) describes the methods used in
their first major behavior setting survey (July 1, 1951-
June 30, 1952). Many features of the survey methods described were used in all subsequent surveys in Midwest (and
in Yoredale), but some have been modified; this chapter
should be scanned but not studied in detail. A better,
more current, description of methods is given in Barker
(1968).

Chapter IV (pp. 84-176) gives the results of the 1951-
52 survey. The catalogue of Midwest community behavior
settings is interesting for at least two reasons: (1)
occupancy times (by town residents only) are reported for
each of the 585 individual settings, and (2) prominent
action patterns and behavior mechanisms are also reported
for each of these 585 settings. Much less detail is reported in Barker (1968) and Barker and Schoggen (1973)--
partly, no doubt, for reasons of space.

Appendix 5 (pp. 491-495) describes the index of interdependence, K, between any pair of behavior settings;
also, the seven subscales on which K is based. This should
be scanned but not studied. Wicker (1979, pp. 206-213) is
much easier to understand. Wicker also notes that, in
practice, K values are calculated only in cases of uncertainty where the surmised values are within a point or two
of the critical value, K = 21. The minimum value of K is
7; the maximum rating on each subscale is also 7. If two
potential settings are very different on two or three subscales, K will almost certainly equal or exceed 21, and the
entities compared will be separate settings.

Appendix 10 (pp. 505-509) lists Town OT for each of
the seven age groups, the two sexes, the three socioeconomic groups of whites, and blacks. For each of these 13
population subgroups, the 10 settings most frequented by
its members are listed along with the percents of that
subgroup's Town OT spent in each setting.

5. Barker, Roger G., 1968, Ecological Psychology:
    Concepts and Methods for Studying the Environment of
    Human Behavior (Stanford, Cal.:   Stanford University
    Press).

Chapters 1, 2 and 3 improve upon earlier statements of the
problems of ecological psychology, defining the ecological

environment, and defining the attributes of behavior settings. Chapter 4 (pp. 35-91) is Barker's definitive description of the method of behavior setting surveys. Chapter 5 (pp. 92-136) reports the results of the survey; Table 5.3 (pp. 110-116) is particularly instructive. Chapter 6 (pp. 137-186) is perhaps the most demanding statement of Barker's theory of behavior settings. It will repay effort, but it will definitely require effort. Chapter 7 (pp. 186-205) overlaps with some other statements by Barker on applications of ecological psychology. The last sentence of the text, on p. 205, contains the earliest use of the term 'eco-behavioral science' I recall seeing in Barker's writings.

6. Barker, Roger G. and Phil Schoggen, 1973, <u>Qualities of Community Life: Methods of Measuring Environment and Behavior Applied to an American and an English Town</u> (San Francisco: Jossey-Bass).

This book contains an enormous amount of information. Many of the tables present four columns of data: Midwest, 1954-55 and 1963-64, and Yoredale, 1954-55 and 1963-64. Thus, it is possible to discuss changes over time in each of the towns and also differences between the towns in each of the two given years.

     Barker and Schoggen introduce a number of terms and concepts not included in any of the earlier books and articles reporting behavior setting surveys. This book and Barker (1968) are the principal starting points for efforts to link the methods and results of behavior setting surveys with official data systems and social system accounts.

7. Barker, Roger G. and Paul V. Gump, eds., 1964, <u>Big School, Small School: High School Size and Student Behavior</u>. (Stanford, Cal.: Stanford University Press).

This book makes extensive applications of the method of behavior setting surveys to 13 high schools ranging in student enrollment from 35 to 2287. The number of behavior settings per school ranged from 60 to 499, and the ratio of students to settings from 0.58 to 4.58.

     Chapter 12, 'Overview and prospects,' by Gump and Barker, is particularly impressive. On page 199 they state:

"The basic unit of the school environment is the behavior setting. To put it plainly: A school is its behavior settings. With this unit and associated measures it is possible to study the school in terms of its first-order reality for its inhabitants."

The book is a classic in the field of research on high schools and their students. In surveying and classifying as many as 499 behavior settings in a high school with 2287 students, Barker and Gump demonstrate that behavior setting surveys can be made in establishments or organizations of large size in any other authority system, also.

8. Barker, Roger G., Louise S. Barker and Dan D. M. Ragle, 1967, 'The Churches of Midwest, Kansas, and Yoredale, Yorkshire: Their Contributions to the Environments of the Towns,' in W. J. Gore and L. C. Hodapp, eds., 1967, Change in the Small Community: An Interdisciplinary Survey (New York: Friendship Press).

This article presents data on church-sponsored behavior settings in Midwest and in Yoredale in 1954-55 and in 1963-64. It demonstrates, as does the article on the Agricultural Extension Service in Barker and Associates (1978), how the contributions of particular organizations to a community can be appraised within the framework of a survey of the community's behavior settings.

APPENDIX II

SELECTED PUBLICATIONS AND
UNPUBLISHED MANUSCRIPTS BY KARL A. FOX
AND ASSOCIATES MAKING USE OF BEHAVIOR SETTING CONCEPTS

I met Roger Barker in 1966 at a workshop on Change in the Small Community, where he and his wife, Louise, presented a paper on 'The Churches of Midwest, Kansas, and Yoredale, Yorkshire: Their Contributions to the Environments of the Towns' (Barker, Barker and Ragle, 1967). This was the first I had heard of Roger Barker, ecological psychology, or the method of behavior setting surveys.

My own paper (Fox, 1967) was ecological in a sense, though I thought of it primarily as an application of central place theory and quantitative geography. In it, I showed how the small town-and-trade area communities studied by Galpin (1915) toward the end of the horse-and-buggy era had been transformed by the automobile into hierarchies of central places (villages, towns, small cities, regional capitals) organized into commuting fields, labor market areas or 'functional economic areas' each extending over several counties or several thousand square miles; one section of my paper was headed 'human ecology at 50 miles an hour.'

As Barker described his 1963-64 surveys of the behavior settings of Midwest and Yoredale, it occurred to me (1) that his method could be extended to yield comprehensive estimates of time use, (2) that it could be combined with consumer expenditure surveys to yield estimates of the simultaneous allocations of time and money, and (3) that it could probably be extended, with the aid of published aggregative data on employment, school enrollment and the like plus some sample surveys, to yield social accounts for successively larger communities and urban-centered regions up to and including the nation as a whole.

I learned later that Barker and Wright (1955, pp. 97-99) had recognized and implemented the first of these ideas as far back as 1951. I knew that an economist, Gary Becker, had formulated the second of these ideas in a theoretical paper published in 1965 and that Bertram Gross (1966) had just published a classic statement on the tasks and

193

prospects of social systems accounting. The important
thing is that Barker's concept of behavior settings seemed
to me equally capable of accommodating and enriching all
three of these emerging fields, which have (since 1966)
received increasing attention from social psychologists,
economists, and sociologists.

That presentation by Roger Barker changed the course
of my scientific career. Not immediately; I had other
lines of research in progress, plus administrative responsibilities. And it was not a conversion experience; I had
been in and around the behavioral sciences much too long
for that. I began to mention Barker's work in papers written in 1967-68 and published in 1969; after that, I don't
recall writing anything in which I did not mention Barker's
work. By 1973-74 I was so far committed to it that the
Author Index of Fox, Social Indicators and Social Theory
(1974b) contained 41 page-references to Roger Barker and 24
to the scientist next in line. My next two research proposals to the National Science Foundation, funded in 1974
and 1976, were specifically based on my efforts to adapt
Roger Barker's concepts, and particularly his concept of
behavior settings, to the potential requirements of social
system accounts and models.

In the section below headed 'References', I have listed eleven publications, including one co-authored with Paul
van Moeseke and two with Syamal K. Ghosh, in which I have
made substantial use of behavior setting concepts. Items 1
through 4 were written during 1967-72 while I was trying to
develop a broad and fairly uniform understanding of the
social sciences; this task was greatly facilitated by the
publication of the International Encyclopedia of the Social
Sciences in 1968. In all four of the items mentioned, I
linked Barker's concept of behavior settings with the ideas
of other social and behavioral scientists (Eric Berne's
transactional analysis, Talcott Parsons's generalized media
of social interchange, Philip Converse's encyclopedia article on time budgets, and others). In 1973 I turned from
reading to writing. The result was Item 5, Social Indicators and Social Theory (1974b). Chapter 5 was entitled
'Time Budgets, Behavior Settings, and Total Income,' and
Chapter 11 ('Elements of an Operational System, I: Individuals, Families, and Organizations in a Small Community')
used behavior setting concepts throughout.

Item 5A is listed because Felson's review essay on Item 5 emphasizes the importance of behavior settings for modeling social processes.

Items 6 through 10 were written from 1976 through 1983 while I was working toward the social accounting framework which is described in the present book. Item 11, addressed to mathematical social scientists, was written in 1984.

In the final section headed 'Reference Notes' I have listed selected chapters from an unpublished manuscript (three volumes) which reported most of the results of the research which my associates and I performed during 1974–80 under National Science Foundation grants SOC 74-13996 and SOC 76-20084 to Iowa State University. Ideas which are illustrated with one or two tables in the present book are backed up by many tables and extensive discussion in the three-volume manuscript.

I expect that a number of articles, and one or more books, will be based on the materials listed. Some of these materials should be of considerable value to statistical agencies as they consider their prospective roles in developing social system accounts.

REFERENCES

1. Fox, Karl A., 1969a, 'Toward a Policy Model of World Economic Development with Special Attention to the Agricultural Sector,' in Erik Thorbecke (ed.), The Role of Agriculture in Economic Development (New York: Columbia University Press).
2. Fox, Karl A., 1969b, 'Operations Research and Complex Social Systems,' Chapter 9 in Jati K. Sengupta and Karl A. Fox, Economic Analysis and Operations Research: Optimization Techniques in Quantitative Economic Models (Amsterdam: North-Holland).
3. Fox, Karl A., 1974a, 'Combining Economic and Noneconomic Objectives in Development Planning: Problems of Concept and Measurement,' in Willy Sellekaerts (ed.), Economic Development and Planning: Essays in Honour of Jan Tinbergen (London: Macmillan).
4. Fox, Karl A. and Paul van Moeseke, 1973, 'Derivation and Implications of a Scalar Measure of Social Income,' in H. C. Bos, H. Linnemann, and P. de Wolff, (eds.), Economic Structure and Development: Essays

in Honor of Jan Tinbergen (Amsterdam: North-Holland
and New York: American Elsevier).

5.   Fox, Karl A., 1974b, Social Indicators and Social
Theory: Elements of an Operational System (New York:
John Wiley).

5A.   Felson, Marcus, 1979, 'How Should Social Indicators
Be Collected, Organized, and Modeled? A Review Essay
on Karl A. Fox, Social Indicators and Social Theory:
Elements of an Operational System,' Contemporary
Sociology 8:40-41.

6.   Fox, Karl A., 1977, 'Measuring Economic and Social
Performance: New Theory, New Methods, New Data,' in
Lectures in Agricultural Economics: Bicentennial
Year Lectures Sponsored by the Economic Research
Service (Washington, D.C.: Economic Research Service,
U.S. Department of Agriculture).

7.   Fox, Karl A., 1980, 'Philosophical Implications of a
System of Social Accounts Based on Roger Barker's
Ecological Psychology and a Scalar Measure of Total
Income,' Philosophica 25:33-54.

8.   Fox, Karl A., 1983, 'The Eco-Behavioural View of Human
Societies and Its Implications for Systems Science,'
International Journal of Systems Science 14:895-914.

9.   Fox, Karl A. and Syamal K. Ghosh, 1980, 'Social
Accounts for Urban-Centered Regions,' International
Regional Science Review 5:33-50.

10.   Fox, Karl A. and Syamal K. Ghosh, 1981, 'A Behavior
Setting Approach to Social Accounts Combining Concepts
and Data from Ecological Psychology, Economics, and
Studies of Time Use,' in F. Thomas Juster and Kenneth
C. Land (eds.), Social Accounting Systems: Essays on
the State of the Art (New York: Academic Press).

11.   Fox, Karl A., 1984a,b, 'Behavior Settings and Eco-
Behavioral Science: A New Arena for Mathematical
Social Science Permitting a Richer and More Coherent
View of Human Activities in Social Systems:
        Part I, Concepts, Measurements, and Linkages to
Economic Data Systems, Time-Allocation Matrices, and
Social System Accounts, Mathematical Social Sciences
7 (2): 117-138.
        Part II, Relationships to Established Disci-
plines, and Needs for Mathematical Development,'
Mathematical Social Sciences 7 (2): 139-165.

REFERENCE NOTES

Fox, Karl A. (ed.), 1980, <u>Measurement and Valuation of</u>
<u>Social System Outcomes</u> (a three-volume series):
<u>Volume I, Comprehensive Social Systems Accounting:</u>
<u>Basic Units and Concepts at Local, Regional,</u>
<u>National, and World Levels.</u> Volume II, <u>Comprehen-</u>
<u>sive Social Systems Accounting: Quantification and</u>
<u>Implementation Based on Published Data.</u> Volume III,
<u>Comprehensive Modeling of Social Systems: Static</u>
<u>and Dynamic Theory, Operational Models, and Data</u>
<u>Needs.</u> Unpublished manuscript, Department of
Economics, Iowa State University.

<u>Volume I. Selected Chapters</u>:

2. Establishing a World Perspective, I: Rural Development Planning in Developing Countries (Karl A. Fox
and Syamal K. Ghosh). 70 pp.
3. Establishing a World Perspective, II: Alternative
Conceptualizations and Models (Karl A. Fox). 80
pp.
4A. BEA Economic Areas and National Metropolitan
Regions, I: Relationships Among Economic and Demographic Variables, 1960-64 (Karl A. Fox). 45 pp.
4B. BEA Economic Areas and National Metropolitan
Regions, II: Relationships Among Earnings in
Economic Sectors and Subsectors and the Usefulness
of Residentiary and Export-Base Classifications,
1969 (Karl A. Fox). 38 pp.
4C. BEA Economic Areas and National Metropolitan
Regions, III: (a) Partitioning BEA Areas into SMSA
and Non-SMSA Components; (b) National Metropolitan
Regions as Bases for Transportation Planning, Social
Accounts and Models, and World Data Systems (Karl A.
Fox). 44 pp.
5A. Functional Economic Areas, I: (a) Properties,
Origins and Disaggregation into Subareas; (b) Disag-
gregation of Standard Metropolitan Statistical Areas
into Census Tracts (Karl A. Fox). 65 pp.
5B. Functional Economic Areas, II: (a) Reports and
Recommendations of the Social Science Research
Council Committee on Areas for Social and Economic
Statistics, 1967; (b) Economic Structure, Labor

Force, and Other Aspects of Functional Economic
Areas in Agricultural Regions (Karl A. Fox). 54
pp.

9. The Fox-Barker (FB) Data Set: An Interim Report
(Karl A. Fox). 67 pp.

10. Additional Aspects of Barker's System and Proposed
Extensions (Karl A. Fox). 59 pp.

11. Behavior Settings as Basic Elements in a System of
Social Accounts: Some Conceptual and Measurement
Problems (James R. Prescott). 55 pp.

12. Purpose and Predictability in the Environment of
Human Behavior: Further Comments on Roger Barker's
Work and Its Influence (Karl A. Fox, Walter G.
Ollor, and Syamal K. Ghosh). 15 pp.

13. The Use of DOT-HAJ (Dictionary of Occupational
Titles and Handbook for Analyzing Jobs) Data and
Concepts for Measuring Behavior Capacities (Karl A.
Fox, Syamal K. Ghosh, and Walter G. Ollor). 69 pp.

Volume II. Selected Chapters:

2. Classification and Measurement of Jobs and Workers
(Karl A. Fox and Syamal K. Ghosh). 66 pp.

3. Expenditures of Time and Energy (Karl A. Fox).
53 pp.

4. Comprehensive Measures of Human Activities in
Behavior Settings (Karl A. Fox). 46 pp.

6. Combining Economic and Behavioral Aspects of
Accounts for a Small Community: An Overview (Karl
A. Fox). 41 pp.

7. Accounts for Private Enterprises Consistent with
Barker's Data and also with Business Accounting
Procedures (Syamal K. Ghosh and Karl A. Fox). 40
pp.

8. Accounts for Nonmarket Organizations (Syamal K.
Ghosh and Karl A. Fox). 31 pp.

9. The Barker-Schoggen View of a Small Community: An
Interpretation of Selected Data from Barker and
Schoggen's Qualities of Community Life (1973) (Karl
A. Fox). 39 pp.

10. Social Accounts for a Small Community: Some
Remaining Problems (Karl A. Fox and Syamal K.
Ghosh). 50 pp.

11. Some Temporal and Spatial Problems in Developing
    Social Accounting Systems (James R. Prescott). 46
    pp.
12A. An Overview of the Des Moines BEA Economic Area, I:
    (a) The Area in National and World Perspectives; (b)
    Demographic and Economic Structures of Subareas and
    Counties (Karl A. Fox, Syamal K. Ghosh, and Walter
    G. Ollor). 80 pp.
12B. An Overview of the Des Moines BEA Economic Area, II:
    (a) Populations of Incorporated Places, Retail
    Sales, and Trade Center Hierarchies; (b)
    Possibilities for Applying Barker's Concepts of
    Authority Systems, Genotypes, Occupancy Times, and
    Inhabitant-Setting Intersections (Karl A. Fox,
    Syamal K. Ghosh, and Walter G. Ollor). 84 pp.
13A. Estimating the Values of Behavior Inputs Made by the
    Labor Force of the Des Moines BEA Economic Area, I:
    (a) The Use of DOT-HAJ Data and Concepts for
    Measuring Behavior Inputs; (b) Occupational Distri-
    butions of Employed Workers by Subareas and Indus-
    tries, 1970 (Karl A. Fox, Syamal K. Ghosh, and
    Walter G. Ollor). 81 pp.
13B. Estimating the Values of Behavior Inputs Made by the
    Labor Force of the Des Moines BEA Economic Area, II:
    (a) The Effects of Differences in Occupational Mix
    upon Average Values of Selected DOT and Census Vari-
    ables; (b) Provisional Estimates of the Values of
    Behavior Inputs Used in Gainful Employment, 1970
    (Karl A. Fox, Syamal K. Ghosh, and Walter G. Ollor).
    77 pp.
14. Estimating the Values of Behavior Inputs Made by the
    Entire Populations of the Des Moines BEA Economic
    Area and Its Subareas (Karl A. Fox, Syamal K. Ghosh,
    and Walter G. Ollor). 41 pp.
15. Prospects for a Comprehensive System of Social
    Accounts Linking Barker's Concepts with Published
    Data Systems (Karl A. Fox, Syamal K. Ghosh, and
    Walter G. Ollor). 26 pp.

Volume III. Selected Chapters:

3. A Dynamic Theory of Behavior Settings in a Small
   Community (Jati K. Sengupta). 48 pp.

 4. Structure, Stability, and Efficiency of the Distri-
    bution of Behavior Capacity in a Community (Jati K.
    Sengupta). 38 pp.
 5. A Theory of Allocation of Behavior Capacity in a
    Community (Jati K. Sengupta). 46 pp.
 6. Translating Behavior Setting Concepts into Measure-
    Theoretic Form (Arnold M. Faden). 12 pp.
10. Dynamic Models of Demographic and Social Change
    (Karl A. Fox and Syamal K. Ghosh). 19 pp.
11. Examples of Data Available and Needed at the
    National Level (Karl A. Fox). 53 pp.
12. Examples of Data Available and Needed for Specific
    Regions: BEA Economic Areas and Their Subareas;
    Standard Metropolitan Statistical Areas and Their
    Census Tracts (Karl A. Fox, Syamal K. Ghosh, and
    Walter G. Ollor). 57 pp.
14. Comprehensive Modeling of Social Systems: Static
    and Dynamic Theory, Operational Models, and Data
    Needs (Karl A. Fox). 11 pp.

AUTHOR INDEX

201

SUBJECT INDEX

'Access' and 'basic
    amenities' (OECD social
    indicators,) implica-
    tions for streets,
    sidewalks, and public
    utilities in Midwest
    town, 93-94
Access to, or proximity of,
    selected services (OECD
    social indicator), as
    related to stores,
    schools, and service
    establishments of
    Midwest town, 91-93
Access to outdoor space,
    37, 41, 90, 101
Action pattern ratings, 52,
    172
  subscales, 26
    evaluation and appreci-
      ation, 26
    participation, 26, 33
    supply, 26, 33
    teaching and learning,
      26
Action patterns, and
    purpose-oriented
    buildings, see
    Buildings, purpose-
    oriented
Action patterns, in
    behavior settings, 4,
    7, 24-31, 53, 58-59,
    136
  aesthetics, 7, 27-31, 58
  business, 7, 26-31, 58

education, 7, 27-31, 58
government, 7, 27-31, 58
nutrition, 7, 27-31, 59
personal appearance, 7,
    27-31, 59
physical health, 7, 27-
    31, 59
professionalism (profes-
    sional involvement), 7,
    26-31, 59
recreation, 7, 26-31, 59
religion, 7, 27-31, 59
social contact, 7, 26,
    28-31, 59
Adult education, 37, 43
Aesthetics, see Action
    patterns
Affective behavior, see
    Behavior mechanisms
Allocation of time, see
    Living-time
Aptitude, see Worker
    traits
Atypical work schedule, 37,
    44
Authority systems, control-
    ling behavior settings,
    3, 19, 31, 49, 57, 65,
    97, 134
  church, 3, 19, 31, 49,
    57, 97, 134
  government, 3, 19, 31,
    49, 57, 97, 134
  household or family, 50,
    91

205

published, see Data
systems, established
Degree of completeness and
closure, 22-23
of a community, 22-23
of a town and its trade
area, 22-23
Demand,
for participant
functions, 74
for worker functions, 74
Demands, imposed by roles
in behavior setting
programs, 12
Dictionary of Occupational
Titles (DOT), 4, 6, 74-
75, 88, 181, 198-199
Fourth edition (DOT 4),
73, 77, 79-80, 83-84,
87, 181, 198-199
Second edition (DOT 2),
74-75
Supplement to DOT 3, 74,
84, 87, 181
Third edition (DOT 3),
74, 79, 83-84, 181,
198-199
Discouraged workers, 37,
43
Distribution of earnings,
37, 44
Distribution of income, 37,
45
Distribution of wealth, 37,
45
DOT codes, see Codes, in
classifications of jobs
and occupations
DOT occupations, 6, 73-74
in grocery stores, 77-78
in banks, 78
DOT system, see Dictionary
of Occupational Titles;
see also Codes, in
classifications of jobs

and occupations
DOT variables (Y-
variables),
values for major occupa-
tional categories, 84-
88
Duration (D), of a behavior
setting, 17, 18, 24

Eco-behavioral science, 2,
9-10, 32, 154-156, 173,
183-192, 196
Barker's mature view of,
in 1977, 156-158
Barker's statement of
need for, in 1969, 155-
156
defined, 32, 151
independent of psych-
ology, 156
interfaces with other
approaches and disci-
plines, 152-155
relationships to
established disci-
plines, 152-155
Ecological dimension, added
to psychology by Barker
and Wright, 32
Ecological environment, of
human behavior, 12, 17,
63, 111, 150
extent (E) measured in
centiurbs, as function
of number, occurrence
and duration of
behavior settings, 17,
67, 114
size of, in distinctive
urban neighborhoods,
112
size of, occupied (used)
by poor, aged, or
disabled persons, 112
Ecological psychology, 2,

centers
Self-contained community,
13-19, 23, 41
and insights into useful-
ness of corresponding
social indicators at
national level, 15
described at physical,
architectural ecologi-
cal, and behavioral
levels, 15-19
improvements in, 14-15,
41
Serious injuries, 37, 46
Service establishments,
110-127
Short-term disability, 37
42
SIC-type industries, 7, 69,
167
Simulation techniques, 132-
149
in modeling communities,
132-149
in modeling urban-
centered regions, 133-
135
Single leader, within a
behavior setting, 62
occupant of zone 6, 62
Small cities, social
accounts for, 8, 130
SMSAs (Standard Metropolitan Statistical Areas),
social accounts for, 8,
109
SOC codes, see Codes, in
classifications of jobs
and occupations
SOC-DOT ratings, 6, 73, 79-
80, 82-84, 87-88, 171-
172
of worker functions, 6,
73, 79-80, 82-84, 87-
88, 171-172

of worker traits, 73-74,
84, 87-88, 172
Social accounting matrices
(SAMs), 8
Social accounting tables,
for a community, 133
Social change, measurement
of, 3, 49
in terms of introduction
(accretion) and disap-
pearance (erosion) of
genotypes, 3, 49
Social class, in Midwest
town, 54-60
Social concerns, OECD list
of, 35-37, 178
command over goods and
services, 36-37, 45
education and learning,
36-37, 43
employment and quality of
working life, 36-37,
43
health, 36-37, 42
personal safety, 36-38,
45
physical environment, 36-
37, 95
social environment, 36-
37, 45
time and leisure, 36-37,
44
Social contact, see Action
patterns
Social differences between
communities, measure-
ment of, 3, 49
in terms of differences
between their arrays of
genotypes, 3, 49
Social environment, 37, 45
Social indicators, 1, 5, 9,
38
objective, 1, 5, 9, 38
OECD list of, 1, 5, 34,

THEORY AND DECISION LIBRARY

An International Series in the Philosophy and Methodology
of the Social and Behavioral Sciences

Editors:

Gerald Eberlein, *University of Technology, Munich*
Werner Leinfellner, *University of Nebraska*

1. Günther Menges (ed.), *Information, Inference, and Decision.* 1974, viii + 195 pp.
2. Anatol Rapoport (ed.), *Game Theory as a Theory of Conflict Resolution.* 1974, v + 283 pp.
3. Mario Bunge (ed.), *The Methodological Unity of Science.* 1973, viii + 264 pp.
4. Colin Cherry (ed.), *Pragmatic Aspects of Human Communication.* 1974, ix + 178 pp.
5. Friedrich Rapp (ed.), *Contributions to a Philosophy of Technology. Studies in the Structure of Thinking in the Technological Sciences.* 1974, xv + 228 pp.
6. Werner Leinfellner and Eckehart Köhler (eds.), *Developments in the Methodology of Social Science.* 1974, x + 430 pp.
7. Jacob Marschak, *Economic Information, Decision and Prediction. Selected Essays.* 1974, three volumes, xviii + 389 pp.; xii + 362 pp.; x + 399 pp.
8. Carl-Axel S. Staël von Holstein (ed.), *The Concept of Probability in Psychological Experiments.* 1974, xi + 153 pp.
9. Heinz J. Skala, *Non-Archimedean Utility Theory.* 1975, xii + 138 pp.
10. Karin D. Knorr, Hermann Strasser, and Hans Georg Zilian (eds.), *Determinants and Controls of Scientific Developments.* 1975, ix + 460 pp.
11. Dirk Wendt, and Charles Vlek (eds.), *Utility, Probability, and Human Decision Making. Selected Proceedings of an Interdisciplinary Research Conference, Rome, 3–6 September, 1973.* 1975, viii + 418 pp.
12. John C. Harsanyi, *Essays on Ethics, Social Behavior, and Scientific Explanation.* 1976, xvi + 262 pp.
13. Gerhard Schwödiauer (ed.), *Equilibrium and Disequilibrium in Economic Theory. Proceedings of a Conference Organized by the Institute for Advanced Studies, Vienna, Austria, July 3–5, 1974.* 1978, l + 736 pp.
14. V. V. Kolbin, *Stochastic Programming.* 1977, xii + 195 pp.
15. R. Mattessich, *Instrumental Reasoning and Systems Methodology.* 1978, xxii + 396 pp.
16. H. Jungermann and G. de Zeeuw (eds.), *Decision Making and Change in Human Affairs.* 1977, xv + 526 pp.
17. H. W. Gottinger and W. Leinfellner (eds.), *Decision Theory and Social Ethics.* 1978, xxii + 329 pp.
18. A. Rapoport, W. E. Stein, and G. J. Burkheimer, *Response Models for Detection of Change.* 1978, viii + 200 pp.
19. H. J. Johnson, J. J. Leach, and R. G. Muhlmann (eds.), *Revolutions, Systems, and Theories; Essays in Political Philosophy.* 1978, xi + 198 pp.

20. Stephen Gale and Gunnar Olsson (eds.), *Philosophy in Geography.* 1979, xxii + 470 pp.
21. Maurice Allais and Ole Hagen (eds.), *Expected Utility Hypotheses and the Allais Paradox: Contemporary Discussions of Decisions Under Uncertainty With Allais' Rejoinder.* 1979, vii + 714 pp.
22. Teddy Seidenfeld, *Philosophical Problems of Statistical Inference: Learning from R. A. Fisher.* 1979, xiv + 246 pp.
23. L. Lewin and E. Vedung (eds.), *Politics as Rational Action.* 1980, xii + 274 pp.
24. J. Kozielecki, *Psychological Decision Theory.* 1982, xvi + 403 pp.
25. I. I. Mitroff and R. O. Mason, *Creating a Dialectical Social Science: Concepts Methods, and Models.* 1981, ix + 189 pp.
26. V. A. Lefebvre, *Algebra of Conscience: A Comparative Analysis of Western and Soviet Ethical Systems.* 1982, xxvii + 194 pp.
27. L. Nowak, *Property and Power: Towards a Non-Marxian Historical Materialism.* 1983, xxvii + 384 pp.
28. J. C. Harsanyi, *Papers in Game Theory.* 1982, xii + 258 pp.
29. B. Walentynowicz (ed.), *Polish Contributions to the Science of Science.* 1982, xii + 291 pp.
30. A. Camacho, *Societies and Social Decision Functions. A Model with Focus on the Information Problem.* 1982, xv + 144 pp.
31. P. C. Fishburn, *The Foundations of Expected Utility.* 1982, xii + 176 pp.
32. G. Feichtinger and P. Kall (eds.), *Operations Research in Progress.* 1982, ix + 520 pp.
33. H. W. Gottinger, *Coping with Complexity.* 1983, xv + 224 pp.
34. W. Gasparski and T. Pszczołowski (eds.), *Praxiological Studies.* 1983, xiv + 418 pp.
35. A. M. Yaglom and I. M. Yaglom, *Probability and Information.* 1983, xx + 421 pp.
36. F. M. Wuketits, *Concepts and Approaches in Evolutionary Epistemology.* 1984, xiii + 307 pp.
37. B. F. Stigum and F. Wenstøp (eds.), *Foundations of Utility and Risk Theory with Applications.* 1983, x + 492 pp.
38. V. V. Kolbin, *Macromodels of the National Economy of the USSR.* 1985, forthcoming.
39. H. J. Skala, S. Termini, and E. Trillas (eds.), *Aspects of Vagueness.* 1984, viii + 304 pp.
40. G. L. Gaile and C. J. Willmott (eds.), *Spatial Statistics and Models.* 1984, x + 482 pp.
41. J. van Daal and A. H. Q. M. Merkies, *Aggregation in Economic Research.* 1984, xiv + 321 pp.
42. O. Hagen and F. Wenstøp (eds.), *Progress in Utility and Risk Theory.* 1984, xii + 279 pp.